The Transformative Daf

MOSAICA PRESS

RABBI DANIEL FRIEDMAN

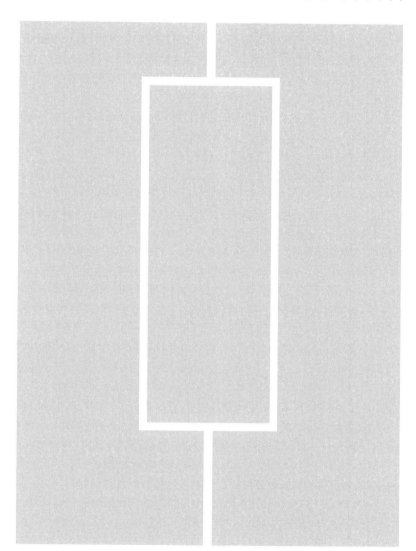

The Transformative Daf

Tractate Kesubos | Volume 2: Daf 58–112

ISBN: 978-1-957579-27-6

Published by Mosaica Press, Inc.
www.mosaicapress.com
info@mosaicapress.com

In memory of my grandfather

Avraham ben Zvi Hersch

Lovingly remembered by

Jonathan and Nina Herbst

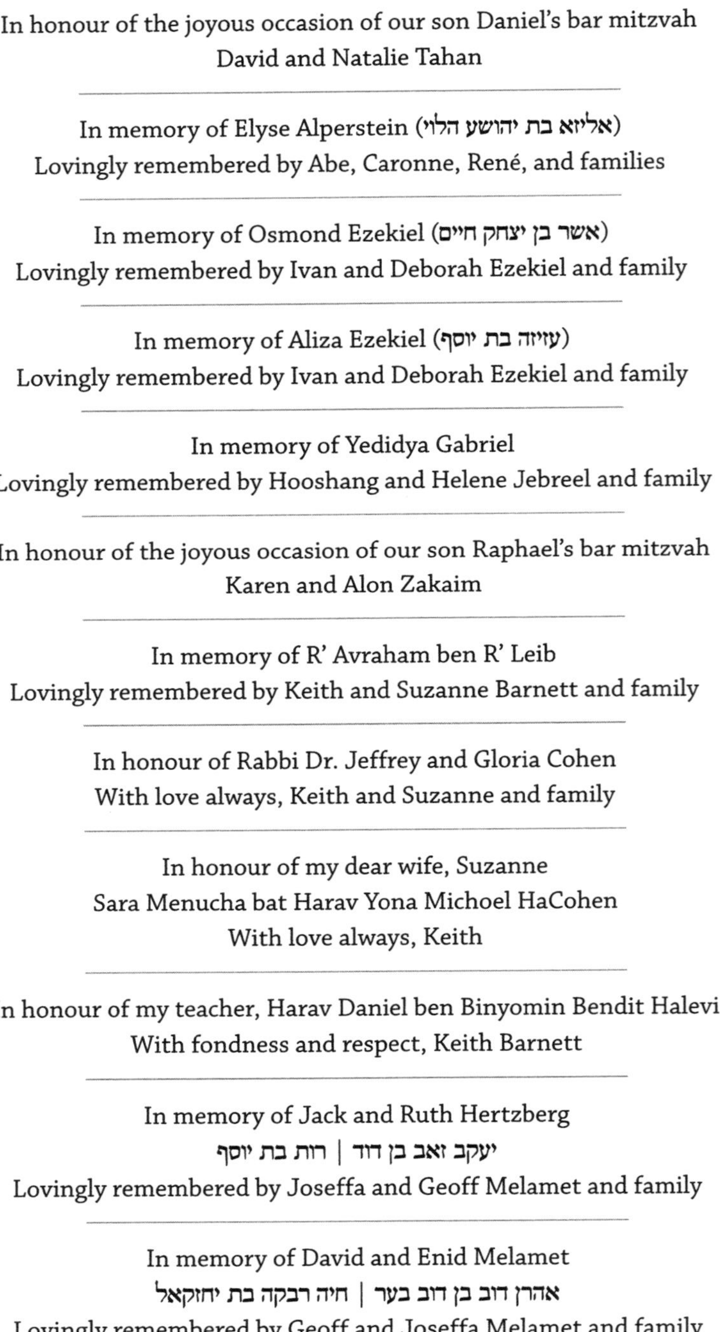

In honour of the joyous occasion of our son Daniel's bar mitzvah
David and Natalie Tahan

In memory of Elyse Alperstein (אליזא בת יהושע הלוי)
Lovingly remembered by Abe, Caronne, René, and families

In memory of Osmond Ezekiel (אשר בן יצחק חיים)
Lovingly remembered by Ivan and Deborah Ezekiel and family

In memory of Aliza Ezekiel (עזיזה בת יוסף)
Lovingly remembered by Ivan and Deborah Ezekiel and family

In memory of Yedidya Gabriel
Lovingly remembered by Hooshang and Helene Jebreel and family

---

In honour of the joyous occasion of our son Raphael's bar mitzvah
Karen and Alon Zakaim

In memory of R' Avraham ben R' Leib
Lovingly remembered by Keith and Suzanne Barnett and family

In honour of Rabbi Dr. Jeffrey and Gloria Cohen
With love always, Keith and Suzanne and family

In honour of my dear wife, Suzanne
Sara Menucha bat Harav Yona Michoel HaCohen
With love always, Keith

In honour of my teacher, Harav Daniel ben Binyomin Bendit Halevi
With fondness and respect, Keith Barnett

In memory of Jack and Ruth Hertzberg
יעקב זאב בן דוד | רות בת יוסף
Lovingly remembered by Joseffa and Geoff Melamet and family

In memory of David and Enid Melamet
אהרן דוב בן דוב בער | חיה רבקה בת יחזקאל
Lovingly remembered by Geoff and Joseffa Melamet and family

BETH DIN ZEDEK
ECCLESIASTICAL JUDICATURE OF THE
CHICAGO RABBINICAL COUNCIL

בית דין צדק דק"ק שיקגו והגליל
דמועצת הרבנים דשיקגו

בס"ד

הרב גדלי' דוב שווארץ זצ"ל, ראב"ד מלפנים
RABBI GEDALIA DOV SCHWARTZ *of blessed memory*
Rosh Beth Din Emeritus

הרב ישראל מאיר קרנו זצ"ל, ראב"ד מלפנים
RABBI ISRAEL M. KARNO *of blessed memory*
Av Beth Din Emeritus

הרב חיים דוד רגנשברג זצ"ל, מייסד הבד"ץ
RABBI C. DAVID REGENSBERG *of blessed memory*

הרב יונה ריס, אב"ד
RABBI YONA REISS
Av Beth Din

הרב אברהם מרדכי אברמסון
RABBI ALAN M. ABRAMSON
Menahel

כ"ג ניסן, אסרו חג הפסח תשפ"א

<u>כתב המלצה</u>

Our esteemed colleague Rabbi Daniel Friedman שליט"א has written a lucid and lyrical book, Daf Yomi, that extracts nuggets of wisdom and pearls of perspicacity from the pages of the Talmud. As an experienced and successful shul Rabbi, Rabbi Friedman has a special talent for connecting with his audience, whether through the written word or the spoken sermon, in a fashion which is משיבת/ נפש של אדם ([illegible]), capable of restoring a person's spiritual well-being, and intellectual appreciation of the Torah's values and teachings. One cannot help but be enriched by Rabbi Friedman's combination of psychological acuity, human compassion, and religious fervor.

והנני מברכו בברכת התורה, שימשיך להגדיל תורה ולקדש שם שמים ברבים,

ידידו ומוקירו,

Yona Reiss

2701 W. Howard Street, Chicago, Illinois 60645-1303
Phone & Fax: 1-773-250-5482 bethdin@crcweb.org

מוסדות אור שמח מרכז טננבאום ע.ר. 58-00-21343-00
רח' שמעון הצדיק 22-28 ירושלים ת.ד. 18103
טל: 02-581-0315

Nissan 5781

MICHTAV BRACHA

Chazal say, "Great is learning because it leads to [virtuous] action" (*Kiddushin* 40b). Ramban writes in his celebrated letter that after learning anything in Torah, one should seek some way to apply that teaching to one's life. Every part of Hashem's Torah is precious beyond measure, but many, perhaps most, of us have some difficulty finding this application. While there are many passages in Tanach and Talmud where the practical lessons are clear, with many others, the message is obscure and elusive.

Rabbi Daniel Friedman has performed a truly valuable service in providing some badly needed assistance. He has authored a book going through the 2,700 plus pages of the Babylonian Talmud, extracting from each *daf* lessons that can be applied to real life. Some stress practical behavior, such as fixing negative character traits and acquiring and developing virtuous ones, others are inspirational, and still others provide a broader philosophical perspective that can help us in our life's journey to become true *avdei Hashem*. Those who study the *daf yomi* will walk away with practical guidance that will elevate the *ruchniyus* in their lives; for those who do not yet study the *daf*, there is the additional benefit of giving them a way to participate in this wonderful global learning endeavor.

Rabbi Friedman deserves our heartfelt gratitude for producing a work that is so helpful on both a practical and inspirational level. May he have much *hatzlachah* both in the dissemination of this book and in all of his *avodas ha'kodesh.*

With Torah blessings,
Yitzchak A. Breitowitz
Rav, Kehillat Ohr Somayach, Yerushalayim

Table of Contents

Preface

Welcome to *The Transformative Daf: Kesubos*, part 2.

What's the purpose of a *ketubah*?[1] On a basic level, it provides a bride with financial security should the marriage go awry, God forbid. Additionally, it contains the husband's commitment to taking care of all his wife's needs during the marriage. But shouldn't it be obvious that he will take care of her? Offering her a document seems to cheapen and "transactionalize" this auspicious moment!

Let's think about our foundational document, the Torah. Which is our primary Torah, the *Torah She'bichsav*, the Written Torah, or the *Torah She'baal Peh*, the Oral Torah? Think about it this way: Could you practice Judaism with the Written Torah alone? No. Could you practice with the Oral Torah alone? Yes. Well, if that's the case, why do we need a Written Torah at all? We could simply have received the Oral Torah and that would tell us everything we need to know about serving Hashem!

There's something, however, about a written document that gives it an element of permanence. Think about any agreement between two people. As much as they trust one another, the stability comes from the

---

1 While we have employed "*Kesubos*" as the tractate title, throughout the book the marriage document is referred to as the "*ketubah*," since that spelling appears officially in various English dictionaries.

line, "Could I have that in writing?" That's the strength of the Written Torah. It anchors the Oral Torah and gives it permanence.

And that's what the *ketubah* symbolizes. It fortifies the marriage. It anchors the marriage. It binds husband and wife to one another, signed and sealed. Likewise, when we stood at Mount Sinai and the Almighty took us unto Him to be His bride, He wrote a *ketubah* called the Written Torah. It's our document attesting to our unbreakable bond with our Groom and His everlasting commitment to take care of our every need. May you feel the power of His blessing and tender loving care every moment of your life!

A huge thank you to the generous patrons of this volume: Jonathan and Nina Herbst, David and Natalie Tahan, Keith and Suzanne Barnett, René and Lance Anisfeld, Ivan and Deborah Ezekiel, Geoff and Joseffa Melamet, Isaac and Helene Jebreel, and Alon and Karen Zakaim. May Hashem bless you in all your endeavors, and grant you good health, abundant *parnassah*, and everlasting *nachas*!

Thank you to all the people who have a *chelek* and a *zechus* in this *sefer*. Of course, as always, the greatest appreciation goes to my dear wife and soul mate, Rabbanit Batya Yocheved. As Rabbi Akiva announced to his students: "What is mine and yours is truly hers."

My special dedication of this volume goes to Rabbi Meir Shapiro of Lublin. There are very few people in our history who have been the cause of as many hours of Torah learning as the founder of the *daf yomi* movement. I, along with hundreds of thousands of Jews, owe an eternal debt of gratitude to you, Rav Meir, *zt"l*.

Once again, thank you to Rabbis Doron Kornbluth and Yaacov Haber and everyone at Mosaica Press for going above and beyond every step of the way. Special thanks to Mrs. Sherie Gross, Rabbi Robert Sussman, and the entire fantastic editorial team. And finally, thank you to the Ribbono Shel Olam for all the blessings in my life. I feel humbled to be the vehicle for these teachings.

Rabbi Daniel Friedman
Shevat 5782
Teaneck

DAF 58

Access the Excess

Yitzchak is getting old. Fearing that his final days are approaching, he calls upon his favored son, Eisav, desiring to bless him. Rivkah overhears Yitzchak's instructions to their son and intercepts the call. She quickly commands their other son, Yaakov, to imitate his brother and seize the blessings. We know that Yitzchak was blind, but how was our wise patriarch unable to distinguish between his righteous and undeserving sons?

The *Alshich* explains that Yitzchak knew exactly who his two sons were. He knew that Yaakov loved learning Torah and that Eisav loved the nightlife and fast camels. And so, he reasoned that if Eisav enjoyed the pleasures of this world and Yaakov enjoyed spirituality, the easiest solution to providing for both of his children was to offer Eisav the bounty of this physical world and save the pleasures of Heaven for Yaakov. Therefore, first he called in Eisav in order to bless him with all the material wealth of this physical world. Later, he would call in Yaakov in order to bless him with Heavenly wealth.

But Rivkah disagreed…

מַתְנִי׳ הַמַּקְדִּישׁ מַעֲשֵׂה יְדֵי אִשְׁתּוֹ הֲרֵי זוֹ עוֹשָׂה וְאוֹכֶלֶת הַמּוֹתָר רַבִּי מֵאִיר אוֹמֵר הֶקְדֵּשׁ רַבִּי יוֹחָנָן הַסַּנְדְּלָר אוֹמֵר חוּלִּין: גְּמָ׳ הַמּוֹתָר רַבִּי מֵאִיר אוֹמֵר הֶקְדֵּשׁ אֵימַת קָדוֹשׁ רַב וּשְׁמוּאֵל דְּאָמְרִי תַּרְוַיְיהוּ מוֹתָר לְאַחַר מִיתָה קָדוֹשׁ רַב אַדָּא בַּר אַהֲבָה אָמַר מוֹתָר מֵחַיִּים קָדוֹשׁ.

> ***Mishnah:*** *If one consecrates his wife's earnings, she may continue to work and sustain herself from her earnings. With regard to the excess, Rabbi Meir says: It is consecrated, and Rabbi Yochanan HaSandlar says: It is not consecrated.*
>
> ***Gemara:*** *The excess, Rabbi Meir says: It is consecrated. When does it become sacred? Rav and Shmuel both said: The excess is sacred after death. Rav Ada bar Ahavah said: The excess is sacred from life.*

According to Jewish law, a husband is obligated to support his wife financially. In order to promote marital harmony, the Rabbis enacted that the wife should, nonetheless, engage in a certain minimal amount of paid work (because idleness is psychologically unhealthy[1]) and that her basic (and any excess) earnings be pooled in his overall family budget.

Our Mishnah deals with a case where the husband (presumably not needing her income) consecrates all her earnings, which means that they are dedicated to the Holy Temple. The *Chasam Sofer* explains that it is as if the husband declares, "May your hands be dedicated to the One who created them." When he makes such a pledge, she is not bound by his declaration, and she may continue to consume her earnings. Otherwise, she would have no incentive to work. Only after her passing would he inherit those funds, at which point his pledge to consecrate would be effective.

But let's say that she was making more than the basic salary. Consecrating the funds wouldn't disincentivize her desire to work because she has chosen to work over and above the basic requirement anyway. And so, the Mishnah wants to know: Would her excess funds become consecrated? Rabbi Meir says they would be. The Gemara then questions at what point Rabbi Meir would deem the excess funds sacred. "Rav and Shmuel both said: The excess is sacred after death. Rav Ada bar Ahavah said: The excess is sacred from life."

Our Sages compare the relationship between God and Israel to a marriage. When we stood at Sinai and accepted the Torah, it was like

---

1 *Kesubos* 59b.

taking a ring, as the Almighty betrothed us to Him. When we work, we dedicate our efforts to Him. But the Mishnah says even though He might consecrate the work of our hands, we may still enjoy this world during our lifetime. Only afterwards do they become consecrated, and in Heaven we will enjoy the consecrated fruits of our labor.

Our Sages declare, "All Israel have a share in the World to Come, as it says: Your nation is all righteous; they shall inherit the land forever, the creation of My planting, the work of My hands, in which I take pride."[2] That sounds really beautiful, doesn't it? Every single Jew is going to Heaven. But it begs the question: If everyone is going to end up in the same place, why bother making any religious effort in this world?

Let's talk about our reward after we die. According to Rav and Shmuel that's when the excess becomes sacred. After we pass from this world into Heaven, every Jewish person will experience an excess that is consecrated for all eternity: excess joy, excess happiness, excess abundance, excess prosperity. In the spiritual realm, there is no shortage of reward. Even regarding those who appear to act contrary to God's will in this world, our Sages tell us that they are "filled with mitzvos like a pomegranate [is filled with seeds]!"

How amazing! But here's the thing: Why wait to consecrate the excess until after you die? Why not consecrate the excess even during your lifetime? When you accept the challenge to consecrate your hands to their Creator, "the excess is sacred from life." Notice that Rav Ada doesn't use the same language as Rav and Shmuel. They say that the excess is sacred "after" death. The contrasting opinion should be that the excess is sacred *during* the person's lifetime. Instead, Rav Ada says that the excess is sacred *from* life." That means that when you choose to live a life consecrated to Heaven, your excess occurs from that very life itself!

Why does Rivkah insist on Yaakov receiving the berachos from Yitzchak? Because she wasn't satisfied with reserving the Heavenly blessing for him. She wanted Yaakov—as heir to the family's values—to

---

2 *Sanhedrin* 90a.

receive the blessings of both this world and the World to Come. Recalling the prophecy she received when her children were still in the womb, she decided that the Children of Israel deserved abundant reward for all their righteous efforts.

She reasoned like this: If we were to receive reward only in the next world, people would feel disenchanted with good behavior. Imagine if all the good people, who were destined to be rewarded in Heaven, endured lives of misery in this world. Who would buy into such a system? Very quickly, people would get the message that bad behavior pays and that only the wicked prosper. And so, Rivkah resolved to capture the blessings of both the physical and spiritual realms for her son who had dedicated his life to Hashem.

Was Rivkah right or was Yitzchak? Clearly, Yitzchak's subsequent warm interaction with Yaakov, as he blessed him and bid him farewell upon his departure to Aram, demonstrated his acknowledgment of Rivkah's wise determination. Ultimately, she sealed the deal, guaranteeing "excess" from life itself for her progeny who dedicate their lives to the service of Hashem.

"All Israel" may have a share in the World to Come—everyone will enjoy excess in *Olam Haba*—but if you commit your hands to your Creator, you will enjoy excess in this world: excess *nachas*, excess *simchah*, excess berachah, excess *shalom*, excess self-fulfillment, and excess greatness! The Almighty is ready to open up His storehouse to bless you with excess abundance and prosperity! May you access the excess both in this world and in the next!

DAF 59

Cure for Insomnia

A man planted a beautiful garden. He sourced his flowers from the most exotic places around the world. Every blade of grass, every shrub was manicured to perfection. It took two years from start to finish. When it was finally complete, it was an award-winning masterpiece. Admirers came from far and wide for the grand opening to experience the unique array of colors and designs, and smell the extraordinary aroma emanating from the tropical plants.

Proud of his achievement, he decided it was time to take a well-earned break. He booked a vacation abroad for three months and locked the gate to the garden to ensure nobody would disturb its beauty while he was away.

Three months later, he returned. Upon opening the gate to the garden, he was shocked to find his extraordinary garden a complete mess. The flowers were drooping, the grass was overgrown, and weeds and thorns had filled every empty space between the exotic plants. He was devastated! How could this have happened? He was so careful to make sure to lock the gate so that everything would remain in its pristine state!

> רַבִּי אֱלִיעֶזֶר אוֹמֵר אֲפִילּוּ הִכְנִיסָה לוֹ מֵאָה שְׁפָחוֹת כּוֹפָהּ לַעֲשׂוֹת בַּצֶּמֶר שֶׁהַבַּטָּלָה מְבִיאָה לִידֵי זִימָּה רַבָּן שִׁמְעוֹן בֶּן גַּמְלִיאֵל אוֹמֵר אַף הַמַּדִּיר אֶת אִשְׁתּוֹ מִלַּעֲשׂוֹת מְלָאכָה יוֹצִיא וְיִתֵּן כְּתוּבָּה שֶׁהַבַּטָּלָה מְבִיאָה לִידֵי שִׁיעָמוּם.
>
> *Rabbi Eliezer says: Even if a bride brought one hundred maidservants into the marriage, the husband may oblige her to*

> *knit because idleness leads to licentiousness. Rabban Shimon ben Gamliel says: Likewise, one who vows that his wife should not work must divorce her and give her the ketubah payment because idleness causes mental health issues.*

What happened to the beautiful garden? Why didn't the man return to find his garden the way that he had left it? Of course, we all know that a garden requires constant care and attention. You cannot simply leave it alone, believing that it will remain in its pristine state. It must be maintained daily. The flowers must be watered. The grass must be mowed. Weeds and thorns must be pulled and removed. Otherwise, it will deteriorate in no time at all.

Likewise, explains Rabbi Yosef Gikatilla, when one's life is idle, it does not simply remain frozen in time.[1] Whatever achievements and strength of character that have been developed begin to deteriorate. The flowers droop, the grass overgrows, and weeds and thorns appear in the person's mind and body. Just imagine a triathlete who has exercised and worked on his muscles for years. When he stops working out, his body does not remain 'as is.' Before long, the muscle withers away, or worse yet, turns to fat. After three months of zero exercise, the individual can hardly run around the block, let alone compete in a triathlon!

Many people look forward to early retirement. Many people yearn for days off and extended vacation time. But we weren't placed on this earth to idle away our time. Too much free time is not healthy for the mind or soul. Certainly, we all need time to wind down and relax, on a daily, weekly, and annual basis. On the other hand, choosing to do nothing constructive in life, says the Talmud, has dire consequences. Boredom leads to inappropriate conduct. Boredom leads to a deterioration in mental acumen.

Think about a *shiur* that you attended last week. Now think about a *shiur* that you attended last year. Which one do you remember more clearly? Unless that *shiur* from last year happened to be one of those

---

1 *Sefer Hameshalim*, cited in *Mesivta* Gemara, *Kaftor Vaferach*.

uniquely unforgettable moments, your ability to recall last week's material is far greater than your ability to quote from the *shiur* that was given a year ago. So, effectively, you're constantly in a state of forgetting. With each passing day, we forget more and more of what we learned in the past.

I used to own a car with a leaky oil tank. When I filled it up, I couldn't tell that there was a leak, it was ever so tiny. But the mechanic found the tiny crack that was letting the oil drip out ever so slowly. It would have been too expensive to replace, he said. It made more sense just to make sure I constantly topped it up with engine oil.

That's what happens to our minds. They're constantly losing the Torah—and any other skills and expertise—that we've acquired over the course of our lives. We don't notice the leak because it's ever so tiny. But it's there. And unless we're constantly topping it up with new knowledge, our "machines" will eventually stop working properly. In fact, Rabbeinu Yonah teaches that the Creator intentionally fashioned our minds that way.[2] Had we been able to remember everything that we ever learned, without ever forgetting any material, we would eventually master the entire Torah. That would lead to boredom, resulting in the dire consequences of our Mishnah.

Some people have trouble sleeping. Baruch Hashem, that's never been an issue for me. Most of the time, as soon as my head hits the pillow, I'm out. But occasionally that doesn't happen. What do I do? I take the advice of the *Orchos Tzaddikim*.[3] He understands the obligation to "toil in it day and night" to mean that when you're lying in bed, you should be uttering or thinking about Torah. Isn't that powerful? Essentially, he's saying that even at the end of a long hard day's work, one can be guilty of idleness, if you're lying in bed doing nothing. Personally, that advice has done wonders for my sleep-ability. Inevitably, no sooner have I started reviewing the day's *daf* in my mind, than I'm fast asleep before I know it!

---

2 *Avos*, ch. 1.

3 *Shaar HaTorah*.

The Almighty placed you in this world to be productive. If you are still here, that means that there is still more to do, more to accomplish. Every moment in life is precious. May you merit the strength to recharge your batteries very quickly and move on to the next great project and achievement!

DAF 60

Wake Up and Smell the Coffee

Yitzchak is eagerly waiting for his son to return and receive the blessings. Sure enough, sooner than expected, the "firstborn" enters with a meal for his father. Yitzchak is a little confused about his son's presentation and aura.

"You're back very quickly!" he tells his son.

"Yes, Father," the son responds, "God showed me the way and accelerated my mission."

That's kind of strange, Yitzchak thinks to himself. *Since when does Eisav talk about God like that? But I've verified his identity. Only Eisav has hairy arms. So, it's definitely Eisav.*

"The voice," concludes Yitzchak, "is the voice of Yaakov. But the hands are the hands of Eisav. Come a little closer, my son."

Yaakov approaches his father and Yitzchak exclaims, "See, the aroma from my son; it's like a field blessed by Hashem!"

> הָכִי אָמַר שְׁמוּאֵל כָּל זְמַן שֶׁמַּכִּירָהּ הָהִיא דַּאֲתַאי לְקַמֵּיהּ דִּשְׁמוּאֵל אֲמַר לֵיהּ לְרַב דִּימִי בַּר יוֹסֵף זִיל בִּדְקֵהּ אֲזַל אוֹתְבַהּ בְּדָרֵי דְנְשֵׁי וְשַׁקְלֵיהּ לִבְרַהּ וְקָמְהַדַּר לֵיהּ עֲלַיְיהוּ כִּי מְטָא לְגַבַּהּ הֲוָת קָא מְסַוֵּי לְאַפַּהּ כְּבַשְׁתִּנְהִי לְעֵינַהּ מִינֵּיהּ אֲמַר לַהּ נְטֹף עֵינִיךְ קוּם דְּרֵי בְּרִיךְ סוּמָא מְנָא יָדַע אָמַר רַב אָשֵׁי בְּרֵיחָא וּבְטַעְמָא.
>
> *This is what Shmuel said: Whenever he [a child] recognizes her [a mother may no longer refuse to nurse her child]. Once, a mother [who refused to feed her child and insisted on a wet*

> *nurse] appeared before Shmuel. He said to Rav Dimi bar Yosef: Go and investigate. He went, placed her in a row of women, and took her son and passed the baby before them. When he reached her, he looked at her face with joy, and she averted her eyes from him. He said to her: Lift up your eyes, arise, and take your son. How does a blind baby recognize his mother? Rav Ashi said: By smell and taste.*

The Gemara discusses a case where a couple was getting divorced. The mother no longer wanted to nurse their child and was insisting that her ex-husband hire a wet nurse for the baby. Shmuel teaches that if the baby was old enough to recognize his mother, then she is required to continue nursing him. How do you tell? This may be the first instance of a "police lineup." Rav Dimi had a number of women stand in a row and passed the baby before them until he recognized his mother. She tried to avoid his gaze, but he knew who his mother was. Rav Ashi adds that even a blind child can recognize its mother utilizing taste and smell.

Sometimes in life, it feels like our "Parent in Heaven" has averted His eyes from us. Crisis may strike in any area of life, and things don't turn around as quickly as we would have hoped. Our Sages call this *hester panim*—the concealment of God's face. The individual who is suffering may have done nothing wrong. Consequently, when that happens, some people conclude that God is not in control, and they begin to question their faith. Ultimately, however, our response must be to scream out to our Father in Heaven and say, "Raise your eyes and tend to your child!" Just like a mother and father would never forsake their child, God would never forsake His children. He loves us dearly, greater than the love of any mortal parent, and He wants to hold us close and be there for us.

Hester panim, of course, is really only from our perspective. From Heaven's perspective, everything God does is good. It may appear to us as if God has turned away His gaze, but He is always intimately engaged with every one of His children. We are the ones who are blind to His providence. So how does a "blind" child recognize His parent? Answers Rav Ashi: By taste and smell.

Our Sages tell us that although we can't see God, we can taste Him and smell Him.[1] What does it mean to taste and smell God?

King David declares, "Taste and see that God is good!"[2] The *Malbim* explains that Torah is sweet and enjoyable even to our earthly physical senses. We don't always appreciate the taste of Torah and so each morning we ask Hashem, "Please make the words of Your Torah sweet in our mouths." But if Torah is already sweet, why do we need to ask Hashem that He make the Torah sweet for us?

The answer should be obvious. The most precious tastes in life require acquiring. If you give a $300 bottle of wine to someone who has never tasted wine before, you're pouring that wine down the drain. To them, it tastes the same as a $10 bottle. What's more, both bottles probably taste bitter to them because they haven't developed a taste for wine, let alone a good wine. If that's true of a physical pleasure like wine, then it's certainly true of Torah, the ultimate spiritual pleasure. The more Torah you learn, the more you are able to savor the sweet taste of Torah.

Once you've developed a taste, you will begin to "see" God. I remember vividly my "aha" moment sitting in yeshiva in Israel. I was learning a *Tosafos*, when everything fell into place. It was magical. All of a sudden, the lights came on inside my mind and soul. Everything made sense and became absolutely clear and true. Just like our fine wine example, it's impossible to describe to someone who hasn't experienced it. But at that moment, God's presence became clear to me like never before in my life. That's the meaning of tasting Hashem.

How about smelling God?

When Yaakov approached his father, Yitzchak exclaims, "See the aroma from my son; it's like a field blessed by Hashem!" While this statement has deep layers of meaning, on a simple level, Yaakov had just returned from the field (or so Yitzchak believed) and had a pleasant aroma about him, having spent time amongst the sweet-smelling vegetation.[3] Yitzchak might have simply said, "See the aroma from my

---

1 *Shemos Rabbah* 17:2.

2 *Tehillim* 34:9.

3 *Ibn Ezra, Radak.*

son; it's like a [fresh] field!" But he didn't suffice with that declaration. He added an important clause, recognizing that the aroma was "blessed by Hashem."

The second way we perceive God in this world is by appreciating the beautiful world that He created. It's not just a tree; it's a Divinely fashioned tree. It's not just an aromatic flower; it's a Divinely infused aromatic flower. To remind us that even smells emanate from Hashem, we even have a berachah that we make upon smelling nice aromas. We're all familiar with the formula from the *Havdalah* service.

But that's not the only occasion that we should make the berachah. Anytime that we derive pleasure from the beautiful smells God imbued in Creation, we should bless Him. In fact, just like there are different berachos over different foods, we make different berachos over different smells! The berachah that we're all familiar with is the catch-all version, "Who creates various aromas." It's the equivalent of the *shehakol* berachah. But really, we should be familiar with the special blessings over aromatic plants and aromatic trees. Because each beautiful smell is a reminder that the Creator went to great lengths to provide a beautiful and pleasure-filled world for us. When we "wake up and smell the coffee" or "stop and smell the roses," we realize that the Almighty tends to and cares constantly for every detail of Creation.

Our Father in Heaven never forsakes His children. When it seems that He has concealed His face, turn to Him as a child does to a parent and demand that He tend to His children. May you forever experience Hashem's providence via all your five senses!

DAF 61

Can We Have a Quiet Shabbos?

Achav was a wicked king who lived during the time of Eliyahu HaNavi. He had sinned and led the country in idolatrous practices. As a result of his sins, famine and drought had come to the Land of Israel. One day, Eliyahu said to Achav, "As Hashem lives, the God of Israel, Whom I serve, there will be no dew or rain except at my bidding." Achav was understandably unimpressed and sought to kill the prophet.

God told Eliyahu, "Leave this place, turn eastward, and go into hiding by the Wadi Cherith, which is east of the Jordan. You will drink from the wadi, and I have commanded the ravens to feed you there." He proceeded to do as Hashem had instructed and off he went to Wadi Cherith. Every morning and evening, ravens brought him bread and meat and he drank from the wadi.

After some time, the wadi dried up because there was no rain in the land. The word of Hashem then came to him and said, "Go at once to Zarephath of Sidon, and stay there. I have instructed a widow there to feed you." So, he went at once to Zarephath. When he came to the entrance of the town, a widow was there gathering wood. He called out to her, "Please bring me a little water in your pitcher, and let me drink."

As she went to fetch it, he called out to her, "Please bring along a piece of bread for me."

"As Hashem, your God, lives," she replied, "I have nothing baked, nothing but a handful of flour in a jar and a little oil in a jug. I am just gathering a couple of sticks, so that I can go home and prepare it for me and my son. We shall eat it and then we shall die."

"Don't be afraid," said Eliyahu to her, "Go and do as you have said, but first make me a small cake from what you have there and bring it out to me. Then make some for yourself and your son. For thus said Hashem, the God of Israel: The jar of flour shall not empty out and the jug of oil shall not fail until the day that Hashem sends rain upon the ground." She went and did as Eliyahu had spoken, and she and he and her household had food for a long time. The jar of flour did not empty out, nor did the jug of oil fail, just as Hashem had spoken through Eliyahu.

After a while, the little boy fell sick, and his illness grew worse, until he had no breath left in him. She said to Eliyahu, "What harm have I done you, O man of God, that you should come here to recall my sin and cause the death of my son?"

"Give me the boy," he said to her; and taking him from her arms, he carried him to the upper chamber where he was staying and laid him down on Eliyahu's own bed. He cried out to Hashem and said, "O Hashem, my God, will You bring calamity upon this widow whose guest I am, and let her son die?" Then he stretched out over the child three times, and cried out to Hashem, saying, "O Hashem, my God, let this child's life return to his body!" Hashem heard Eliyahu's plea. The child's life returned to his body, and he was resuscitated.

Eliyahu picked up the child and brought him down from the upper room to the main room, and gave him to his mother. "See," said Eliyahu, "your son is alive." And the woman answered Eliyahu, "Now I know that you are a man of God and that the word of Hashem is truly in your mouth."[1]

אָמַר רַב יִצְחָק בַּר חֲנַנְיָא אָמַר רַב הוּנָא הַכֹּל מְשַׁהִין בִּפְנֵי הַשַּׁמָּשׁ חוּץ מִבָּשָׂר וְיַיִן אֲבוּהּ בַּר אִיהִי וּמְנְיָמִין בַּר אִיהִי חַד סָפֵי מִכֹּל מִינָא וּמִינָא וְחַד סָפֵי מֵחַד מִינָא מָר מִשְׁתַּעֵי אֵלִיָּהוּ בַּהֲדֵיהּ וּמָר לָא מִשְׁתַּעֵי אֵלִיָּהוּ בַּהֲדֵיהּ הָנְהוּ תַּרְתֵּין חֲסִידֵי וְאָמְרִי לַהּ רַב מָרִי וְרַב פִּנְחָס בְּנֵי רַב חִסְדָּא מָר קָדֵים סָפֵי

1 *Melachim I* 17.

וּמָר מְאַחַר סָפֵי דְּקָדֵים סָפֵי אֵלִיָּהוּ מִשְׁתַּעֵי בַּהֲדֵיהּ דִּמְאַחַר סָפֵי לָא מִשְׁתַּעֵי אֵלִיָּהוּ בַּהֲדֵיהּ.

Rav Yitzchak bar Chananiah quoted Rav Huna: All foods may be withheld from before the waiter [until the guests have eaten] except for meat and wine. Regarding Avuah bar Ihi and Minyamin bar Ihi, one of them would give his waiter from every kind of food that he ate, while the other one would only share one of the dishes with him. Eliyahu conversed with the former Sage, but Eliyahu did not converse with the latter Sage. And there were two pious men, some say they were Rav Mari and Rav Pinchas the sons of Rav Chisda: One Sage would feed the waiter before the meal, and the other Sage would give him afterwards. The one who gave earlier, Eliyahu conversed with him. But the one who gave it later, Eliyahu did not converse with him.

Why did the widow merit to have her son resurrected? Because she was prepared to give food to a hungry stranger even before she had fed her own family. The *Ben Ish Chai* points to this story and explains why Eliyahu appeared to the Sage who would feed his hungry waiter before himself.[2] He adds that the first story of the Sages must have taken place on Shabbos, when it is proper to partake of various delicacies. After *Havdalah*, he explains, we sing about Eliyahu HaNavi, as he writes a report of all the merits that we accrued over Shabbos, including the special foods that we ate. If we shared our delicacies with others, that's double points!

God gave us this world to enjoy. But more importantly, He placed us on Earth to make this world a better place and become net contributors. Every opportunity for enjoyment is an equal opportunity for contribution. It's a mitzvah to enhance our Shabbos meals with delicious dishes that we wouldn't partake of during the week. But it's an even bigger mitzvah to share those delicacies with other people.

---

2 *Ben Yehoyada.*

We all love having guests at our Shabbos tables. But sometimes, we're so busy running around all week long that we just want some peace and quiet on Shabbos. We feel like just having the meal and putting our feet up and relaxing. Who needs the hassle of a meal that lasts three hours? Why bother with the fancy crockery and all the clean-up, when we can just eat off disposables because it's "just us?" Especially after a year of eating alone during the pandemic, it's a real effort to bother with thinking about Shabbos guests.

But that's the true delight of Shabbos. Yes, Hashem wants us to enjoy His delicacies. But even more, He wants to see us "break (our) bread" with someone else. For some people, the challenge is to part with some of their personal delights to share with guests. For others, the challenge is to part with their precious R&R time to spend their Shabbos with others.

Nonetheless, it's undoubtedly worth the effort. Having guests changes the entire tenor of the meal for yourself and the kids. The Shabbos meal shouldn't be a quick in and out. It should look different from the rest of the week, replete with *zemiros* singing, *divrei Torah*, and yes, even just schmoozing. That's all part and parcel of the delight of Shabbos. And having guests ensures the meal becomes more than just dinner. It becomes an experience.

But of course, our Gemara is about much more than just having your friends over. That's important. However, it's also important to remember those less fortunate. Whether that's someone in shul who you think might not have anyone with whom to spend Shabbos. Or even your own domestic help. Who did Eliyahu appear to? The Sages who thought about their waiters and wanted to make sure that they felt appreciated and cared for.

How do we treat those who work for us? Whether they're our professional employees or domestic help, we must never forget that they are equal human beings created in the image of God. They have feelings and needs, and one must always be sensitive to them and mindful of their spirit.

Sometimes, we reason to ourselves: Well, compared to where they came from, life is great. Back in their home country, they barely had enough to feed their families, now they enjoy Western life, they get days off, and they even have extra money to send back home in the form of remittances. They should be more than grateful for what we have given them!

That's not an acceptable attitude. Listen to the sage teachings of the Talmud: You are not even allowed to make their mouths water while they're serving you. You need to feed them first. Before the guests arrive and they're serving everyone, they get to eat the Shabbos delicacies! They are holy human beings and must be treated with the utmost dignity and sensitivity.

Every human being is equal in the eyes of the Almighty. Never take your good fortune for granted. You must be forever grateful for His bounty and never feel that you are better than the next person who has not been similarly endowed. May you share Heaven's bounty with all of Hashem's children, taking it to a whole other level on Shabbos!

DAF 62

Oy Vay Iz Mir

Following Yosef's revelation of his true identity to his brothers, the entire family comes down to live in Egypt. Upon Yaakov's arrival in the country, he is brought before Pharaoh, who asks him a strange question.

"How old are you?" inquires the king.

"My days in this world have been few and difficult," responds the patriarch, "and they have not reached the days of my forebears."

The *Daas Zekeinim* teaches that Yaakov shouldn't have responded so resentfully. As a result of his negative response, a number of years were ultimately deducted from his life. In the end, his years, indeed, failed to reach those of his forebears.

But what even prompted the strange question from Pharaoh?

> אָמַר רַב אֲנָחָה שׁוֹבֶרֶת חֲצִי גּוּפוֹ שֶׁל אָדָם שֶׁנֶּאֱמַר וְאַתָּה בֶן אָדָם הֵאָנַח בְּשִׁבְרוֹן מָתְנַיִם וּבִמְרִירוּת תֵּאָנַח וְרַבִּי יוֹחָנָן אָמַר אַף כָּל גּוּפוֹ שֶׁל אָדָם שֶׁנֶּאֱמַר וְהָיָה כִּי יֹאמְרוּ אֵלֶיךָ עַל מָה אַתָּה נֶאֱנָח וְאָמַרְתָּ אֶל שְׁמוּעָה כִּי בָאָה וְנָמֵס כָּל לֵב וְרָפוּ כָל יָדַיִם וְכִהֲתָה כָל רוּחַ וְכָל בִּרְכַּיִם תֵּלַכְנָה מַּיִם.
>
> *Rav said: Sighing breaks half of a person's body, as it is stated: "Sigh, therefore, you son of man, with the breaking of your loins; sigh so bitterly." And Rabbi Yochanan said: Sighing breaks even a person's entire body, as it is stated: "And it shall be, when they say to you: 'Why are you sighing?' That you shall say: 'Due to the tiding, for it comes, and every heart*

> *shall melt, and all hands shall be slack, and every spirit shall be faint, and all knees shall drip with water.'"*

The *Daas Zekeinim* suggests that Yaakov looked much older than he actually was. And that's OK. Premature aging often happens whether we choose it or not. But it was something more than just a few white hairs that prompted Pharaoh's enquiry. Rabbi J.J. Schacter explains that Yaakov's response demonstrates that Yaakov's demeanor and self-presentation as he entered the room gave off the impression of a very old man. We might not be able to control how many wrinkles we have, but we can control how we hold ourselves. Yaakov gave off the impression of being old and tired, which was how he responded to Pharaoh's question.

Really, there's nothing wrong with sighing. And it's completely understandable when a person sighs and groans when he's experiencing great pain. But all too often, people moan and groan when they have so much to be grateful and happy about. Our Gemara teaches that the very act of sighing can be detrimental to one's physical health. Sighing can put a person into a mood of self-pity and hopelessness. When that happens, the body follows the emotions and one's suffering becomes a self-fulfilling prophecy.

A sigh doesn't make you feel any better. When you sigh, you resign yourself to defeat, and your body follows suit. If instead, you jump for joy, you awaken and release endorphins into the body and you begin to heal yourself from whatever is troubling you. What's more, you inspire others to live their lives with happiness and passion—they think to themselves, "Wow, look at her. She's dealing with that terrible illness, and she's still so full of life! I had better fix my attitude!"

When you smile, the whole world smiles with you. When you kvetch and *krechtz*, it doesn't necessarily lead to others kvetching and *krechtzing*, but after a while, you begin to wonder why people aren't running to spend time with you. Some people have extremely challenging lives, but you'd never know it. You see them every day, every week, and they're smiling, cheerful, standing tall. Only their closest relatives and friends know what's really going on in their lives—the medical report, the financial troubles, the challenges with their children.

Sighing doesn't help the situation. It only makes you feel worse. And it makes others around you uncomfortable. May you live with optimism and positivity even in your darkest hour, and may it lead to healing and prosperity throughout your life!

DAF 63

Love Your Fellow as Yourself

Rabbi Akiva began as a shepherd of the rich and powerful Kalba Savua. Rachel, the daughter of Kalba Savua, saw that Rabbi Akiva was humble and refined. She said to him, "If I marry you, will you go to learn Torah?"

"Yes," he replied. They married secretly and she sent him off to learn. But her father heard about it and expelled her from his house. He vowed that she would never benefit from his estate.

Rabbi Akiva went and sat for twelve years in the study hall. When he returned, he brought twelve thousand students with him. As he approached, he heard an old man saying to Rachel, "How long will you remain a living widow?"

She said to him, "If he would take my advice, he would stay for another twelve years." When Rabbi Akiva heard this, he said, "She's just given me permission," and off he went to learn for a further twelve years. When he returned, he brought twenty-four thousand students with him.

Rachel heard and went out to greet him. Her neighbors said, "Borrow some nice garments for the occasion!"

"He knows exactly who I am," she replied, "our relationship is higher than mere clothing." As she approached, his attendants pushed her away as they did not know who she was. He declared, "Leave her! My Torah and yours are really all hers!"

שְׁמַע אֲבוּהָ דַּאֲתָא גַּבְרָא רַבָּה לְמָתָא אָמַר אֵיזִיל לְגַבֵּיהּ אֶפְשָׁר דְּמֵפַר נִדְרַאי אֲתָא לְגַבֵּיהּ אֲמַר לֵיהּ אַדַּעְתָּא דְּגַבְרָא רַבָּה מִי נָדַרְתְּ אָמַר לוֹ אֲפִילּוּ פֶּרֶק אֶחָד וַאֲפִילּוּ הֲלָכָה אַחַת אֲמַר לֵיהּ אֲנָא הוּא נְפַל עַל אַפֵּיהּ וְנַשְּׁקֵיהּ עַל כַּרְעֵיהּ וִיהַב לֵיהּ פַּלְגָא מָמוֹנֵיהּ.

Her father heard that a great man came to the town. He said, "I will go to him. Maybe he will nullify my vow." He came to him. Rabbi Akiva said to him, "Did you vow thinking that he would become a great man?" He said to him, "If I had believed he would know even one chapter or even one halachah I would not have vowed." He said to him, "I am he." He fell on his face and kissed his feet and gave him half of his money.

When Kalba Savua first heard that his daughter had married a simple shepherd boy, he was incensed. What a stain on his family's fine reputation! And Rachel, of all people? It made no sense. She was a *baalas middos*, a girl of such wonderful, refined character traits! How could she do this to the honor of her family? He immediately cut her off and vowed that she would never get a penny from him.

But as time passed, he began to regret his rash decision. A daughter is a daughter, after all. It was more of a shame to the family to see her wandering around town in rags. And so, one day, he hears that a great sage by the name of Rabbi Akiva is coming to town. Here was his opportunity to consult with the sage and have his vow annulled. Unbeknownst to him, Rabbi Akiva was none other than the shepherd boy whom he had dismissed all those many years ago.

He comes before the Sage and pours out his heart. Rabbi Akiva asks him, "Did you consider the meaning of your vow if your son-in-law ended up being a *gadol*?"

"Without a doubt," replied Kalba Savua, "I was upset that my daughter would marry a complete ignoramus. If he could learn even so much as one chapter or even one halachah, there's no way I would have made such a vow!"

"Well in that case," Rabbi Akiva responded, "your vow is null and void. I am the man you vowed about."

Let's take a moment to think about Rabbi Akiva's incredible response. At this point in his life, did he need Kalba Savua? Certainly not. He was the greatest Sage of his generation. He was surrounded by adherents who would have taken care of all his worldly needs. Given such newfound stature, many in his place would have been dismissive of Kalba Savua.

"All those years when my wife was destitute," he might have answered, "you didn't care. Now that we no longer need your assistance, now you come to us?" But that wasn't his response. Not only did he forgive him, but he helped his father-in-law find ways to assuage the guilt of his earlier decision. Essentially, he said to him, "You were right that your daughter deserved better than an ignoramus. We know that you never really meant what you said, did you?"

How often do we harbor ill feelings over things people said or did to us? If we would only place ourselves in their shoes and try to understand why they acted the way that they did, we'd be able to resolve matters and get it off our own chest and theirs. They might have acted inappropriately, like Kalba Savua. Even if Akiva had remained an ignoramus, it was still no reason for Kalba Savua to disown his daughter. But even still, we must seek ways to allow the other person to save face, as Rabbi Akiva did.

That's the greatest test. To forgive a person when there's absolutely nothing in it for you. Rabbi Akiva and Rachel didn't need her father's money. They didn't need his fame. They didn't need his favors. And so, the forgiveness was completely pure and altruistic. But they didn't stop there. Not only did Rabbi Akiva forgive, but he constructed the forgiveness in a way that ensured Kalba Savua wouldn't continue to feel foolish and sheepish every time that he saw Rabbi Akiva and Rachel. That's true forgiveness!

Rabbi Akiva is famous for saying that one of the greatest principles in the Torah is "Love your fellow as yourself." It's one of the biggest because it's so hard. We're all easy on ourselves. We find ways to excuse our behavior. The challenge is to employ those same "excuses" and "justifications" when we think about the way others have acted. That's the meaning of loving them as yourself.

We all have people in our lives who have wronged us. It's a big mitzvah to forgive them. It's an even bigger mitzvah to forgive them in a way that makes them feel that they never erred to begin with. May you forever display the benevolence of Rabbi Akiva!

DAF 64

Overpopulation

Yaakov is married to Rachel and Leah and working as a shepherd for his father-in-law, Lavan. That, of course, was not the original plan. He had intended to marry Rachel, but, unbeknownst to him, Lavan had replaced her under the chuppah with Leah. Upon finding out about Lavan's trickery, Yaakov resolves to work however long and hard he needs to in order that he can marry both sisters.

Life in their new home opens idyllically, as the sisters are a model of sibling love and care. But, before long, relationships start to strain, as fertile Leah gives birth to one baby after another, while Rachel remains barren. Despite her selfless righteousness, the agony begins to wear on her. One day, in a moment of exasperation, she confronts Yaakov and exclaims, "Bring me children, for if not, I am dead!"[1]

What does Rachel mean by this poignant declaration?

אָמַר רַב טוֹבִי בַּר קִיסְנָא אָמַר שְׁמוּאֵל כּוֹתְבִין אִגֶּרֶת מָרֶד עַל אֲרוּסָה וְאֵין כּוֹתְבִין אִגֶּרֶת מָרֶד עַל שׁוֹמֶרֶת יָבָם בְּמַאי אוֹקִימְתַּהּ לְהָא דִשְׁמוּאֵל בְּשֶׁתָּבְעָה הִיא הַאי כּוֹתְבִין אִגֶּרֶת מֶרֶד עַל אֲרוּסָה לַאֲרוּסָה מִיבְּעֵי לֵיהּ הָא לָא קַשְׁיָא תְּנִי לַאֲרוּסָה מַאי שְׁנָא שׁוֹמֶרֶת יָבָם דְּלָא דְּאָמְרִינַן לַהּ זִיל לָא מִפַּקְדַתְּ אֲרוּסָה נָמֵי נֵימָא לַהּ זִיל לָא מִפַּקְדַתְּ אֶלָּא בְּבָאָה מֵחֲמַת טַעֲנָה דְּאָמְרָה בָּעֵינָא חוּטְרָא לִידָא וּמָרָה לִקְבוּרָה.

---

1 *Bereishis* 30:1

> *Rav Tovi bar Kisna quoted Shmuel: The court writes a letter of rebellion about a betrothed woman [refusing to complete the marriage]. But it does not write a letter of rebellion about a widow awaiting her uncompleted levirate marriage. In which case did you establish that teaching of Shmuel? If it is a situation where she asked to marry him and he did not want to, then why phrase it, "The court writes a letter of rebellion 'about' a betrothed woman"? It should have said instead, "Write a letter of rebellion 'for' a betrothed woman [meaning it is written on her behalf against her husband]." This is not difficult. We can amend the text to read: For a betrothed woman. But what is the difference between [a betrothed woman and] a widow awaiting her levirate marriage? Because we may say to her, "Depart, you have no obligation to procreate." But then in the case of a betrothed woman too, let us likewise say to her, "Depart, you have no obligation." Rather, the case where a letter of rebellion is issued concerns a woman who comes with a claim, saying, "I want a staff in my hand and a hoe for burial."*

The classic adage that "you can't be half pregnant" doesn't apply to marriage. Nobody gets married from one day to the next—first you get engaged, then you get married. That's not only true of modern marriage. Ancient marriages had a similar two-step process, called *eirusin* and *nisuin*. The big difference, however, is that *eirusin* would bind the couple to one another, such that a *get* was necessary if the relationship went awry. Our Gemara discusses a couple who is in limbo because the husband has not completed the *nisuin*. The wife may demand that the court write an injunction against her husband because he is impeding her ability to have children who will support her in her old age and take care of her burial needs.

Tosafos[2] states that there are other claims that the woman may assert, such as Rachel's contention that being "childless is akin to death."[3]

---

2 *Yevamos* 65a.

3 *Rashi* to *Bereishis* 30:1.

The commentators emphasize, however, that she must offer some sort of reason for seeking to procreate. Merely "desiring to have children" is not sufficient reason to compel the court to get involved in their marital impasse.[4]

The *Netziv* explains that some people have children to satisfy their own pleasure.[5] That's why Elkanah, the father of Shmuel the Prophet, responded to his barren wife Chanah, "Why are you sad? Am I not better than ten children?"[6] If it's all about the pleasure that we will derive from children, then there are other ways to have fun. Chanah subsequently dedicates her son to the service of Hashem, thereby demonstrating that she had not sought a child for her own benefit. Like our matriarch Rachel, Chanah wanted a child in order to "live." Rabbi Yaakov Tzvi Mecklenburg explains that "living" means living to fulfill one's ultimate purpose in this world.[7]

In the commentaries' discussion of our Gemara, we encounter three approaches to procreation. Some people have children because they want children, just like they want other pleasures in life. That, say the commentators, is insufficient basis for the courts to get involved. The next level is the person who has children in order that those children can take care of him in his later years and beyond. That's a satisfactory rationale, but it's not the ideal reason to bring children into this world. The highest level is one who gives birth in order to populate the Earth with souls in human bodies serving Heaven. We want to create "lives"—individuals who are not here to satisfy our own pleasures, but seeking to bring pleasure to the Creator.

Historically, one of the main reasons that people had children was in order to be supported in their old age. Nowadays, with the advent of state support systems, that expediency has diminished. We live in a day and age when begetting children is truly optional. And so, it comes as no surprise when "responsible" activists call for a curb on childbearing.

---

4 Cited in *Oz V'Hadar Mesivta, Yalkut Biurim*, p. 100, note 60.

5 *Bereishis* 30:1.

6 *Shmuel* I 1.

7 *Hakesav V'Hakabbalah, Bereishis* 1:30.

Without a spiritual purpose, extra human beings are an unnecessary burden on a planet with "limited resources."

If you are a believer, however, you know that the Almighty created this world for His service. He has promised to provide for all His children for all eternity. That doesn't mean that we may abuse the bountiful Earth with which He has endowed us. But as long as we are respecting the planet, the resources will never run dry. And the more children that we have, the greater the glory we bring to the Creator.

In fact, our Sages tell us that Mashiach will not come until all the souls have been born into bodies. And so, every child we bring into the world is a step closer to the messianic era. That's a powerful thought. Some people think: Well, I don't have the personal wherewithal to have more kids. Will I have enough time for each of my children? Will I have the money to send them to the right schools? Can I guarantee they'll turn out OK if I spread myself too thin?

The answer to all of the above is: yes, Hashem will give the personal and financial resources that you need. But, beyond that, even if they don't all end up as "chips off the old block," the mere introduction of life into this world is already a fulfillment of the Divine will and one step closer to Mashiach!

Above all, children should never get the impression from their parents that they were brought into this world simply as accessories and indulgences for their parents' lives. Why would children feel the need to respect the people who imposed life upon them just to satisfy their parents' own desires? Your children should be brought up with the knowledge that you have granted them the greatest gift—the gift of life—the ability to serve the Creator. When they receive that message, their lives will be filled with awe and respect for the two holy mortals who enabled them to fulfill their mission in the universe. May you merit begetting many healthy children, physically and spiritually!

DAF 65

Tuning In to Your Spouse

After a year in the ark, Noach finally steps out into a new world. He praises God and offers a sacrifice of thanks. Hashem is pleased with Noach's efforts and makes a covenant never to destroy the world again. The rainbow would be the eternal symbol of that covenant. Whenever the Almighty is unhappy with our behavior, He produces the rainbow, thereby reminding us to improve our ways and "reminding" Himself that He will always forgive us for our iniquities.

Unfortunately, it does not take long for Noach to debase himself in iniquity. Following his initial spiritual euphoria, "Noach, the man of the Earth profaned himself and planted a vineyard." He gets drunk and becomes the Torah's eternal symbol of the tragic consequences of compromising one's self-control. The aftermath of his conduct leaves a stain on the family that would reverberate for many generations.

> תָּנָא כּוֹס אֶחָד יָפֶה לָאִשָּׁה שְׁנַיִם נִיוּוּל הוּא שְׁלֹשָׁה תּוֹבַעַת בַּפֶּה אַרְבָּעָה אֲפִילּוּ חֲמוֹר תּוֹבַעַת בַּשּׁוּק וְאֵינָהּ מַקְפֶּדֶת אָמַר רָבָא לֹא שָׁנוּ אֶלָּא שֶׁאֵין בַּעְלָהּ עִמָּהּ אֲבָל בַּעְלָהּ עִמָּהּ לֵית לַן בָּהּ.
>
> *One cup of wine is proper for a woman. Two is dishonorable. Three cups cause her to explicitly ask for her husband's intimacy. Four cause her to approach a mule. Rava clarified: That is only when her husband is absent, but when her husband is present, there is no concern.*

This is one of those pieces in the Gemara that we may be tempted to brush past quickly and assume that we have advanced from the thinking of our ancestors. But every word of the Gemara is precious and meaningful. When we encounter a teaching that does not sit well with us, it is incumbent upon us to work harder to appreciate the timeless wisdom of our Sages. Let's explore this lesson on two levels: first, we'll endeavor to understand the matter on a basic, literal level. Then we'll broaden it to our relationship with Hashem.

All the pleasures of this world may be used in one of two ways: either we sanctify them for the service of Heaven, or we aim simply to fulfill our physical desires. Wine is the ultimate example of a food that could go either way. It could be used for *Kiddush*, or it could be used to bring out the worst in us.

We know that drinking a glass of wine has health benefits; it reduces stress levels and maintains cardiac health. But one cup is all that's needed, says the Gemara. Any further imbibing is indulgent and therefore dishonorable. Regardless of one's gender, one needs to be cognizant of the right amount of wine to consume to maximize one's mission on Earth, and at what point one might put oneself over the edge and detract from one's service of Heaven.

Wine is the most precise example of a worldly pleasure that could go either way because it's black and white. A little ice cream is OK to enjoy. Three servings of ice cream are an unnecessarily gluttonous decision, but won't really impair your capacity to serve Hashem, at least not in the short term. Too much wine, however, impedes your cognitive aptitude and inhibits your ability to focus on your Divine mission.

Continuing with the sequence of the Gemara, what happens after a wife drinks more than two cups? She begins to make demands on her husband that she would not previously have made explicitly. But why is that so terrible? Surely, she's only asking him to fulfill his marital duty!

Here's the issue the Gemara is concerned about. Marriage is not a transaction. It's an emotional bond. It's the deepest of all relationships. Unlike the bond with a child, the marital relationship must be earned. In order to get there, you need to be able to tune into your spouse's needs and desires. The wife shouldn't need to ask her husband to be there for her. He should simply know. The Torah calls this the mitzvah of *onah.*

A husband must be so in tune with his wife's needs and wants that she doesn't need to spell them out to him. He should be there for her every desire without her needing to ask or say anything at all. The fact that she needs to drink to remove her inhibitions and make him aware of her needs is worse than dishonorable. His lack of sensitivity and awareness have pushed her to turn to foreign stimulants. And sadly, the Gemara warns of dire consequences if, even after she's spelled it out to him, he's still not listening. As an aside, Rava notes that only if he is absent will she look elsewhere, but if he is present, even if he is not as aware as he should be, we need not be concerned.

Regrettably, more than a statement about the wife's ability to hold her alcohol, our Gemara is an indictment of her inattentive husband. But if that's the case, why does the Gemara mention the wife's drinking pattern and not the husband's?

The answer, as we know, is that women don't need to be told to be in tune with their husband's needs and wants—their natural intuition and nurturing nature cause them to be constantly aware. For men this trait doesn't come naturally, so much so that men wonder why their wives expect them to just know how they're feeling and what they need.

But that's your job as a husband—to train yourself to be in tune with your wife's needs and wants. It's not easy, and it's not natural for males, but it's the key to a successful marriage. The way to get there is to constantly keep your wife at the forefront of your mind. Every other thought, you should be asking yourself, "What could I do now to make my wife happy?"

One way to tune in to your wife's needs and wants is simply to be "present" by staying in touch throughout the day. You might go through a day hardly thinking about your spouse. How about you touch base every time you conclude an event or appointment in your schedule? That's a great start to making her feel that she is your number one priority, the number one thought on your mind!

But of course, every time we learn about the relationship between husband and wife, we are reminded of our Sages' teaching that Hashem took us unto Him as His wife at Sinai. Let's think about the meaning of our Gemara for us, as the "wife" of the Almighty.

Judaism is not an ascetic religion. Hashem gave us pleasures in this world to enjoy. To enjoy, most certainly, but not to overindulge. That's the meaning of one cup of wine being appropriate. We enjoy the pleasures of this world in moderation. Overindulgence is not a sin, but it is dishonorable, because we're taking ourselves off the track of our Divine mission. We're distracting ourselves away from the reason that we're here on Earth.

What happens after "three cups?" The more that we indulge in the pleasures of this world at the expense of our spiritual pursuits, the more materialistic we become. And we start demanding physical and material satisfaction from our Heavenly Husband. Instead of trusting that He knows exactly what we need, we become more and more dissatisfied with our lot in life and get upset at Him when we're not getting what we want. The final step, God forbid, is when we become so overindulgent in worldly desires that we are no longer satisfied with kosher pleasures, and we seek to satisfy our cravings outside our holy marriage with Hashem.

Let's conclude today's intense subject matter with an important note about men's and women's drinking patterns. The Gemara notes from the story of Chanah, the mother of Shmuel the Prophet, that our women were not known as drinkers. Accused by Eli the Kohen Gadol of arriving drunk to the *Mishkan*, it subsequently becomes clear that he had misinterpreted her actions and the Divine message that he received via the *Urim V'Tumim*. What's more, as our Gemara points out, the story continues with Chanah's husband Elkanah drinking, but not her. After learning our Gemara, it's important to recall that all the instances of drunkenness in the Torah are men, from Noach to Lot to Nadav and Avihu.

As a husband or a wife, you must be so dedicated and bound to your spouse that you can be there for your spouse's every need and want even without your spouse asking. May you learn to be forever in tune with your spouse!

DAF 66

Your Preservation Salt

Rabban Yochanan ben Zakkai was once riding on a donkey departing Jerusalem, accompanied by his disciples. They encountered a young lady who was so poor that she lived by gathering barley from among the dung of the animals of the locals. Upon noticing him approach, she cried, "Rebbi, please give me something to eat!"

Not recognizing the unfortunate maiden, he asked, "My daughter, who are you?"

"I am the daughter of Nakdimon ben Gurion [the great philanthropist who sustained the inhabitants of Jerusalem during the Roman siege]," she replied.

Shocked to find her in such a destitute state, he gasped, "My daughter, where did all the money of your father's household disappear to?"

אָמְרָה לוֹ רַבִּי לָא כְּדֵין מָתְלִין מַתְלָא בִּירוּשָׁלַיִם מֶלַח מָמוֹן חֶסֶר וְאָמְרִי לַהּ חֶסֶד וְשֶׁל בֵּית חָמִיךְ הֵיכָן הוּא אָמְרָה לוֹ בָּא זֶה וְאִיבֵּד אֶת זֶה אָמְרָה לוֹ רַבִּי זָכוּר אַתָּה כְּשֶׁחָתַמְתָּ עַל כְּתוּבָּתִי אָמַר לָהֶן לְתַלְמִידָיו זָכוּר אֲנִי כְּשֶׁחָתַמְתִּי עַל כְּתוּבָּתָהּ שֶׁל זוֹ וְהָיִיתִי קוֹרֵא בָּהּ אֶלֶף אֲלָפִים דִּינְרֵי זָהָב מִבֵּית אָבִיהָ חוּץ מִשֶּׁל חָמִיהָ בָּכָה רַבָּן יוֹחָנָן בֶּן זַכַּאי וְאָמַר אַשְׁרֵיכֶם יִשְׂרָאֵל בִּזְמַן שֶׁעוֹשִׂין רְצוֹנוֹ שֶׁל מָקוֹם אֵין כָּל אוּמָּה וְלָשׁוֹן שׁוֹלֶטֶת בָּהֶם וּבִזְמַן שֶׁאֵין עוֹשִׂין רְצוֹנוֹ שֶׁל מָקוֹם מוֹסְרָן בְּיַד אוּמָּה שְׁפָלָה וְלֹא בְּיַד אוּמָּה שְׁפָלָה אֶלָּא בְּיַד בְּהֶמְתָּן שֶׁל אוּמָּה שְׁפָלָה וְנַקְדִּימוֹן בֶּן גּוּרְיוֹן לָא עֲבַד צְדָקָה וְהָתַנְיָא אָמְרוּ עָלָיו עַל נַקְדִּימוֹן בֶּן גּוּרְיוֹן כְּשֶׁהָיָה יוֹצֵא מִבֵּיתוֹ לְבֵית הַמִּדְרָשׁ כְּלֵי מֵילָת הָיוּ מַצִּיעִין תַּחְתָּיו וּבָאִין עֲנִיִּים וּמְקַפְּלִין אוֹתָן מֵאַחֲרָיו אִיבָּעֵית אֵימָא

לִכְבוֹדוֹ הוּא דַּעֲבַד וְאִיבָּעֵית אֵימָא כִּדְבָעֵי לֵיהּ לְמִיעְבַּד לָא עֲבַד כִּדְאָמְרִי אִינָשֵׁי לְפוּם גַּמְלָא שִׁיחְנָא.

She said to him, "Rebbi, do they not say the proverb in Jerusalem: Salt for wealth is lacking [chaser]?" And some say the proverb asserts that kindness [chessed] is salt for wealth. [He replied,] "But the money of your father-in-law's house, where is that?" She said to him, "This one came and destroyed that one." She said to him, "Rebbi, do you remember when you signed on my marriage contract?" He said to his students, "I remember that when I signed on the marriage contract of this woman, and I read in it, it listed a million gold dinars as a dowry from her father's house, aside from what was promised her from her father-in-law." Rabban Yochanan ben Zakkai cried and said: How fortunate are you, Israel, for when Israel performs the will of the Omnipresent, no nation or tongue can rule over them; and when Israel does not perform the will of the Omnipresent, He delivers them into the hand of a lowly nation. Not only are they delivered into the hand of a lowly nation, but even into the hand of the animals of a lowly nation! But did Nakdimon ben Gurion not perform charity? Isn't it taught, they said about Nakdimon ben Gurion that when he would leave his home to go to the study hall, fine woolen garments were laid beneath him to walk on, and subsequently, the poor would come and fold them up from behind him to keep? Perhaps, we could suggest that he acted that way for his own honor. Or, alternatively, perhaps he did not do as much as he should have done, as they say: according to the camel is the load.

This tragic story takes place in the aftermath of the Roman conquest of Jerusalem. Rabban Yochanan ben Zakkai has saved Torah Judaism and he pays a visit to Jerusalem from his yeshiva in Yavneh. On his way home, he sees the daughter of Nakdimon ben Gurion who was one of the wealthiest Jews of the era. She's looking through the scraps to find something to eat. And Rabban Yochanan's disciples are totally bewildered by what they're seeing. Her father was such a great philanthropist! Is this how Heaven repaid his generosity?

The Gemara concludes that while he donated abundantly, he had the ability to give much more. "According to the camel is the load." What may be a heavy burdensome load for one camel takes no effort whatsoever for his fellow camel. Undoubtedly, compared to everyone else, Nakdimon was an extraordinary philanthropist, but our Divine service is not about comparing ourselves to anyone else. Compared to what he could have given, he had not been sufficiently generous.

Many people's first question when asked for tzedakah contributions is: What are other people giving? And they are proud if they are able to match other top givers. Nakdimon ben Gurion not only matched other top givers, but he was always on the top of the organizational dinner and synagogue capital campaign lists. But that wasn't good enough—true, he was one of the top givers, but even those magnificent contributions were just a proverbial drop in the bucket. When his fellow Jerusalemites were suffering, he should have given until it hurt. Nakdimon may have been proud of the fact that he was the biggest contributor, but he had much greater capacity to give.

In life, there is only one person in your race: You. Once you start comparing yourself to others, you've gone to run a different race than the Almighty intended for you. As challenging as it may sound, one hundred dollars that one person gives to the campaign may be a more generous than the larger dollar figure of his neighbor. It all depends how much effort each has had to expend to earn and part with their money.

And the same is true of all mitzvos. Never compare yourself to anyone else. It doesn't matter how often your neighbor is attending minyan or going to a *shiur*. He's not running your race. It doesn't matter how many Shabbos guests he's inviting. Or how many times he's returned your *simchah* invitation. He's not running your race.

Nakdimon's daughter understood this. Our Sages explain her pithy comment that "kindness is salt for wealth" to mean that just like when you first salt meat it appears to detract from the meat by removing all its moisture, over the long term, the salt, which initially shrank the meat, is what preserves it. Likewise, giving tzedakah might appear to deplete one's freshwater reserves today, but ultimately, it preserves one's wealth. The key factor to remember, however, is that many people don't even have the meat to begin with. And even those who do have the meat often don't have enough to preserve it. Nakdimon was unable to preserve his assets because he failed to add sufficient salt. Instead of parting with his tzedakah in a timely manner, he thought the meat would stay forever moist.

Heaven has endowed each of us with specific blessings. If you've been blessed with a sharp mind, your preservation salt is to learn more Torah. If you've been blessed with great emotional IQ, your preservation salt is constantly to seek ways to help others and make them feel special. If you've been blessed with excellent interpersonal skills, your preservation salt is to take leadership positions on shul, school, and charitable boards and committees.

The great Chasidic master, Reb Zushe of Anipoli, famously related, "After 120, when I reach the Heavenly court, they won't ask me, 'Why weren't you as great as Avraham Avinu? Why weren't you as great as Moshe Rabbeinu?' No, they will ask me, 'Why weren't you as great as Zushe?'"

Your neighbor's commitment level doesn't make any difference to your service of Heaven. There is only one person running your race: You. And only you know if you're running your personal best. May you merit never looking over your shoulder at anyone else and running your best race through life!

DAF 67

Where's Your Bread Buttered?

A man once knocked on the door of Hillel the Elder.

"How may I help you?" asked the sage.

"I've come for tzedakah," the man replied.

"Tzedakah?!" Hillel responded incredulously, "just last month, did I not see your carriage rolling down the street replete with horses and servants?"

"Yes, indeed," said the downtrodden man, "but, sadly, I have lost it all."

"I'm sorry my dear sir," said Hillel, "but if that's the case, then we must make sure you are provided with all you are lacking. I will arrange for you to have your horse and servant!"

One time Hillel did not find a servant to run before the man. And so, Hillel himself ran in front of him for about three miles!

תָּנוּ רַבָּנַן דֵּי מַחְסוֹרוֹ אַתָּה מְצֻוֶּה עָלָיו לְפַרְנְסוֹ וְאִי אַתָּה מְצֻוֶּה עָלָיו לְעַשְּׁרוֹ אֲשֶׁר יֶחְסַר לוֹ אֲפִילּוּ סוּס לִרְכּוֹב עָלָיו וְעֶבֶד לָרוּץ לְפָנָיו אָמְרוּ עָלָיו עַל הִלֵּל הַזָּקֵן שֶׁלָּקַח לְעָנִי בֶּן טוֹבִים אֶחָד סוּס לִרְכּוֹב עָלָיו וְעֶבֶד לָרוּץ לְפָנָיו פַּעַם אַחַת לֹא מָצָא עֶבֶד לָרוּץ לְפָנָיו וְרָץ לְפָנָיו שְׁלֹשָׁה מִילִין הָהוּא דַּאֲתָא לְקַמֵּיהּ דְּרָבָא אָמַר לוֹ בַּמֶּה אַתָּה סוֹעֵד אָמַר לוֹ בְּתַרְנְגוֹלֶת פְּטוּמָה וְיַיִן יָשָׁן אֲמַר לֵיהּ וְלָא חָיְישַׁתְּ לְדוּחְקָא דְּצִיבּוּרָא אֲמַר לֵיהּ אַטּוּ מִדִּידְהוּ קָאָכֵילְנָא מִדְּרַחְמָנָא קָאָכֵילְנָא דְּתָנֵינָא עֵינֵי כֹל אֵלֶיךָ יְשַׂבֵּרוּ וְאַתָּה נוֹתֵן לָהֶם אֶת אָכְלָם בְּעִתּוֹ בְּעִתָּם לֹא נֶאֱמַר אֶלָּא בְּעִתּוֹ מְלַמֵּד שֶׁכָּל אֶחָד וְאֶחָד נוֹתֵן הַקָּדוֹשׁ בָּרוּךְ הוּא פַּרְנָסָתוֹ בְּעִתּוֹ אַדְּהָכִי אֲתַאי אֲחָתֵיהּ דְּרָבָא דְּלָא חָזְיָא

לֵיהּ תְּלֵיסְרֵי שְׁנֵי וְאַתְיָא לֵיהּ תַּרְנְגוֹלֶת פְּטוּמָה וְיַיִן יָשָׁן אָמַר מַאי דְּקַמָּא אֲמַר לֵיהּ נַעֲנֵתִי לְךָ קוּם אֱכוֹל.

The Sages taught: "Enough for his deficiency..." teaches that you are commanded with respect to the pauper to support him, but you are not commanded with making him wealthy. But the verse continues "...which is deficient for him," implying even a horse upon which to ride and a servant to run in front of him [if that's what he was previously accustomed to]. A certain person came before Rava. He said to him, "On what do you normally dine?" He said to him, "On a fattened hen and aged wine." He said to him, "And are you not concerned about being a burden on the community?" He said to him, "Is that to say that it is from their funds that I eat? I eat from the support of the Almighty, as we already learned that in the verse, 'The eyes of all wait for You, and You give them their food in his time.' It does not say 'at their time,' rather 'in his time.' This teaches that the Holy One, blessed be He, gives each and every one his sustenance at his time." Meanwhile, Rava's sister, who had not seen him for thirteen years, came. And she brought him a fattened hen and aged wine. Rava said, "What just happened here?" Rava said to him, "I spoke too soon. Arise and eat!"

How much tzedakah is considered adequate when we're giving to a poor person? Says the Gemara, it all depends. For someone who was always poor, it's enough to give him the basics. But for someone who was once wealthy, for whom the wheel of fortune turned, the basics are insufficient. Obviously, as long as we have the wherewithal to do so, we are obligated to provide for that individual to the extent that he enjoyed in the good old days.

That's powerful and counterintuitive. Who would have thought that we would have such a duty? And yet, that's how far we must go. Of course, it parallels the mitzvah "Love your fellow as yourself." Imagine, God forbid, that you found yourself in a financial bind because you had gone "all in" on a major investment, only to see it go south. As terrifying as that may sound, we have all heard of people who have lost it all. Just as we would want our friends to step in and carry us through the storm if it happened to us, we are expected to carry our fellow through such a crisis. While that does not necessarily necessitate the underwriting of lavish vacations, there are certain minimum needs of a wealthy individual who is experiencing a cash crunch or worse, including private school tuition, mortgage payments, etc. Those expenses might be luxuries for most of the population, but for this individual they are essential. If Hillel was willing to pay for his fellow's horse and servant, then covering this family's private school fees doesn't sound entirely outlandish.

But the fellow who once visited Rava really nailed it. When the man requested good meat and wine as he was accustomed to consuming, Rava tried to put him in his place and suggest that such a demand was an unnecessary burden on the community. The man, however, wasn't deterred.

"Am I eating your food?" he cried, "I'm eating the Almighty's food!" Lo and behold, as they were talking, Rava's sister suddenly showed up, bringing with her a fattened chicken and aged wine. Rava was astonished and immediately handed over the gift to his guest.

Pay close attention to the incredible unwavering faith of this individual. God may have removed his revealed immediate source of parnassah, but he knew that our Father in Heaven never forsakes His children. Cognizant of the mitzvah in the Torah, he went to Rava and asked for community funding. When Rava hesitated, he wasn't concerned. If Rava and the community would not provide, Hashem would find other ways to provide for him. Sure enough, no sooner had he uttered those words than Hashem provided.

In the face of such a heavy loss, many people would become depressed and completely forsake any devotion to Heaven. They would tell themselves that God is not in control. And yet, this righteous individual continued to believe that Hashem is the sole provider and that he was not subject to the whims of mortal man. He knew that it wasn't the people who would grant his needs; they were just God's messengers, just like his former clients and customers were God's messengers. But the Almighty has limitless messengers. The ultimate *emunah* is the wholehearted acceptance that even if everything looks bleak, God can and will provide for you on the same level that He provided for you when—according to the natural order—things were going well.

Some people are great at maintaining their trust in Hashem when the going is good. But when the curveball comes in their lives, they suddenly begin to question Heaven's providence. Others forget God when the going is good, believing that they've achieved it all on their own. It's only when life gets tough that they begin to turn their eyes Heavenward, begging God for salvation. The key to spiritual and material fulfillment is to maintain a strong, deep relationship with the Almighty at all times, through thick and thin.

God always provides. Sometimes it's more evident than other times in life. But as long as you remember where your bread is truly buttered, you will never go hungry. Not only will you not go hungry, but you will continue to eat a daily meal fit for a king. Because you deserve it. You are a prince and princess of the Supreme King of Kings. May you merit the Almighty's eternal revealed blessing and trust in Him every step of the way!

DAF 68

Fake It till You Make It?

Rabbi Chanina would send a certain poor family four *dinars* every Erev Shabbos. One week, his wife brought over the gift. However, upon her return, Rabbi Chanina noticed the look of displeasure on her face. "What's the matter?" he inquired.

"These fraudsters don't need our charity," she replied.

"What makes you so sure?" her husband asked.

"As I was approaching," Mrs. Chanina responded, "they were discussing which tablecloths to put out: 'Shall we use the silver cloths this week or the gold ones?' I couldn't believe what I was hearing!"

"Fear not," replied Rabbi Chanina, "For this is what Rabbi Elazar taught: We must give thanks to the swindlers who ask for charity that they do not need because were it not for them, who command our attention and receive our charity, we would be sinning every day in failing to properly support the truly poor, as it is stated: 'Beware that there be not a base thought in your heart, saying: The seventh year, the year of sabbatical, is at hand, and your eye be evil against your needy brother, and you will not give him, and he will cry to the Lord about you, and there will be sin upon you.' Because fraudsters like these folks wrongly take charity, it's unsurprising that many people don't always give so readily to those who are truly in need. At least now, they have a valid excuse!"

וְתָנֵי רַבִּי חִיָּיא בַּר רַב מִדִּיפְתִּי רַבִּי יְהוֹשֻׁעַ בֶּן קׇרְחָה אוֹמֵר כׇּל הַמַּעֲלִים עֵינָיו מִן הַצְּדָקָה כְּאִילּוּ עוֹבֵד עֲבוֹדָה זָרָה כְּתִיב הָכָא הִשָּׁמֶר לְךָ פֶּן יִהְיֶה דָבָר עִם

לְבָבְךָ בְלִיַּעַל וְגוֹ׳ וּכְתִיב הָתָם יָצְאוּ אֲנָשִׁים בְּנֵי בְלִיַּעַל מָה לְהַלָּן עֲבוֹדָה זָרָה אַף כָּאן עֲבוֹדָה זָרָה תָּנוּ רַבָּנַן הַמְסַמֵּא אֶת עֵינוֹ וְהַמַּצְבֶּה אֶת בִּטְנוֹ וְהַמְקַפֵּחַ אֶת שׁוֹקוֹ אֵינוֹ נִפְטָר מִן הָעוֹלָם עַד שֶׁיָּבֹא לִידֵי כָּךְ הַמְקַבֵּל צְדָקָה וְאֵין צָרִיךְ לְכָךְ סוֹפוֹ אֵינוֹ נִפְטָר מִן הָעוֹלָם עַד שֶׁיָּבֹא לִידֵי כָּךְ.

Rabbi Chiya bar Rav of Difti taught: Rabbi Yehoshua ben Korchah says: One who averts his eyes from the obligation to give charity is considered to have worshipped idols. It is written here concerning charity: "Beware that there be not a base thought in your heart," and it is written there concerning idolatry: "Certain base people have gone astray." Just as there, the word connotes idol worship, so too, here, it implies idol worship. The Sages taught: One who fakes a blind eye, or one who bloats his stomach as if he were sick, or one who pretends to have a damaged leg [in order to benefit dishonestly from charity] will not depart from the world before he comes to this same plight. More generally, one who receives charity and does not need it, his end will be that he will not depart from the world before he comes to this [state of actually needing charity].

"How much money did you make this year?" Have you ever considered the religious problem inherent in that question? You didn't make any money this year. God provided you with the money, as the Torah warns us against the attitude of: "my strength and the power of my hand made this wealth for me." That's why refusing to give charity is likened to idolatry. The only impediment to giving away one's money to someone in need is the false belief that you made the money and that this other fellow should make his own money. Once one acknowledges that it is Hashem Who makes our money and we are mere stewards of His bounty, charitable giving comes naturally.[1]

But when it comes to our hesitancy to give, our Sages recognize that the reticence to part with our "personal hard-earned cash" is only half the problem. The other half of the problem lies with the recipients, many of whom probably shouldn't be accepting charity. It's painful

---

1 *Yalkut Gershuni* cited in *Oz V'Hadar Mesivta, Kaftor Vaferach.*

when we learn, as Rabbi Chanina's wife did, that there are beneficiaries who are less destitute than they pretend to be. How do we deal with that challenge?

The *Shomer Emunim*[2] notes that the Torah commands us, "Give to him readily and have no regrets when you do so, for in return, Hashem, your God, will bless you in all your efforts and in all your undertakings. For there will never cease to be needy ones in your land, which is why I command you: you shall surely open your hand to the poor and needy kinsman in your land."[3] We have a mitzvah to "surely open" our hands to those who we believe to be poor and needy. If they have not acted with propriety, then they'll be answerable to Heaven. From our perspective, however, we have fulfilled the mitzvah of "surely open," and so you really never need to worry about having mistakenly given tzedakah to an undeserving recipient.

From the perspective of the recipient, however, it's actually quite scary. The Gemara teaches that one who takes charity without needing it will eventually be reduced to a point where they do in fact need the charity. I say it's scary because we think of the charity recipient as the tzedakah collector going door-to-door begging for alms. But that's not the only instance of people living off the charity of the community. Sadly, there are too many individuals who could and should be paying substantially more in the way of yeshiva day-school tuition fees, synagogue dues, and the like. It goes without saying that most people who ask for a break are decent, honest folks who sincerely cannot afford to pay the entire bill. But those who have the means to pay but ask for a discount just because they want a bargain, need to think about the charitable funds that need to be raised to cover the shortfall. If we have the wherewithal to pay what the good people of the financial committees have calculated to be the correct cost, then we should be paying the full amount.

And, of course, it goes without saying that the same is true of honestly completing and paying our taxes. The worst kind of *chillul Hashem* is when we hear in the news that someone who purports to be a frum

---

2 *Maamarei Hatzedakah.*

3 *Devarim* 15:10.

person is found to have cheated on his taxes on wrongly claimed government funding. That money doesn't grow on trees. It belongs to the people, and if someone submits a false claim by misstating his financial situation, the Gemara makes it clear that it doesn't portend well for the individual's future financial security, God forbid. Let's always strive to make a *kiddush Hashem* by being model citizens and members of society.

The good news is that everything in this world was created in equilibrium. If you appreciate that feigning poverty leads to poverty, then you'll love this next story:

> *In the early years of the Chassidic movement, there was a good deal of opposition from certain circles that felt that Chassidism was being too innovative in its approach to Judaism. They adopted all manner of stringency in mitzvos, along with extended prayer sessions. And, among other things, they were accused of feigning piety. "Look at these Chassidim," the Misnagdim [opponents] would say, "even the most unlettered, simplest of them davens for hours on end. Who do they think they are?"*
>
> *Rabbi Dov Ber, the Maggid of Mezritch, was the successor to the Baal Shem Tov, the founder of Chassidism. Exclaimed the Maggid, "Even if the accusations of the Misnagdim are true about many of my Chassidim, I am not concerned. For if the Gemara declares that one will not die without experiencing a negative practice that he has faked, then how much more so will a person not leave this world without experiencing a positive practice to which he has pretended to aspire! They might not yet be as pious as they demonstrate, but I know that one day, during their lifetimes, they will indeed be the Chassidim who they yearn to be!"*

Many people mistakenly believe that the feeling must come first, before they can observe the mitzvos. That's not Judaism's approach. The Talmud declares, "A person should always perform a mitzvah for the wrong reasons, because out of the wrong reasons will eventually come the right reasons." The *Sefer Hachinuch* explains that one's actions influence one's values.

It's not about faking it till you make it. It's about believing deep down that it's really the right thing to do. And by doing, you will train your value system to follow suit until it becomes a natural, comfortable part of who you are. May you forever train yourself to be the Jew you know you truly are!

DAF 69

Shivah Is Spiritually Intense

Rav Anan once sent the following letter to Rav Huna: "Huna, our friend, we wish you peace. When this woman bearing this letter comes before you, provide her one-tenth of her father's estate."

Rav Huna opens the letter and reads it in the presence of Rav Sheshes, his disciple. Rav Huna then says to him, "Go and give the following response to Rav Anan." Sensing that Rav Sheshes would be hesitant to relay the sharp language of the reply, Rav Huna then warns him, "And whoever does not say to him my exact words shall be excommunicated!"

"Here's what I want you to tell him," says Rav Huna, "Anan, Anan, should the one-tenth be provided from real estate or from movable property? And, incidentally, tell me who sits at the head in the house of a *marzeicha*?"

Off Rav Sheshes goes to see Rav Anan and he gently relays the message to him, "My Master is a teacher, but Rav Huna is the teacher of the teacher. Moreover, he readily excommunicates whoever does not convey his exact message. Thus, were it not for the fact that he would excommunicate me, I would not repeat his words: "Anan, Anan, should the one-tenth be provided from real estate or from movable property? And, incidentally, tell me who sits at the head in the house of a *marzeicha*?"

Rav Anan approaches Mar Ukva to consult with him about Rav Huna's reply. He says to him, "Let the Master see how Rav Huna sent me an offensive message, addressing me as Anan, Anan. And what's he talking about this business with a *marzeicha*? I've never heard of the word!"

"My dear friend, please tell me," Mar Ukva responds, "how did this matter unfold?"

Rav Anan replies, "Here's what happened," and Rav Anan proceeds to share the details with Mar Ukva.

Mar Ukva listens carefully and then says, "I hear you. But tell me, a man who does not even know what a *marzeicha* is has the audacity to write a letter to Rav Huna addressing him as Huna, our friend?"

מַאי מַרְזֵיחָא אֵבֶל דִּכְתִיב כֹּה אָמַר ה׳ אַל תָּבֹא בֵּית מַרְזֵחַ וְגוֹ׳ אָמַר רַבִּי אֲבָהוּ מִנַּיִן לְאָבֵל שֶׁמֵּיסֵב בָּרֹאשׁ שֶׁנֶּאֱמַר אֶבְחַר דַּרְכָּם וְאֵשֵׁב רֹאשׁ וְאֶשְׁכּוֹן כְּמֶלֶךְ בַּגְּדוּד כַּאֲשֶׁר אֲבֵלִים יְנַחֵם יְנַחֵם אֲחֵרִים מַשְׁמַע אָמַר רַב נַחְמָן בַּר יִצְחָק יְנֻחָם כְּתִיב מָר זוּטְרָא אָמַר מֵהָכָא וְסָר מִרְזַח סְרוּחִים מַר וָזָח נַעֲשָׂה שַׂר לִסְרוּחִי.

What is a marzeicha? A mourner, as it is written: "For so says the Lord: Enter not into the house of mourning [marze'iach]." Rabbi Avahu said: From where is it derived that a mourner sits at the head? As it is stated: "I chose out their way, and sat as chief, and dwelled as a king in the army, as one that would comfort [yenachem] the mourners." But the word yenachem implies comforting others [and not the mourner being comforted]! Rav Nachman bar Yitzchak said: Read it as if it were written "would be comforted [yinachem]." Mar Zutra said: Derive the custom from here: "And the revelry [mirzach] of those who stretched themselves shall pass away [sar]." [The word mirzach may be read as two words: Bitter [mar] and flustered [zach], and the word sar has a homonym that means ruler.] One who is bitter and flustered [i.e., the mourner], is made the ruler of those who sit [i.e., he sits at the head].

Let me tell you about my friend Moshe. He grew up in a traditional Israeli family. After the army, like many Israelis, he hopped on a plane and set off to see the world. Sadly, whatever Jewish observance that had not dissipated while he was in the army quickly vanished during his travels. He ended up meeting a very nice, but completely non-observant, Jewish girl in Canada, whom he married.

One day, he received the sad news that his father had passed on. Unfortunately, he couldn't make it to Israel in time for the funeral and so, he ended up sitting *shivah* at home in Canada. During the *shivah* period Moshe became a whole new person. The ritual gave him a weeklong period of introspection and, contemplating the temporary nature of life on this earth, spurred him on to recommit to keeping Shabbos and maintaining a kosher home.

Why does the mourner sit at the head? Because, at that moment, he is at the most intense moment of spiritual connection in this world. Mourning the loss of a loved one is like holding the loved one's hand as he crosses over from this world into the next. At that brink, one experiences the most powerful challenge. How do I continue alone without my dear one? Where do I go from here? What is the meaning of this immense change in my life? What is the meaning of our short time on Earth?

That's why we encounter vastly different reactions to the death of a loved one. Some people undergo a metamorphosis and conclude that life is incredibly short and temporary. At that intense moment, they decide to rededicate themselves to Heaven and pledge to redouble their efforts for Torah and mitzvos. That's what happened to my friend Moshe.

But that's not always the case. The loss of a loved one, especially if it was unexpected, can be extremely challenging. Many mourners will struggle with their faith on the brink.

Nevertheless, every mourner sits at the head. We hold him in the utmost esteem as he finds himself at that intense spiritual point, so close to Heaven. We don't judge, we simply sit in reverence and awe and try to share in his loss by providing consolation and simply being there during his time of need.

Nobody looks forward to tragedy in his life. We hope that life will be as pain-free as possible. But loss and mourning are a part of life. When a loved one passes away, you are the closest you can be on this Earth to Heaven. Your purpose in life is to take those moments and develop your soul, mightier and stronger. It's not an easy time for any mourner. But as difficult as it may be, our mission at that moment is to channel our faith and become closer to the Divine, carrying it through the ensuing days and years of our lives.

Why didn't Rav Anan know the meaning of the word *marzeicha* and why did Rav Huna use that particular word to test him? As the verses from the Prophets demonstrate, the word can mean a "mourner," but it is also related to the word for "revelry." The passing of the righteous from this world to the next is a bewildering period. On the one hand, we believe that our loved one is "in a better place." On the other hand, for those who remain here in this world, the loss is indescribable. How do we explain those two concomitant beliefs and feelings?

Only someone on the level of Rav Huna can reconcile that intense spiritual moment. Perhaps, his remark to Rav Anan meant to say: Before you start trying to figure out how much inheritance this woman is entitled to, a good rabbi and spiritual guide will feel her pain and help her transition through this overwhelming physical and spiritual ordeal. Once you've truly understood the dichotomy and confusion of the *marzeicha,* then we can discuss halachic matters as equals.

Shivah is an extreme moment of intense spirituality. When you find yourself on the brink, carry that moment into the rest of your life. And if you're visiting a mourner, seat him at the head and revere him for the deep spiritual experience that he is undergoing. May you maximize your short time on Earth and be sensitive and understanding to all!

DAF 70

Martyrdom of Fools

Avraham is in a quandary. Sarah doesn't like the influence that his older son, Yishmael, is having on their son, Yitzchak, and is insisting that it is time for Hagar and Yishmael to leave the patriarch's household. "Everything Sarah says to you, hearken unto her voice," the Almighty declares. And so, Avraham obediently sends Hagar and Yishmael off into the desert.

Can you imagine how painful that was for Avraham? To evict his own flesh and blood from his home? Undoubtedly, in his mind, any fatherly impact that he would have upon his child would cease at that moment. Who knew what would become of Yishmael? Indeed, whatever does become of Yishmael after such an agonizing moment in their lives?

The next time we encounter Yishmael in the Torah is at his father's funeral. The Torah tells us that he was buried by his two sons Yitzchak and Yishmael. Our Sages tell us that Yishmael did *teshuvah* later in life and therefore merited to be mentioned as he paid his final respects to his father.

What prompted his *teshuvah*?

> תְּנַן מִי שֶׁהָיָה מוּשְׁלָךְ בְּבוֹר וְאָמַר כָּל הַשּׁוֹמֵעַ קוֹלוֹ יִכְתּוֹב גֵּט לְאִשְׁתּוֹ הֲרֵי אֵלּוּ יִכְתְּבוּ וְיִתְּנוּ.
>
> *If a man was thrown into a pit and said that anyone who hears his voice should write a get [bill of divorce] for his wife, they should indeed write it and give it [to her].*

A fellow is trapped in a deep pit and thinks to himself, "I'm going to die down here, and nobody will know what happened to me. My poor wife will remain an *agunah*. Let me shout out to passersby. Perhaps, someone will hear my voice and accept my instructions to write a *get* for my wife. Our Sages permitted such a designation. However, the *Shulchan Aruch* adds, "Some say this law applies only when they saw the figure of a man or even a faint resemblance, otherwise we suspect it to be a *sheid* [demon]."[1]

Let's take a moment to think about this strange scenario. The fellow is trapped in a pit. Why doesn't he scream for help for someone to come and save him? Instead, he's so selfless that all he can think about it is, "How will this dire situation impact my wife?" And so, he responds by protecting her future by arranging a *get* for her. But is that really the best way to protect her? Of course not. If he would be saved, he would have far greater ability to care for her needs for years to come. In his mind, he has acted selflessly, thinking about others' needs before his own. But, by placing her needs before his own, ultimately, he's not helping either of them.

Sadly, many people selflessly put the needs of their loved ones before their own, acting almost like a martyr for the other person. They think that they're doing the right thing, but it's not always so straightforward. Sometimes, stepping back and letting go would be far more helpful to both of them.

Picture the following situation: Herschel is fifty years old. He still lives at home with his parents. Actually, he hasn't always lived with them. For a time, he had his own apartment, took care of himself, and rarely even called his parents. But Herschel has a gambling problem. Time and again, he has lost everything, getting deeper and deeper into debt and eventually declaring bankruptcy. Unable to cover his basic costs, ten years ago he moved back in with his parents. Initially, he was still working, but after a while, he got laid off and never got around to looking for a new job. He just had no motivation. With a roof over his

---

1 *Even Ha'ezer* 141:19.

head and three meals a day, a phone line, and internet connection, what more could he ask for in life? Meanwhile, Herschel's parents Yankel and Rivkah are in their late seventies and still going to work every day to ensure that they have enough money to take care of themselves and Herschel.

One day Herschel's aunt, Leah, has had enough of witnessing their upside-down life. "Why don't you kick him out already, Rivkah?" Leah asks her sister, wondering why Herschel does nothing all day.

"I would never do that," Rivkah replies, "he's my son!"

That was our patriarch Avraham's attitude toward Yishmael. He couldn't ever imagine evicting him. But that wasn't the only problem. Yishmael's waywardness was due, in part, to Avraham's extraordinary kindness.[2] Think about the following example: If a child asks a parent for a knife, how should he be responded to? The correct response is to refuse the knife to the child, of course. But, sometimes, misplaced kindness results in the parent saying yes, thinking that he wants to make the child happy. It would seem that Avraham, in his quest to please his child, said 'yes' far too often, leading to a child who was spoiled and undisciplined. It took the painful decision to send him away for Yishmael to mature and learn to create his own limits. And the more he matured and set his personal limits, the more he understood his purpose in this world. Until, by the end of Avraham's life, Yishmael had become a decent, moral human being.

Until Avraham let Yishmael go, they were really both suffering. They just didn't know it. However, once Avraham took that courageous step, as painful as it may have been, it was the first step toward Yishmael's growth and maturity. Avraham might have thought that he was helping Yishmael by selflessly giving and giving, but not only did it hurt Avraham and everyone else in the family, it wasn't helping Yishmael either.

The fellow in the pit, who selflessly offers a *get* to his wife, epitomizes this attitude of self-sacrifice to make the other person happy. But it's really just a martyrdom of fools. He believes that he's helping her, but

---

2 *Igeres Hakodesh* 2 (of the *Baal Hatanya*).

he's not really helping her; the best way to help his wife would be to figure out how to get out of the pit and return to his wife and children. Right now, he needs to put himself first. Doing so is ultimately the best solution not just for himself, but for everyone involved.

Rivkah wakes up each day and believes that she is acting selflessly by going out to work and supporting Herschel. But all she's really supporting is his habit—of uselessness. That's not doing him any favors. It's a martyrdom of fools. If she would force him to leave, he would be forced to get his life back on track.

You were placed on this earth to help others, but you always need to check and ask yourself whether you are indeed helping them or simply providing a crutch for them to avoid helping themselves. If you are suffering while the other person is living it up at your expense, you're not doing him or yourself any favors. Just like that man in the pit who was almost a "shadow" of his former self, sometimes a person can become so selfless that he forgets who he is.

It might be a child to whom you are giving money far beyond the parental duty years. It might be a friend who is dragging you down with his negative energy while you are constantly there to support him. It might be an employee or a colleague who is not pulling his weight—by constantly picking up the pieces and covering for his negligence, it might not be helping anyone.

Don't be a martyr of folly. Sometimes the best assistance you can give someone is to let go and watch with consternation as he figures out his issues. May you merit climbing out of the pit and watching others climb out of theirs!

DAF 71

Does the Husband's Minhag Override His Wife's?

The first couple of years of our marriage we spent Pesach with my parents in Sydney and my wife's parents in New York. After that, we moved to Edmonton, and as rabbi and rebbetzin, we were the ones making Pesach and conducting the Seder. One of the customs with which my wife had grown up was to pass the Seder plate over everyone's heads. I told her it was beautiful, but it wasn't our family *minhag*, to which she replied, "My father always did it. I think it's one of the highlights of the Yom Tov. If you're not going to do it, I'll do it myself." I wasn't going to argue with her. And so, for the next few years, that became the practice in our home.

But then, one day, I realized how immature I had acted.

> אָז הָיִיתִי בְעֵינָיו כְּמוֹצְאֵת שָׁלוֹם אָמַר רַבִּי יוֹחָנָן כְּכַלָּה שֶׁנִּמְצֵאת שְׁלֵמָה בְּבֵית חָמִיהָ וּרְדוּפָה לֵילֵךְ וּלְהַגִּיד שִׁבְחָהּ בְּבֵית אָבִיהָ וְהָיָה בַיּוֹם הַהוּא נְאֻם ה' תִּקְרְאִי אִישִׁי וְלֹא תִקְרְאִי לִי עוֹד בַּעְלִי אָמַר רַבִּי יוֹחָנָן כְּכַלָּה בְּבֵית חָמִיהָ וְלֹא כְּכַלָּה בְּבֵית אָבִיהָ.
>
> *"Then I was in his eyes as one that found peace," Rabbi Yochanan expounds: Like a bride who is considered perfect in her father-in-law's house and is eager to go and relate her praise in her father's house. "And it shall be on that day, says Hashem, that*

> *you will call Me "My Husband [ishi]," and you will no longer call Me "My Master [baali]." Rabbi Yochanan expounds: Like a bride in her father-in-law's house and not like a bride still in her father's house.*

There are two words for husband in Hebrew: *baal* and *ish*. The former connotes ownership, while the latter connotes partnership. When you get married, there's a sense of winning a prize. You own something that nobody else can have. But true love must transition from that feeling of acquisition to a feeling of partnership.

The initial phase of marriage is a period of transition. Suddenly, you have to live with another human being and adjust to all of his sentiments, behaviors, and quirks. What's more, not only do you have a new spouse, but you have to deal with a whole new family, as well, and all their sentiments, behaviors, and quirks. That can be a real challenge for some, who say to themselves, "Well, I married him, I didn't marry his family."

The Torah does not accept that response. We have a duty to respect our in-laws.[1] Respect for in-laws is a much more difficult mitzvah than respect for parents. You need to work on yourself to make it happen. The in-law relationship is unnatural. It's not unreasonable to want to resist embracing your spouse's quirky family. It's not what you're used to. But working your hardest to become part of the family and treating them as your own flesh and blood goes a very long way in becoming one with your spouse.

Sometimes, if your spouse has issues with his parents, it can be doubly challenging. You find yourself walking a fine line between supporting your spouse emotionally, while at the same time being extremely careful to treat your in-laws with the utmost honor. It's really not OK for your spouse to talk negatively about his parents, but it's certainly far worse if you were to weigh in. The truth is, irrespective of whatever issues your spouse might have with them, you are eternally indebted to

---

1 *Shulchan Aruch, Yoreh Deah* 240.

your in-laws. After all, they created this incredible individual whom you call your husband or wife!

One of the ways that we can honor our in-laws—and bring incredible joy to our spouse—is in the arena of family *minhag*. Why was I opposed to my wife's *minhag* of the Seder plate? Because it wasn't *my* family's *minhag*. And so, I felt justified telling her that it would not be *our* family *minhag*.

But then, one day, I had a huge awakening. Was the Seder plate ritual my father-in-law's *minhag*? Hardly. My *shver* is a dyed-in-the-wool Litvak. He hails from the royal Rabbinic families of Bialystok. Admittedly, over the years, he's adopted more and more Chassidic practices as his sons went in that direction. But a Sephardi Jew, he certainly is not. So why does he pass the Seder plate over the heads of all the participants?

Because that's what his Algerian wife wanted him to do. That's what her family did. And for her, that's an essential part of the Seder.

My error of judgment stemmed from a misunderstanding of the nature of family *minhag*. Anytime two people get married, unless they grew up next door to one another, they're bound to come into the marriage with different *minhagim*. And so, in order to preserve *shalom bayis,* at a certain point in history the Rabbis ruled that the newly married couple should adopt the *minhagim* of the husband's family.

But here's where I think many people stumble. When must we fall back on this Rabbinic enactment? When we have two *minhagim* that contradict one another. The simplest example is *nusach ha'tefillah*—the siddur formula that we utilize to daven from. When an Ashkenazi boy marries a Sephardi girl, they must choose which *nusach* to teach their children. It can't be both. It's one or the other. And so, our Rabbis ruled that we follow the *minhag* of the father.

Many *minhagim*, however, pose no potential for contradiction whatsoever. When my father-in-law adopted the practice of passing the Seder plate over everyone's heads, did it negatively impact any of his own customs? No, it didn't. It simply added. In such a case, there's no reason to cancel out the wife's *minhagim*. Combining each family's rituals only serves to enhance the new home. That's the ultimate meaning of *shalom bayis*. Once that realization dawned on me, it was a game-changer. Now,

I can't wait to see the smile on my wife's face as I jump up to fulfill the mitzvah of "pass-over!"

In our tradition, you don't just marry the person. You marry into a family. That means doing your very best to please not only your spouse, but also his parents. The goal is to reach a point where you can say with pride, "Then I was in his eyes as one that found peace." You want to make your spouse so happy that she runs back to her parents relating how elated that she feels about the home that you've created together.

That doesn't just mean introducing your spouse's family rituals. It means acting like a son or daughter to your in-laws. It means caring for them as their own child would. And sometimes, it even means filling in the gaps where your spouse might not be doing enough for his parents.

Call your mother-in-law regularly. Send her flowers for Shabbos. Ask your father-in-law about the family customs and rituals. Be the one who organizes their surprise wedding anniversary. No matter how your spouse feels about his parents, he will unconsciously begin to admire and love you more intensely than ever!

Marriage is about the coming together not just of two individuals; it is the coming together of two lives. Those lives include different experiences, backgrounds, and families. May you merit embracing your spouse's parents and siblings, becoming a regular, equal member of the family, and ultimately joining in true unity with your spouse!

DAF 72

Guarantee a Minyan at Your Shivah House

Story #1: After decades of barrenness, our forefather Avraham and Sarah had a baby boy, Yitzchak. He was immediately given a bris, but they decided to delay the grand celebration until the day he was weaned.[1] You can imagine who attended that event. This was no tent-in-the-wilderness affair. Dignitaries and VIPs, noblemen and women from across the known world were all there. After all, apart from the miracle of the occasion, Avraham and Sarah were well known amongst the royals of the day.

Who exactly was there? That, the Torah does not tell us.

Story #2: Iyov has experienced extraordinary success in his life. A beautiful family, a great career, a life dedicated to Torah, mitzvos, and community, who could ask for more? And then, one day, he loses it all. His wife and children die. He himself becomes very sick. He loses his fortune. He is sitting *shivah* for his family, and his friends come to visit him: "Eliphaz the Temanite, Bildad the Shuhite, and Tzophar the Naamathite, they gathered together to come to lament with him and console him."[2]

---

1 *Bereishis* 21:8.

2 *Iyov* 2:11.

Certainly, it was kind of them to pay their respects, but do we really need to know the precise identity of who signed the visitor registry at the *shivah* house?

> מַתְנִי׳ הַמַּדִּיר אֶת אִשְׁתּוֹ שֶׁלֹּא תֵּלֵךְ לְבֵית הָאֵבֶל אוֹ לְבֵית הַמִּשְׁתֶּה יוֹצִיא וְיִתֵּן כְּתוּבָּה מִפְּנֵי שֶׁנּוֹעֵל בְּפָנֶיהָ: גְּמָ׳ בִּשְׁלָמָא לְבֵית הַמִּשְׁתֶּה אִיכָּא נוֹעֵל בְּפָנֶיהָ אֶלָּא לְבֵית הָאֵבֶל מַאי נוֹעֵל בְּפָנֶיהָ אִיכָּא תָּנָא לְמָחָר הִיא מֵתָה וְאֵין כָּל בְּרִיָּה סוֹפְדָהּ וְאִיכָּא דְּאָמְרִי אֵין כָּל בְּרִיָּה סוֹפְנָהּ תַּנְיָא הָיָה רַבִּי מֵאִיר אוֹמֵר מַאי דִּכְתִיב טוֹב לָלֶכֶת אֶל בֵּית אֵבֶל מִלֶּכֶת אֶל בֵּית מִשְׁתֶּה בַּאֲשֶׁר הוּא סוֹף כָּל הָאָדָם וְהַחַי יִתֵּן אֶל לִבּוֹ מַאי וְהַחַי יִתֵּן אֶל לִבּוֹ דְּבָרִים שֶׁל מִיתָה דִּסְפַד יִסְפְּדוּנֵיהּ דִּקְבַר יִקְבְּרוּנֵיהּ דִּידַל יְדַלּוּנֵיהּ דְּלַוַּאי יְלַוּוּנֵיהּ דִּטְעַן יִטְעֲנוּנֵיהּ.
>
> **Mishnah:** *One who swears his wife from attending a shivah house or wedding celebrations must divorce her and give her the ketubah payment because he is inappropriately restricting her movement.*
>
> **Gemara:** *Granted, when he forbids her from going to a wedding, he may be accused of unreasonable restriction, but when he forbids her from going to a shivah house, what does the restriction concern? He taught: In the future she too will die, and no person will eulogize her [just as she did not do so for others]. And some say: No person will pay attention to her [due to her exclusion from the community]. It was taught: Rabbi Meir used to say: What is the meaning of that which is written: "It is better to go to a house of mourning than to go to a house of feasting, since that is the end of all men, and the living will take it to heart"? What will the living take to heart? Matters of death. When you eulogize others, others will eulogize you. When you bury others, others will bury you. When you weep for others, others will weep for you. When you escort others to the grave, others will escort you. When you bear the pall of others, others will bear your pall.*

While the names of Iyov's friends might no longer mean very much to us, Rabbeinu Bachya teaches that we are provided with the names for a reason.[3] True, many a nobleperson would have attended Avraham's party, but that's of little long-term consequence. Everyone likes a good party. However, parties don't change us. *Shivah* houses do. Walking into a house of mourning and contemplating our short time on Earth has the power to be transformational. That's why the names of Iyov's friends matter. Ultimately, their lives were impacted for eternity, in contrast with Avraham's guests who came and went. That's the literal meaning of "the living will take it to heart."

Our Gemara takes King Solomon's teaching in a slightly different direction. Why should you attend a *shivah* house? Because—inevitably—one day, that will be you. If you attend *shivah* houses, others will attend yours. You never have a problem getting a minyan at the *shivah* house of the individual who always attended everyone else's *shivah* during his lifetime.

Some people hold the mistaken belief that if they don't know the family so well, it would be an intrusion to visit their *shivah* house. Quite the contrary! Think about how touching it is for a family when an individual, whom they hardly know, takes time out of his day to stop by for a few minutes to pay his respects to their dearly departed loved one. That's a true fulfillment of the mitzvah of comforting the bereaved. You're not there because you have to be there, you're there purely to fulfill the mitzvah and bring comfort to others in their time of distress.

But then the Gemara expands on this idea and teaches us that every step of the way we must endeavor to go the extra mile for others. When we make the effort for others in need, they will be there for us when our time of need arrives. Let me tell you about a shul member whom I had many years ago:

"Nobody cares about me!" complained Rachel. "I've been ill and haven't been to shul for weeks now, and you're the only person to call me, Rabbi. Why doesn't anybody ever come and visit me? Why does nobody offer to help me?"

---

3 *Bereishis* 21:8.

I thought back to a conversation I had with Rachel a number of years prior. We needed volunteers to help out with our Chanukah carnival and so I gave her a call.

"I don't volunteer anymore," she replied.

"Why not?" I asked, quite surprised at her firm response.

"Well, some years back, I helped out with a community project, and I didn't get so much as a thank you from anybody for all my hard work. I decided right then and there that I was done giving to the community."

The Gemara emphasizes that as we treat others, so may we expect to be treated ourselves. If you want others to call and visit when you take ill, make sure you are visiting the sick today, while you are healthy. You want others to pay you a *shivah* visit when you lose a loved one? Make sure you're going to their *shivah* houses.

I once knew this fellow who became ill, and anytime people would ask him how he was doing, you could expect a ten-minute response detailing every ailment in his body. Nobody really wanted to hear all the minute details, but they listened. Not only did they listen, but he was never short of visitors and people bringing him food and taking him to the doctor. Why? Because when he was well, he was always there for others. He was an incredible community volunteer. He was always trying to help people personally. He might have been a little socially awkward, but everyone knew that his heart was in the right place. So, when his time of need came, everyone rushed to be there for him.

While you certainly should be helping others because it's the right thing to do, remember that what goes around comes around. One day, when you may need the assistance, others will be there for you. May you merit being that person that everyone can always count on, personally and communally!

DAF 73

How Many Spouses Do You Have?

When our patriarch Yaakov meets Lavan's daughters, Leah and Rachel, he knows instantly that Rachel is the one for him. Wary of the cunning of her father, however, Rachel devises a sign-language system to exchange with Yaakov under the chuppah to confirm it is indeed her. At the eleventh hour, however, she realizes that Lavan has no intention of giving her away that night. Concerned for her sister's public embarrassment, Rachel conveys the signs to Leah.

Sure enough, when Yaakov encounters Leah at the wedding ceremony, she responds successfully with the prearranged signs. The next morning, even though Yaakov is devastated to find that he was deceived by Lavan, he is nonetheless in awe of the extraordinary kindness of Rachel. Her selflessness only makes her even more desirable in his eyes and he insists on marrying both sisters.

But one day, sweet, kind, gracious Rachel reveals a whole other side of herself to Yaakov. Watching her sister give birth to one child after another, she corners her husband and cries at him to give her a child. Yaakov is shocked at her outburst and angrily responds, "Am I in place of God, Who has withheld the fruit of the womb from you?"

מַתְנִי׳ הַמְקַדֵּשׁ אֶת הָאִשָּׁה עַל מְנָת שֶׁאֵין עָלֶיהָ נְדָרִים וְנִמְצְאוּ עָלֶיהָ נְדָרִים אֵינָהּ מְקוּדֶּשֶׁת כְּנָסָהּ סְתָם וְנִמְצְאוּ עָלֶיהָ נְדָרִים תֵּצֵא שֶׁלֹּא בִּכְתוּבָּה: גְּמָ׳ אִיתְּמַר קִידְּשָׁהּ עַל תְּנַאי וּכְנָסָהּ סְתָם רַב אָמַר צְרִיכָה הֵימֶנּוּ גֵּט וּשְׁמוּאֵל

אָמַר אֵינָהּ צְרִיכָה הֵימֶנּוּ גֵּט אָמַר רַבָּה מַחְלוֹקֶת בְּטָעוּת אִשָּׁה אַחַת כְּעֵין שְׁתֵּי נָשִׁים.

Mishnah: *One who betroths a woman on condition that she has no vows of abstinence in effect, and subsequently discovered that she has such vows, she is not betrothed [i.e., the marriage is nullified]. If he married her without conditions and it was subsequently discovered that she had vows, she may be divorced without payment of her ketubah obligation [since he discovered a crucial issue about which he had not initially been informed].*

Gemara: *If he betrothed her on condition, but married her without conditions, Rav says she would require a get, and Shmuel says she does not require a get [i.e., the marriage is nullified]. Rabbah taught: They are debating a case where there was an error made with one woman who is [really] like two women.*

When a person gets married, he is entitled to know about any major baggage that his spouse is carrying. It would be grossly inappropriate to get married and hide the fact that you'd been in jail or that you had a terminal illness, God forbid. While these are extreme examples, the list of pertinent matters that should be discussed prior to getting married is extensive. One such issue, says the Mishnah, is that of vows of abstinence.

Let's say the wife can't stand the smell of meat and she's vowed not only to be vegetarian, but that there will be no meat whatsoever in her home. If she didn't inform her husband of this stipulation prior to the marriage, he would have every right to say he married her with an information deficiency. He would be entitled to end the marriage because he couldn't imagine Shabbos without *fleishig* cholent.

The Gemara then presents a scenario whereby, initially when they were betrothed, he knew that she had made certain vows. But then, based on their conversation, he assumed that she'd annulled them prior to the wedding day, only to find out that she still had vows in effect. The husband now wants out of the marriage. According to Rav, he must divorce her, because he knew about the vows to begin with. According to Shmuel, the marriage is annulled, because he was under the erroneous impression that the vows had been nullified.

Eventually, Rabbah explains that the case is a little more complicated than that. What actually happened was that he married a "woman who was really like two women." *Rashi* explains that she is like two women because he actually married her twice.

Here's what happened: The man initially betrothed his wife knowing that she had vows in effect. For whatever reason, they decided not to proceed and so they were divorced from their betrothal stage of marriage. They subsequently had a change of heart, and decided once again to get married. This time, they complete the wedding ceremony. At that point, he realizes that her vows are still in effect. Rav says that a *get* is required because he knew about her vows prior to the marriage. Shmuel, however, says that the marriage is null and void because he clearly had no intention of completing a marriage with a woman who had vows in effect.

While Rabbah's meaning of a "woman who was really like two women" is that the man married the same woman twice, the idea of a spouse who appears to be two separate characters will probably sound familiar to most. You get married to an individual based on certain personality traits that he exhibits. But before long, you start to wonder what happened. Your new spouse seems like a completely different person from the individual whom you thought you'd married.

While our Sages are critical of Yaakov's unsympathetic overreaction to Rachel's cry for help, we can all relate to it. Here he was thinking he'd married this sweet, kind, selfless soul who never thought about her own needs. After all, she was the heroine who made the ultimate sacrifice by sharing the signs with her sister! And so, her sudden outburst seemed so out of character to Yaakov. He was completely caught off guard, especially if she'd been bottling up her pain for so long. Who was this woman? She didn't seem to be the Rachel whom he had married!

But all of us, men and women, go through cycles: emotional cycles, physical, biological cycles, spiritual cycles. It's unreasonable to expect that your spouse will always be the incredibly sweet, pleasant, calm person whom you dated. Because chances are, once your spouse gets to know you, he'll be equally surprised to learn that you're not always as cool, calm, and collected as you were on every date.

Being married means being with the entire person, through the tranquil times and the challenging times. Sometimes, it might feel like you're married to two different people, but remember, you've been blessed with finding a partner who is multi-dimensional, not the same dull person day-in day-out.

As a loving spouse, you need to learn to ride the wave and recognize when your spouse needs you the most. When your spouse overreacts to something you say or do, don't argue back. When your spouse is experiencing a low moment or a tough day, don't disappear when he needs you more than ever. When your spouse is experiencing emotional highs and lows, think of it as a gift from Heaven designed to teach you to be more patient and understanding, to teach you empathy, and to teach you how to maintain your own balance and equilibrium in the face of stress and adversity.

You married your spouse to serve him in his entirety, through every facet of who he is. We all have highs and lows; a loving spouse is always there no matter what happens. May you grow to love every aspect and manifestation of your spouse's character and personality!

DAF 74

Spiritual Check-Up

A number of years ago, a colleague in a large shul told me about a new initiative that he had embarked upon to stay in touch with his many congregants. He called it the annual "spiritual check-up." Just like you go to see your doctor for an annual physical check-up, he encouraged his congregants to meet with him at least once a year for a spiritual check-up.

Those meetings provided the opportunity to touch base, particularly with those whom he would only see a couple of times a year on the High Holy days and at *simchahs*. All too often, a rabbi does not even hear when a congregant is unwell or has a family *simchah* or crisis. The spiritual check-up was an opportunity to receive timely updates on his congregants' lives. Thus, he was able to be with them in their times of joy and advise them in their times of need.

> תָּנוּ רַבָּנַן הָלְכָה אֵצֶל חָכָם וְהִתִּירָהּ מְקוּדֶּשֶׁת אֵצֶל רוֹפֵא וְרִיפֵּא אוֹתָהּ אֵינָהּ מְקוּדֶּשֶׁת מָה בֵּין חָכָם לְרוֹפֵא חָכָם עוֹקֵר אֶת הַנֶּדֶר מֵעִיקָּרוֹ וְרוֹפֵא אֵינוֹ מְרַפֵּא אֶלָּא מִכָּאן וּלְהַבָּא.
>
> **רש"י:** עוקר הנדר מעיקרו—שהרי פותח לה בחרטה אדעתא דהכי מי קא נדרת והיא אומרת לו לא וחכם אומר לה הרי הוא בא לך לידי כך הילכך לאו נדר הוא ומותר לך נמצא כמי שלא היה עליה בשעת קידושין.
>
> *The Rabbis taught: If she went to a sage who released her from her vows, they remain married. But if she went to a doctor who healed her, the marriage is still void. What is the difference*

between a sage and a doctor? The sage has the power to uproot the vow from its inception; the doctor can only cure the malady going forward.

Rashi: *For he [i.e., the sage] offers her an opening of remorse, saying, "Did you vow knowing this?" And she replies, "No." And the sage says, "It has brought you to this. Therefore, it is not a vow, and it is permissible to you." Consequently, it is as if she had no vows in effect at the time of the wedding.*

When two people get married, there's an assumption that they tell one another about any major issues with which they're personally dealing prior to the wedding. Otherwise, the agreement to marry would be somewhat fraudulent. The Mishnah teaches that if a man married a woman with the understanding that she had no pre-existing vows of abstinence and, subsequently, he discovered that she had made vows which remain in effect, the marriage is void, because it was based on misinformation. Similarly, if they were married with the understanding that she had no physical ailments and, subsequently, he discovered health issues of which she had not informed him, the marriage is void.

The Gemara then suggests that they could fix the issues by approaching a physical or spiritual "doctor." If the rabbi annulled the vows or the doctor healed the ailments, would the marriage still be considered null and void? Our Sages rule that the rabbi's annulment could save the marriage, but the doctor's healing would not. Because the doctor's ability to cure only has the power to remedy the ailment going forward. Thus, when they were married the ailment was present because the doctor can't backdate his cure. And so, if this was officially a marriage based on the understanding that there were no physical ailments, we can't change the fact that there were concealed issues at the time of the wedding, thus making it fraudulent and ineffective. Hence, it is null and void.

How about the rabbi's "cure"; why does that save the marriage? Says the Gemara: Because by annulling the vow, he cancels it retroactively, thereby removing it not only going forward, but causing it never to have existed to begin with. Thus, at the time of the wedding, there were effectively no outstanding vows in place. How does he do this? *Rashi* explains that he seeks an opening for the abstainer to express remorse at having uttered the vow, thereby uprooting it from the beginning. In this case, the rabbi would ask, "Had you known that the vow would negate your marriage, would you have made the pledge?" If the response is "no," then it is as if the vow was never made to begin with, because the actual vow was made on a false pretext. Consequently, at the time of the marriage, no vows were in force as the husband had assumed, and the marriage is validated and remains in effect.

The *Yitav Panim* teaches that *teshuvah* works the same way.[1] When a person repents for his misdeeds, not only does he remove them going forward, but he uproots them from the very beginning, causing them to never have existed! How does that work? Hashem is above time, he explains. When that individual sins, Hashem knows that he will eventually do *teshuvah*. That future moment of *teshuvah* is happening right now for Hashem Who is above time. Therefore, even at the time of the sin, it is as if it never happened!

When you sin, you blemish your soul. Just like a physical wound, a spiritual blemish is painful and dangerous, and you're going to want to cure it as quickly as possible. The way to cure a spiritual wound is through *teshuvah*. When you sincerely regret your misdeed, confess your iniquity to God, and promise never to do it again, you cure the blemish on your soul. In Judaism, you can generally achieve that healing on your own, but if you feel you need assistance, you can always ask a rabbi for advice on achieving spiritual healing.

Here's the incredible power of spiritual versus physical healing. When you go to see a doctor, all he can do is cure your malady going forward. He might not even be able to remove all evidence of the original wound—an operation might result in a lifelong scar, and medication might result in side-effects. In contrast, when you achieve spiritual healing, you can completely uproot the problem from its inception, such that it's as if it never happened! What's more, the Talmud tells

1 *Shabbos Shuvah.*

us that an incredibly potent *teshuvah* has the power to transform one's sins into merits! Not only do your spiritual blemishes heal, but they become adornments for your soul!

The power of *teshuvah* is unparalleled. When you turn over a new leaf, you completely eradicate the previous leaf that may have been a little rotten. Sometimes, you can do this by yourself; other times, you might need to seek spiritual advice. Just like you wouldn't hesitate to ask a doctor about your physical ailments, you should never be shy to discuss your spiritual ailments with your rabbi.

When was your last spiritual check-up? Even though it's true that Judaism requires no intermediary to whom to confess one's sins, it does help to have a close relationship with a rabbi who can advise you objectively on how to best accomplish your Divine mission. May you merit spiritual healing and transformation!

DAF 75

A Perfect Spouse

Prior to entering the land of Canaan, Yehoshua sent two spies from Shittim, saying, "Go, spy out the region of Jericho." So they set out, and they came to the house of an innkeeper named Rachav and lodged there. The king of Jericho was told, "Some men have come here tonight, Israelites, to spy out the country." The king of Jericho sent orders to Rachav: "Turn over the men who came to you and entered your house, for they have come to spy out the whole country." The woman, however, had taken the two men and hidden them. "It is true," she said, "the men did come to me, but I didn't know where they were from. And, at dark, when the gate was about to be closed, the men left; and I don't know where they went. Quick, go after them, for you can overtake them." Meanwhile, she took them up to the roof and hid them under some stalks of flax.

So the men pursued the spies in the direction of the Jordan down to the fords, and no sooner had the pursuers gone out than the gate was shut behind them. The spies had not yet gone to sleep when she came up to them on the roof. She said to the men, "I know that Hashem has given the country to you, because dread of you has fallen upon us, and all the inhabitants of the land are quaking before you. For we have heard how Hashem dried up the waters of the Red Sea for you when you left Egypt, and what you did to Sichon and Og, the two Amorite kings.

"Now, since I have shown loyalty to you, swear to me by Hashem that you, in turn, will show loyalty to my family. Provide me with a reliable sign that you will spare the lives of my father and mother, my brothers and sisters, and all who belong to them, and save us from death." The men answered her, "Our persons are pledged for yours, even to death! If you do not disclose this mission of ours, we will show you true loyalty when Hashem gives us the land. When we enter the country, tie this length of crimson string to the window as a sign to protect your home." She let them down by a rope through the window—for her dwelling was at the outer side of the city wall and she lived in the actual wall. She said to them, "Make for the hills, so that the pursuers may not come upon you. Stay there in hiding three days, until the pursuers return; then go on your way."[1]

אָמַר רֵישׁ לָקִישׁ טָב לְמֵיתַב טַן דּוּ מִלְּמֵיתַב אַרְמְלוּ אַבָּיֵי אָמַר דְּשׁוּמְשְׁמָנָא גַּבְרָא כּוּרְסְיַהּ בֵּי חָרָאתָא רָמֵי לַהּ רַב פַּפָּא אָמַר דְּנַפָּסָא גַּבְרָא תִּיקְרֵיֵהּ בְּסִיפֵּי בָבָא וְתֵיתִיב רַב אָשֵׁי אָמַר דְּקַלָּסָא גַּבְרָא לָא בָּעֲיָא טְלָפְחֵי לְקִידְרָא תָּנָא וְכוּלָּן מְזַנּוֹת וְתוֹלוֹת בְּבַעְלֵיהֶן .

Reish Lakish said: It is better to dwell together as two than to dwell [alone as if] a widow. Abaye said: One whose husband is small as an ant, [still does she] place her seat among the noblewomen. Rav Pappa said: One whose husband is a wool comber, calls him to sit with her at the entrance to the house. Rav Ashi said: Even one whose husband is "kalsa" does not require lentils for her pot. It was taught: All of these [women] stray and hang it on their husbands.

This is one of those pieces in the Gemara that clearly requires expounding. The various examples offered by the Rabbis suggest a deeper meaning than meets the eye.

We have five lessons here. The first teaching from Reish Lakish is that it's better to be married than single. While that may sound obvious to many, not everyone believes that axiom. Some people have been single for longer than they anticipated and the older they get, the pickier they are. They become entrenched in their own personality and lack

1 *Yehoshua* 2.

any desire to adjust their lives to make space for another individual. And then, there are those who have had unfortunate experiences in their relationships and assume that all marriages are awful. They see their happily married friends and presume it must be a façade and just a show. Just like they were able to fake it when they were married, pretending to the world around them that life was rosy, everyone else must be in the same boat. The only difference is that these other people must be lacking the courage to walk away.

Reish Lakish teaches that it's not so. Most people who are married actually enjoy being with their spouse most (if not all!) of the time. Marriage might require work, but a couple where each spouse is committed to serving each other will have a wonderful life together. And as true as that might be right now, it only accelerates with age. Who wants to be alone at any point in his life, let alone in his senior years? Whether you are single today because you've decided you think life is easier without accommodating another individual with all his quirks and idiosyncrasies or you've been burned by a bad relationship in the past, Reish Lakish is asking you to reconsider. *It is better to dwell together as two than to dwell as a widow.*

The second lesson comes from Abaye who says that it's OK if your husband is an "ant." Not only is it OK, but having a husband who is an "ant" will seat you alongside nobility. *Rashi* explains that the meaning is that one's spouse is a regular, non-famous, everyday person. If this concern existed in Talmudic times, it is certainly a worry in the twenty-first century. We live in a world where status is measured by the number of social media followers that one has. Fame is equated with success and greatness. To a certain extent, human nature has always been that way, but social media has exacerbated the issue. Abaye comes along and teaches that fame might help you in some areas of your life, but it won't make you a good spouse. The mark of a good spouse is humility. Look for someone who is not constantly trying to outsize everyone else, and you'll have a life of bliss that surpasses even the nobles!

The next lesson is from Rav Pappa who offers that a good spouse is a wool comber. What does a wool comber do? He painstakingly filters out the short fibers from the wool in preparation for the yarn's spinning and the creation of the garment. According to Kabbalah, all good in this world is enmeshed with *kelipos* that must be removed in order to elevate the sparks of goodness. *Kelipah* literally means a shell or a peel—the analogy is one of an orange peel or egg shell, which must be removed in order to reach the goodness beneath. That's what the wool comber is doing, removing the bad fibers in order to refine the good fibers. (Incidentally, we should point out that on Shabbos we're not permitted to remove the bad from the good, because it's an act of "creation"—that's what we were placed in this world to do.) Rav Pappa reminds us that most people look for the easy path in life. Life is about pleasure maximization. But the ideal spouse is the person who is willing to "roll up his sleeves" and work to make this world a better place. That's the person who will "sit with" you "at the entrance to the house." He'll be an equal partner in all the household and family duties and never shirk responsibility. He puts family first and himself second.

Next, we have Rav Ashi who says that a wife whose husband is *kalsa* does not require lentils for her pot. Many of the commentaries translate the word *kalsa* as "shame." However, based on Rav Ashi's reference to the lentils, the *Aruch* relates the word to the Mishnah that discusses the *kalsei ha'keruv*—the section of the vegetables that protect them as they grow.[2] The *Yachin* translates the word as "helmet." All too often, we are impressed by people who are exciting and adventurous. Such people might make for wonderful friends and good company. However, when it comes to choosing a spouse, yes, we must find him fun and exciting to be with, but we must also prioritize the traits of safety, security, and protection. A good spouse is adventurous, but at the same time, measured and considered. The reference to the lentils might be a play on words connecting the two types of vegetables. Lentils are traditionally foods of mourning, symbolizing the circle of life. Rav Ashi appears to be saying that when our spouse is sufficiently protective of the family, he will avoid tragic situations.

The Gemara concludes that these women "stray and hang [depend] it on their husbands." While this teaching is difficult to comprehend, let

2 *Uktzin* 1:4.

us suggest two explanations. The first is that when we choose a good spouse per the descriptions of our Sages, we might make mistakes in life, but that spouse will always be there to depend on. He is forgiving and understanding. While the Gemara uses an extreme term for this idea of straying, it could possibly be a figure of speech to suggest acting erroneously.

The second explanation is related to sustenance. In the story of the spies that Yehoshua sent to Canaan, they stay at the home of a certain "*zonah*." The *Radak* explains that the word has two meanings. Sometimes, it refers to a woman of ill-repute, and other times it means an inn-keeper, and derives from the root word for sustenance (that we employ in the first berachah of *bentching* or *Birkas "Hamazon"*). He suggests that the connection between the two meanings is that both cases imply a person who is available and open to all customers. Perhaps, we could recalibrate that idea and suggest that the double entendre means that she provides sustenance for all. In other words, the root word always implies sustenance.

With that meaning in mind, perhaps we could suggest that the Gemara is the classic adage, "Behind every great man is a great woman." This statement is a little outdated, and nowadays it cuts both ways. Any successful happily married couple will tell you that it's just as true the other way around. Either way, the important principle here is that a good spouse sustains his spouse and gives him all the credit. That might mean supporting the spouse while he's building his career or engaged in full-time *kollel* or academic pursuits or running a political campaign. And, sometimes, it simply means giving a spouse the emotional support and confidence to achieve his dreams.

My wife and I *were* married over twenty years ago. But that's in the past. Today we *are* married. That's a present-tense verb, implying something we must do each and every day. What are the keys to a great marriage? Look for a spouse *and always* strive to be a spouse who is humble, purpose-driven, and measured. Above all, a good spouse endeavors to bring out the very best in his better half without seeking personal accolades. May you forever strive to *be* married!

DAF 76

The Key to Life Is Investment

Obeying the word of his mother, our patriarch Yaakov has just usurped the family blessings from his brother, Eisav. Fearing for the life of her younger son, Rivkah sends him to find a wife in her birthplace of Aram. Despite the urgency of the journey, Yaakov does not depart empty-handed. Yitzchak and Rivkah prepare camel-loads of gifts for Yaakov to take to the family.

Those goods, however, are not destined to make their way to Aram. No sooner has Yaakov hit the road than Eisav's son, Eliphaz, catches up with him in hot pursuit, under strict instructions from his father not to return until he has murdered his uncle, Yaakov. Eliphaz reaches his uncle but cannot bring himself to kill his own flesh and blood.

"What shall I do?" asks Eliphaz, "If I return without having fulfilled my father's bidding, he may very well kill me!"

"Here's what I suggest," Yaakov replies, "take all of my possessions away from me. I shall then be destitute, and one who is poverty-stricken is considered as good as dead. That way, you will be able to tell my brother that you have 'killed' me!"

Eliphaz heeds the words of his uncle, leaving Yaakov penniless as he continues his sojourn toward Aram.

מַחַט שֶׁנִּמְצֵאת בְּעוֹבִי בֵּית הַכּוֹסוֹת מִצַּד אֶחָד כְּשֵׁרָה מִשְּׁנֵי צְדָדִין טְרֵיפָה נִמְצָא עָלֶיהָ קוֹרֶט דָּם בְּיָדוּעַ שֶׁהוּא לִפְנֵי שְׁחִיטָה לֹא נִמְצָא עָלֶיהָ קוֹרֶט דָּם בְּיָדוּעַ שֶׁהוּא לְאַחַר שְׁחִיטָה הוּגְלַד פִּי הַמַּכָּה בְּיָדוּעַ שֶׁשְּׁלֹשָׁה יָמִים קוֹדֶם

> שְׁחִיטָה לֹא הוּגְלַד פִּי הַמַּכָּה הַמּוֹצִיא מֵחֲבֵירוֹ עָלָיו הָרְאָיָה וְאִי יְהַיב טַבָּח דְּמֵי בָּעֵי לְאֵיתוּיֵי רְאָיָה וּמַפֵּיק וְאִי דְּלָא יְהַיב טַבָּח דָּמֵי בַּעַל בְּהֵמָה בָּעֵי לְאֵיתוּיֵי רְאָיָה וּמַפֵּיק וְאַמַּאי סְפֵיקָא בִּרְשׁוּת טַבָּח אִיתְיְילִיד דִּיהַיב טַבָּח דְּמֵי וּמַאי פַּסְקָא סְתָמָא דְּמִילְתָא כַּמָּה דְּלָא יָהֵיב אִינִישׁ זוּזֵי לָא יָהֵיב אִינִישׁ חיותָא .
>
> *If a needle that is found in the thick wall of a slaughtered animal's second stomach has pierced the stomach from only one side, the animal is kosher. If the stomach is pierced from both sides, it is treif. If a drop of congealed blood is found on top of the needle, it is certain that the perforation was created before the slaughtering of the animal [and it is, therefore, treif]. If no drop of blood is found on it, it is certain that it occurred after the slaughtering. If a scab appeared over the wound, it is clear that the puncture happened three days before the slaughtering. If a scab did not appear over the wound, the burden of proof rests upon the claimant. And therefore, if the butcher had already given the money, he needs to bring proof in order to reclaim his money. If the butcher had not already given the money, the owner of the animal must bring proof, and only then can he take his money. But why? The uncertainty was formed in the butcher's possession! Because the butcher had already given the money. But why is that so clear-cut? Because, generally speaking, so long as a person has not yet given the money, a person will not grant the animal [chayusa].*

Following the *shechting* of an animal, the *shochet* must inspect the animal's internal organs for any injuries or blemishes. In order for an animal to be kosher, it is not sufficient that it was properly *shechted*, but it must also have been a healthy, viable animal. If it was sick and fated to die within a year, it is not kosher, despite the *shechitah*.

If you've ever wondered why you couldn't find that needle in the haystack, any *shochet* will know from halachah that it was swallowed by the cow! The Gemara states that if the needle was found lodged in one side of the stomach it would not render the animal *treif*. (While we colloquially use the word "*treif*" to refer to any non-kosher food item, strictly speaking this is the technically correct usage. It refers to an animal that was *shechted* properly, but afterwards found to be non-viable.) The needle in the stomach wall might be uncomfortable, but it would not be life-threatening. If, however, the needle has caused a puncture all the way through the wall of the stomach, the animal is *treif*.

What do we do when a butcher purchases an animal and then, a few days later, he *shechts* it only to find that the animal is *treif*? He would like a refund for having purchased a faulty product. But, for his part, the cattle breeder is claiming that it's been a couple of days and the damage could very well have taken place after the sale. At the time of the sale, the animal was completely healthy, he contends.

The Gemara answers with the classic Talmudic principle that whoever is holding the money has the upper hand. If the other party is attempting to extract the money from him, the burden of proof is on the claimant. And so, if the butcher had not yet paid, the original owner would have to provide proof in order to claim the money owed to him. The Gemara then counters with the principle of "doubt." When did the doubt as to the animal's viability arise? In the domain of the butcher when he cut open the animal to inspect it. At the time of the animal's transfer, there was no doubt. Therefore, he should still be liable to pay the breeder. The Gemara answers that the butcher here has already paid the money, thus giving the breeder the upper hand. How do we know that the money has already been paid? Because that's how the marketplace works. You don't receive the merchandise until you pay.

The Gemara uses an interesting phraseology for this idea: "So long as a person has not yet given the money, a person will not grant the *chayusa*." Giving the money results in getting the *chayusa*. *Chayusa* means animal, but it comes from the word for life. If you want to get the *chayusa*—the life and energy—you need to give the money, you need to be prepared to make the investment.

There's a peculiar connection between life and money. The word *damim* has two meanings, translating both as "money" and "bloods." Explaining the relationship, Rabbi Chaim ben Betzalel, the brother of the *Maharal*, writes that "just like blood is the life-force, similarly a person lives by money, and one who is poverty-stricken is considered as dead."[1]

Often in life, the key to becoming excited and alive about something is investment. The more we invest, the more we become passionate about it. That's the basis of the *korbanos*, the Holy Temple sacrifices. God doesn't need our animals, He doesn't eat! The word *korban* actually translates as "gift," and the original meaning of "sacrifice" was a "sacred gift." It's only in recent centuries that the word in English became associated with the idea of an exchange, for obvious non-Jewish reasons. Truthfully, the meaning is a gift for Hashem. While He, of course, does not require our gifts, He instructed us to invest in our spiritual service, thereby deepening our commitment to Him.

Many people wonder why they're not excited and passionate about their Judaism. It's because they have not invested the time, money, and effort. You want *chayusa*—life and energy—in your Judaism? You need to invest in it. You want to be excited about learning Torah? It doesn't come naturally. It takes an investment of time and effort into figuring it all out. And it takes serious investment in our children's Jewish education. You want to enjoy davening? It takes an investment of time and effort into understanding what you're saying and staying focused on your relationship with Heaven.

Adoption of a child is probably the greatest example of an investment that produces a tangible relationship. This has real halachic consequences. Generally, it is forbidden to be alone with someone who is not your parent, spouse, or child. Likewise, hugging and kissing are prohibited. But what about adopted children?

Rabbi Moshe Feinstein was asked the question, and ruled that being alone with and hugging and kissing an adopted child is permissible.[2] Explained Rav Moshe: When a child is adopted at a young age, one develops a true parent-child relationship, and the assumption is that a parent would never act inappropriately with his child. Just like a biological parent is permitted to be alone with his child, so too, an adopted

---

1 *Igeres Hatiyul, chelek ha'remez dalet.*

2 *Igros Moshe, Even Ha'ezer* 4:64.

parent may generally be alone with his child.[3] Adoptive parents become just like biological parents because they've invested time, money, and effort into their children, developing a natural relationship with them.

Of course, the greatest example of a non-biological relationship that has the potential to become natural is marriage. A person's spouse is not related to him by birth and, yet, they can love each other. How does that happen? When they invest in one another. The more a person gives to another, the more *chayusa* he has for that individual. Judaism doesn't believe in love at first sight. There might be lust at first sight. But love takes investment. Time. Money. Effort. Emotional investment. And slowly but surely the love is developed. And husband and wife become one "life."

You want life, passion, energy? You need to invest. Whether it's your familial relationships or your relationship with your Father in Heaven, the more time, money, and effort that you invest into the relationship, the greater the jubilation and oneness you will feel. May you develop *chayusa* in your physical and spiritual life!

---

3 See also *Tzitz Eliezer* 6:40, 7:44.

DAF 77

Chariot of Fire

When Rabbi Yehoshua ben Levi reached his allotted time on Earth, they said to the Angel of Death, "Go and see how he wishes to be escorted." The Angel of Death went and appeared to him. Rabbi Yehoshua ben Levi said to him, "Show me my place in Heaven."

"Very well," replied the angel.

Rabbi Yehoshua then said to him, "Give me your knife of death, lest you frighten me along the way," which he did. Upon their arrival, he lifted Rabbi Yehoshua above the gate and showed him his final resting place. But, before the angel could stop him, Rabbi Yehoshua had jumped over to the other side. The angel, however, managed to grab him by the corner of his cloak.

Rabbi Yehoshua ben Levi declared, "I swear that I will not come back with you." The angel didn't know what to do, and turned to God for assistance.

The Holy One, blessed be He, said, "If he ever in his life requested to annul an oath, he must return to this world with the Angel of Death, as he can have his oath dissolved this time also. But if he has never requested annulment, he need not return." Since Rabbi Yehoshua had, in fact, never requested dissolution of an oath, he was allowed to stay in Heaven.

The Angel of Death said to him, "At least give me my knife back," but Rabbi Yehoshua refused, as he did not want any more people to die.

A Divine voice emerged and said, "Give it to him, as it is necessary to kill the created beings. Death is the way of the world."

Suddenly, Eliyahu HaNavi took Rabbi Yehoshua by the hand and began to lead him through Heaven, announcing, "Make way for the son of Levi, make way for the son of Levi!" Rabbi Yehoshua ben Levi then encountered Rabbi Shimon ben Yochai sitting on thirteen golden thrones.

Rabbi Shimon asked him, "Are you the son of Levi?"

"Yes, I am," Rabbi Yehoshua replied.

Rabbi Shimon inquired, "Did a rainbow ever appear during your lifetime?"

"Yes, it did," Rabbi Yehoshua replied.

"If that's the case," Rabbi Shimon responded, "you are not the son of Levi." For everyone knows that a rainbow is a sign of Hashem's forbearance. He might wish to destroy humankind due to their iniquities, but He reminds Himself of His promise to Noach never to destroy the world again. The complete *tzaddik* shoulders the burden of his generation and is constantly praying to dispel their sins. Therefore, there is no need for a rainbow during his lifetime, as there are no sins prompting God to consider a restart. Nevertheless, the truth is that no rainbow was indeed seen during Rabbi Yehoshua's lifetime. But his utter humility would not allow him to take any credit for such an extraordinary happening.

Very few individuals in history have entered Heaven alive. Most famous, of course, was Eliyahu HaNavi who ascended to Heaven in a chariot of fire. Thus, it comes as no surprise that he was the one who greeted Rabbi Yehoshua and accompanied him in the supernal world. We are familiar with the miracles that Eliyahu performed during his life on Earth. But what accounted for Rabbi Yehoshua ben Levi's incredible merit to enter Heaven alive?

תַּנְיָא הִקִּיז דָּם וְשִׁימֵּשׁ הָוְיָין לוֹ בָּנִים וִיתִיקִין הִקִּיזוּ שְׁנֵיהֶם וְשִׁימְּשׁוּ הָוְיָין לוֹ בָּנִים בַּעֲלֵי רָאתָן אָמַר רַב פָּפָּא לָא אֲמַרַן אֶלָּא דְּלָא טָעֵים מִידֵּי אֲבָל טָעֵים מִידֵּי לֵית לַן בַּהּ מַאי סִימָנֵיהּ דָּלְפָן עֵינֵיהּ וְדָיְיבִי נְחִירֵיהּ וְאָתְיָא לֵיהּ רִירָא מִפּוּמֵּיהּ וּרְמוּ דִּידְבֵי עִילָּוֵיהּ מַכְרִיז רַבִּי יוֹחָנָן הִזָּהֲרוּ מִזְּבוּבֵי [שֶׁל] בַּעֲלֵי רָאתָן רַבִּי זֵירָא לָא הֲוָה יָתֵיב בְּזִיקֵיהּ רַבִּי אֶלְעָזָר לָא עָיֵיל בְּאַהְלֵיהּ רַבִּי אַמֵּי וְרַבִּי אַסִּי לָא הֲווּ אָכְלִי מִבֵּיעֵי דְּהָהִיא מְבוֹאָה רַבִּי יְהוֹשֻׁעַ בֶּן לֵוִי מִיכְרָךְ בְּהוּ

וְעָסֵיק בַּתּוֹרָה אָמַר אַיֶּלֶת אֲהָבִים וְיַעֲלַת חֵן אִם חֵן מַעֲלָה עַל לוֹמְדֶיהָ אַגּוֹנֵי לָא מַגְנָא כִּי הֲוָה שָׁכֵיב אֲמַרוּ לֵיהּ לְמַלְאַךְ הַמָּוֶת זִיל עֲבֵיד לֵיהּ רְעוּתֵיהּ אֲזַל אִיתְחֲזֵי לֵיהּ אֲמַר לֵיהּ אַחְוִי לִי דּוּכְתַּאי אֲמַר לֵיהּ לְחַיֵּי אֲמַר לֵיהּ הַב לִי סַכִּינָךְ דִּלְמָא מְבַעֲתַתְּ לִי בְּאוֹרְחָא יַהֲבַהּ נִיהֲלֵיהּ כִּי מְטָא לְהָתָם דַּלְיַיהּ קָא מַחְוֵי לֵיהּ שְׁוַר נְפַל לְהָהוּא גִּיסָא נַקְטֵיהּ בְּקַרְנָא דִגְלִימֵיהּ אֲמַר לֵיהּ בִּשְׁבוּעֲתָא דְּלָא אָתֵינָא אֲמַר קוּדְשָׁא בְּרִיךְ הוּא אִי אִיתְּשִׁיל אַשְּׁבוּעֲתָא נֶיהְדַּר אִי לָא לָא נֶיהְדַּר אֲמַר לֵיהּ הַב לִי סַכִּינַאי לָא הֲוָה קָא יָהֵיב לֵיהּ נְפַקָא בַּת קָלָא וַאֲמַרָה לֵיהּ הַב נִיהֲלֵיהּ דְּמִיתַּבְעָא לִבְרִיָּיתָא מַכְרִיז אֵלִיָּהוּ קַמֵּיהּ פַּנּוּ מָקוֹם לְבַר לֵיוַאי פַּנּוּ מָקוֹם לְבַר לֵיוַאי אֲזַל אַשְׁכְּחֵיהּ לְרַבִּי שִׁמְעוֹן בֶּן יוֹחַאי דַּהֲוָה יָתֵיב עַל תְּלָת עֲשַׂר תַּכְטָקֵי פִּיזָּא אֲמַר לֵיהּ אַתְּ הוּא בַּר לֵיוַאי אֲמַר לֵיהּ הֵן נִרְאֲתָה קֶשֶׁת בְּיָמֶיךָ אֲמַר לֵיהּ הֵן אִם כֵּן אִי אַתָּה בַּר לֵיוַאי וְלָא הִיא דְּלָא הֲוַאי מִידֵּי אֶלָּא סָבַר לָא אַחְזֵיק טֵיבוּתָא לְנַפְשַׁאי רַבִּי חֲנִינָא בַּר פָּפָּא שׁוֹשְׁבִינֵיהּ הֲוָה כִּי הֲוָה קָא נָיְחָא נַפְשֵׁיהּ אֲמַרוּ לֵיהּ לְמַלְאַךְ הַמָּוֶת זִיל עֲבֵיד לֵיהּ רְעוּתֵיהּ אֲזַל לְגַבֵּיהּ וְאִיתְחֲזֵי לֵיהּ אֲמַר לֵיהּ שְׁבַקִי תְּלָתִין יוֹם עַד דְּנַהְדַּר תַּלְמוּדַאי דְּאָמְרִי אַשְׁרֵי מִי שֶׁבָּא לְכָאן וְתַלְמוּדוֹ בְּיָדוֹ שַׁבְקֵיהּ לְבָתַר תְּלָתִין יוֹמִין אֲזַל אִיתְחֲזֵי לֵיהּ אֲמַר לֵיהּ אַחְוִי לִי דּוּכְתַּאי אֲמַר לֵיהּ לְחַיֵּי אֲמַר לֵיהּ הַב לִי סַכִּינָךְ דִּלְמָא מְבַעֲתַתְּ לִי בְּאוֹרְחָא אֲמַר לֵיהּ כְּחַבְרָךְ בָּעֵית לְמִיעְבַּד לִי אֲמַר לֵיהּ אַיְיתִי סֵפֶר תּוֹרָה וַחֲזֵי מִי אִיכָּא מִידֵּי דִּכְתִיב בֵּיהּ דְּלָא קַיֵּימְתֵּיהּ אֲמַר לֵיהּ מִי אִיכָּרַכְתְּ בְּבַעֲלֵי רָאתָן וְאִיעֲסַקְתְּ בַּתּוֹרָה.

One who let blood and immediately afterward engaged in marital relations will have weak children. If both of them let blood and then engaged in marital relations, they will have children afflicted with raasan. Rav Pappa said: We said this only if he did not taste anything in between, but if he tasted something we have no issue with it. What are the symptoms of raasan? His eyes water, his nose runs, drool comes out of his mouth, and flies rest upon him. Rabbi Yochanan would announce: Be careful of the flies found on those afflicted with raasan. Rabbi Zeira would not sit in a spot where the wind blew from the direction of someone afflicted with raasan. Rabbi Elazar would not enter the tent of one afflicted with raasan, and Rabbi Ami and Rabbi Asi would not eat eggs from a street on which someone afflicted with raasan lived. Rabbi Yehoshua ben Levi, however, would learn Torah with them, saying: "The Torah is a loving deer and a graceful doe." If it bestows grace on those who learn it, does it not protect them from illness? Rabbi Chanina bar Pappa was a friend of the Angel of Death and would see him frequently. When Rabbi Chanina was on the verge of dying, they said to the Angel of Death: Go and perform his bidding. He went before him and appeared to him. He said to the angel: Leave me for thirty days until I have reviewed my studies, for they say: Happy is he who comes here, to Heaven, with his learning in his hand. He left him, and after thirty days, he again went and appeared to him. He said to the Angel of Death: Show me my place in Heaven. He said to him: Very well. Rabbi Chanina said to him: Give me your knife, lest you frighten me on the way. The Angel of Death said to him: Do you wish to do to me as your friend [Rabbi Yehoshua did and escape]? He said to him: Bring a Torah scroll and see: Is there anything written in it that I have not fulfilled? He said to him: But did you attach yourself to those afflicted with raasan and study Torah, as he did?

In ancient times, it was popular to let blood from time to time. Thank God, we have come a long way: nowadays we understand the value of blood, which the Torah calls "life" itself. The only time we voluntarily release blood is in order to share it with other human beings so we can grant them life. Nevertheless, bloodletting in those days was thought to be important to maintain proper bodily health.

When a person engages in bloodletting—serving his bodily needs—and then immediately proceeds with marital relations, the *Beraisa* warns us that it is dangerous. Intimate relations may be the holiest act or the coarsest behavior. If one's entire intention is the fulfillment of the desires of the flesh—from bloodletting to relations—that will have negative consequences.

Nonetheless, Rav Pappa informs us that doing a mitzvah, as simple as eating in between, will resolve the matter. Why? Eating connects the physical world with the spiritual. When a person eats, the food is transformed into energy that enables him to serve Heaven. One has thus elevated the food from the physical realm to the spiritual realm. And so, at that moment, he's managed to switch gears from serving the flesh to living a Godly existence, and the marital relations will be energized from a pure source.

Engaging in relations purely to serve physical desires, says the Gemara, portends disastrous results for the children who are produced, as they are beginning their lives, their very conception, on the wrong foot. One of the symptoms of *raasan* is flies hovering around. The *Chida* teaches that flies symbolize the *yetzer hara*, our internal tempter.[1] One is afflicted with *raasan* when he only sees (*ro'eh* in Hebrew) temporary pleasures and ignores long-term spiritual concerns.

Rabbi Yaakov Emden writes that most of the rabbis would stay far away from such people for fear that the people's negative spiritual energy might rub off on them.[2] The one exception was Rabbi Yehoshua ben Levi, who maintained that the merit of Torah would protect him. The *L'horos Nossan* explains that a person who is completely devoted to spirituality is unaffected by the impurities of this world.[3] Rabbi Yehoshua's complete divestment from the pleasures of this world made him entirely spiritual, thus enabling him to enter Heaven in his body.

Just like Rav Pappa's example of the mitzvah of eating, our purpose in this world is to fuse the physical with the spiritual. Some people will get caught in the net of physicality and spend a lifetime in pursuit of the desires of the flesh. Others will shun the physical world and create a sanctuary, a sacred space, to devote themselves to spirituality and avoid the world around them. The ultimate Jew goes out into the world, draws down spirituality into the mundane, and elevates the physical.

That was Rabbi Yehoshua. He was not afraid to go out and meet his brothers and sisters who were far removed from spirituality. Because for him, there were no barriers between the physical and spiritual realms. That's the meaning of entering Heaven in a body. When you've elevated your body to such an extent that you've fused the physical and

---

1 *Pesach Einayim.*

2 *Yaavetz, Avodah Zarah* 15b.

3 Intro, part 6.

spiritual worlds, your entire being can enter Heaven. Just like Eliyahu, who dedicated his life to going out into the world and attempting to win back the hearts and minds of his wayward brethren, Rabbi Yehoshua was not afraid to face the world and infuse it with spirituality.

Rav Dessler teaches that the reason for the Angel of Death's inability to overpower Rabbi Yehoshua ben Levi was that in his capacity as the Satan, he had tried numerous times throughout Rabbi Yehoshua's life to entice him to sin.[4] Every time, Rabbi Yehoshua was victorious. When we overcome the Satan's efforts, says Rav Dessler, it's a win-win. As an agent of Heaven, he would also like to see us succeed and pass the tests and trials that he sends our way. The more tests that we pass, the more he is able to challenge us. Consequently, he maintained a debt of gratitude to Rabbi Yehoshua for keeping him in business and allowing him to fulfill his Divine mission!

Once in Heaven, who does Rabbi Yehoshua meet? Rabbi Shimon bar Yochai, the rabbi who spent thirteen years secluded in a cave learning Torah, represented by thirteen golden thrones upon which he sat in Heaven. Originally Rabbi Shimon had only planned to spend twelve years in the cave, but upon his first attempt at re-entry into society he could not relate to regular human beings. He found them too worldly. And so, he returned to the cave for a thirteenth year where he worked on accepting and internalizing the Torah's concept that the Torah was not given to angels, but was meant to be fulfilled here in this world.

Nevertheless, in contrast with many of his colleagues, he still felt that one should be entirely occupied with Torah and not be engaged with earthly pursuits.[5] As far as Rabbi Shimon understood, one could not be a perfect *tzaddik* while out there in the world dealing with materiality and sinful people. "There's no way you could have acted like that and avoided the appearance of the rainbow," was what he was effectively telling Rabbi Yehoshua. Although one can afford to be confrontational in the "ivory tower" of the four walls of the *beis midrash*, rabbis who engaged in outreach like Rabbi Yehoshua, understood that sometimes

---

4 *Michtav Me'Eliyahu* 4:190.

5 *Berachos* 35b.

you just need to smile and avoid unnecessary conflict. And so, Rabbi Yehoshua humbly nodded his head to the rainbow question without debating the matter.

It's a rare individual who can enter Heaven in a body. But that doesn't mean we can't strive to follow Rabbi Yehoshua's example and engage with those who have been afflicted spiritually. Most of our brothers and sisters today weren't fortunate to have been born into observance. And many of those who were given the right opportunities sadly made choices that prioritized their flesh over their spirit. It's not for anyone to judge. But that doesn't mean that we simply turn a blind eye. If we're personally strong enough, then we must do our very best to teach Torah to all.

That's easier said than done. Most people don't like to "stick out like a sore thumb." They'd rather blend in and go with the flow. When they're in their religious communities, they're happy to shine with spirituality, but then they go out into the world and feel awkward and uncomfortable with their religious identity. They'll put on a baseball cap or remove their yarmulke. They'll tuck in their tzitzis. Some might even "order a fruit salad" when they find themselves in a business lunch situation.

That's why the Baal Shem Tov introduced the idea of Chassidim adopting a distinctive form of dress. He wanted to ensure that his followers could never hide their Jewish identity. That's an essential prerequisite to dealing with the physicality and materialism of this world without being influenced and affected. If you want to be able to reach out to our brethren and impact their spiritual lives, first you need to be solid and unwavering in your own identity and commitment.

Hashem placed you into this world to impact the world. When you maintain your personal spirituality in a mundane, physical world, you imbue your physical body with spirituality and transform it into something Divine. May you merit fusing the physical with the spiritual, and entering Heaven in a chariot of fire!

DAF 78

Regurgitating Old Arguments

Just prior to reciting the *Shema* prayer before retiring to bed at night, we recite a prayer in which we forgive all who may have wronged us that day. That way, we can go to bed without holding a grudge against anyone. It is especially important to pay particular attention to your relationship with your spouse. Many spouses make a point of never going to sleep upset with one another—this prayer guarantees that! Here's the prayer:

> *Master of the Universe! I hereby forgive anyone who has angered me, or sinned against me, either physically or financially, against my honor or anything that is mine, whether accidentally or intentionally, inadvertently or deliberately, by speech or by deed, in this incarnation or in any other, any Israelite [is forgiven], and may no man be punished on my account. May it be Your will, Hashem, my God and the God of my fathers, that I shall sin no more, nor repeat my sins, neither shall I again anger You, nor do what is wrong in Your eyes. The sins I have committed, erase in your abounding mercies, but not through suffering or severe illnesses. May the words of my mouth and the thoughts of my heart be acceptable before You Hashem, my Rock and my Redeemer.*

What is the meaning of this prayer and why is it so important?

הָאִשָּׁה שֶׁנָּפְלוּ לָהּ נְכָסִים עַד שֶׁלֹּא תִּתְאָרֵס מוֹדִים בֵּית שַׁמַּאי וּבֵית הִלֵּל שֶׁמּוֹכֶרֶת וְנוֹתֶנֶת וְקַיָּים נָפְלוּ לָהּ מִשֶּׁנִּתְאָרְסָה בֵּית שַׁמַּאי אוֹמְרִים תִּמְכּוֹר וּבֵית הִלֵּל אוֹמְרִים לֹא תִּמְכּוֹר אֵלּוּ וָאֵלּוּ מוֹדִים שֶׁאִם מָכְרָה וְנָתְנָה קַיָּים אָמַר רַבִּי יְהוּדָה אָמְרוּ חֲכָמִים לִפְנֵי רַבָּן גַּמְלִיאֵל הוֹאִיל וְזָכָה בָּאִשָּׁה לֹא יִזְכֶּה בַּנְּכָסִים אָמַר לָהֶם עַל הַחֲדָשִׁים אָנוּ בּוֹשִׁים אֶלָּא שֶׁאַתֶּם מְגַלְגְּלִין עָלֵינוּ אֶת הַיְּשָׁנִים.

If a woman was bequeathed property before she was betrothed, Beis Shammai and Beis Hillel agree that she may sell or give the property as a gift, and the transaction is valid. However, if the property was bequeathed to her after she was betrothed, Beis Shammai say: She may sell it; and Beis Hillel say: She may not sell it. Both agree that if she sold it or gave it away as a gift, the transaction is valid. Rabbi Yehuda said that the Sages said before Rabban Gamliel: Since he merited the woman herself through betrothal, would he not acquire the property from the moment of their betrothal? [Why, then, is her transaction valid?] Rabban Gamliel said to them: We are already ashamed about the new items, and now you also seek to include the old items?

If a woman brings her personal assets into the marriage, they are hers with which to do business. If, however, she came into an inheritance after she was married, Beis Hillel rules that she should not personally deal with those assets. Rather they join the account that she shares with her husband. Nevertheless, if she did use the money, her transactions are valid. The Sages ask why those assets that she owned prior to the marriage do not automatically become part of the family account. Rabban Gamliel responds by expressing wonder at the halachah that even the funds she inherits once married must be shared with her husband, let alone the previously owned assets! In his words, "We are already ashamed about the new items, and now you also seek to include the old items?"

Marriage is the coming together of two different individuals. Our Sages teach that just like no two people have the same face, no two people share the exact same opinions. Consequently, conflict is inevitable in any marriage. The question is not whether there will be conflict, but how we deal with the conflicting opinions. The challenge of marriage is to learn how to work together in a spirit of compromise, partnership, and the desire to choose the path that is best not for either spouse, but for the family as a whole. And it's not as if once you've figured it out, marriage is smooth-sailing and conflict-free. New issues will always arise that will continue to challenge the couple's ability to negotiate calmly and peacefully.

But here's what you need to know about conflict in marriage: Nobody gets it right on day one. Just like anything of value in life, the more you work at it, the better the spouse that you'll become. And hopefully, with each dispute, you're able to resolve the issues. Sometimes, that will entail compromising. Other times, it will entail apologizing. And still other times, it will entail simply accepting the other person's position. The key to a successful marriage is to move on from that issue, however it's been resolved.

Sadly, some people are resistant when it comes to learning how to be a good spouse. One of the great pitfalls of marriage is the inability to let go of old issues. Matters that were already resolved and put to bed are regurgitated and rehashed over and over again. Anytime a new issue arises, some spouses have the tendency to start bringing up the old issue. But as Rabban Gamliel emphasizes, "We are already ashamed about the new items, and now you also seek to include the old items?"

Why is the nightly forgiveness prayer so essential? Because if you've utterly forgiven your spouse for everything on a daily basis, that means it's impossible to ever bring up past arguments. They're completely gone. Your spouse may have said or done things in the past that upset you. But if you forgave him—which you should daily—you must never ever bring it up again. As the Sages tell Rabban Gamliel, the new issues are embarrassing enough as it is, without having to re-impose the old issues! You should be embarrassed to bring up old issues—it reflects poorly on you; it means you never really forgave your spouse and that he can't really trust you to put things in the past behind you.

What's interesting about the prayer is that the last few lines switch gears. It's no longer about forgiving others, but about asking God to forgive you. What's the connection? The reason for this additional piece is to remind us that if we want Hashem to forgive and forget our past iniquities, then we'd better be serious when we pledge to forgive and forget what others have done to us. When we are completely committed to putting the past behind us in our relationships with our fellow human beings, God will do likewise in His relationship with us.

Don't bring up old issues. Forgive your spouse daily and bury old issues never to be heard of again. May you merit a beautiful relationship filled with love and constant forgiveness!

DAF 79

Multicolored Identity

Our forefather Yaakov is living in Canaan and rearing his large family in the family shepherding business. The apple of his eye is his son Yosef, the first son of his beloved wife Rachel, whose role is to help out the sons of Yaakov's wives Bilhah and Zilpah. But Yosef is a little wet behind the ears and not always so diplomatic in his dealings with his brothers. He earns the ire of his brothers; first, when he speaks ill of them to their father, and second, when he begins to have dreams of grandeur.

Nevertheless, Yaakov can't help but love Yosef more than all his other children. Not only is he Rachel's child, but he was born to him later in life and holds a special place in his heart. To demonstrate his special love for Yosef, Yaakov makes him a *passim* coat.

What exactly is a *passim* coat?

הָרוֹצָה שֶׁתַּבְרִיחַ נְכָסֶיהָ מִבַּעְלָהּ כֵּיצַד הִיא עוֹשָׂה כּוֹתֶבֶת שְׁטַר פַּסִּים לַאֲחֵרִים דִּבְרֵי רַבָּן שִׁמְעוֹן בֶּן גַּמְלִיאֵל וַחֲכָמִים אוֹמְרִים רָצָה מְצַחֵק בָּהּ.

If a woman seeks to shelter her property from her husband [-to-be], how does she proceed? She composes a "passim" document to others. This is the statement of Rabban Shimon ben Gamliel. And the Sages say: If the recipient would want, he could laugh off her eventual claim.

In the story of Yosef and his brothers, what does the word *passim* mean? According to the *Chizkuni*,[1] *passim* comes from the word "*piusim*," meaning "appeasement." Yaakov wanted to show Yosef a little extra love to make up for all the bullying he was getting from his brothers. That's how *Rashi* understands the word here in the Gemara. The purpose of the contract is to appease the third party to accept the assets under their name and keep them outside the reach of the newlyweds' joint bank account.

The *Radak* translates *passim* in Yosef's story as it's popularly understood. It was a coat of many colors. According to that understanding of the word, one might explain our Gemara as follows: A multicolored contract masquerades as something that it is not. Officially, the property is being transferred to a third party, but it's a sham transaction that the woman never truly intends to affect. As the Sages say, it's laughable and not to be taken seriously.

Why is it called a multicolored contract? Because this woman is presenting a certain identity to one person (her husband) and another identity to someone else. She presents different faces depending upon whom she's dealing with. In the end, the Sages laugh her off and tell her that her ruse won't work. Upon embarking on marriage, we must be prepared to be completely open and honest with our spouse.

Many people compartmentalize their life and wear different faces and identities depending on where they are and whom they are dealing with. They'll act pious in the synagogue and community, but then throw off the yarmulke and become ruthless and less-than-ethically-stellar in the workplace. They'll keep the most scrupulously kosher homes, but then order a salad in a non-kosher restaurant. They'll preach about showing kindness to the stranger and the oppressed, but then treat their own family members with disrespect.

Who are you? Are you the same person in shul as you are at home, and as you are at work? Or do you have a multicolored identity? Do you compartmentalize your life into different contracts or are you the

---

1 *Bereishis* 37:3.

same person, no matter who is watching? Don't be laughable in the eyes of Heaven! Be true to yourself and true to those around you by maintaining your face of righteousness and piety wherever you go!

When my friend, Rabbi Jonathan Gross of Baltimore, is asked, "Where are you a rabbi?" he responds, "Wherever I go!" May you merit being a sincere and transparent Yid wherever you go!

DAF 80

Cost-Benefit Analysis

We all know the famous story of the fellow whose boat capsizes in the middle of the Mediterranean Sea. Despite all attempts at search and rescue, he is nowhere to be found, and everyone assumes the worst.

Three years later, a ship is passing by a desert island in the Mediterranean and they see a man desperately trying to get their attention. Lo and behold, it's the fellow whose boat capsized. He appears to be in good health, and he's even managed to build himself a modest home and another couple of buildings.

"Who are those houses for?" the captain of the ship asks him.

"Oh, no," replies the fellow, "they're not homes. I've built myself two shuls."

"Two shuls?" the captain exclaims. "Whatever would you need two shuls for? Surely one would suffice. You're only one person!"

"Well, my friend," says the man smugly, "that's the shul I daven in. The other is the shul I would never ever step foot in!"

הָהִיא אִיתְּתָא דִּנְפַלוּ לַהּ אַרְבַּע מְאָה זוּזֵי בֵּי חוֹזָאֵי אֲזַל גַּבְרָא אַפֵּיק שֵׁית מְאָה אַיְיתַי אַרְבַּע מְאָה בַּהֲדֵי דְּקָאָתֵי אִיצְטְרִיךְ לֵיהּ חַד זוּזָא וּשְׁקַל מִנַּיְיהוּ אֲתָא לְקַמֵּיהּ דְּרַבִּי אַמֵּי אֲמַר לֵיהּ מַה שֶּׁהוֹצִיא הוֹצִיא וּמַה שֶּׁאָכַל אָכַל.

There was once a woman who inherited four hundred zuz in Bei Chozai. Her husband set out to claim the money, but laid out six hundred of his personal funds for travel expenses, as he

> *brought back the four hundred. On the way home he needed a zuz, which he took from the money that he had collected. He came before Rabbi Ami for a ruling. He said to him: What you spent, you spent; and what you ate, you ate.*

In this story, it was nice of the husband to go off traveling to fetch the inheritance money for his wife, but he spent more in the process than he actually collected. What was the point of that? Clearly not much of a businessman, he failed to perform a cost-benefit analysis prior to setting out on his journey.

Every decision we make in life entails a cost-benefit analysis. Or at least, it should. Unfortunately, most of the time we tend to jump into what sounds like a good idea without considering whether the cost might outweigh the benefit.

Sure, it's wonderful to attend charity dinners every night, but if that means we're never spending time with the family, how charitable are we really acting? Sure, it's great to attend twenty *shiurim* a week, but if that means one never has time to review what one has learned, how much has one accomplished?

Every night before going to sleep, one should make a *cheshbon ha'nefesh*, which literally means "accounting of the soul," but roughly translates to a personal cost-benefit analysis. Ask yourself: What spiritual investments did I make today? Were they worth the effort that I put in? Ideally, we should subject ourselves to this self-analysis each day. And then, during the month of Elul, as we approach the New Year, we should perform a similar cost-benefit analysis for our accomplishments over the course of the past year. And at the end of these daily and annual assessments, if you discover that you've invested more in terms of time and effort than you've gotten out of it, it's time to be honest with yourself and reassess the best way to maximize results.

Practically speaking, how does this cost-benefit analysis work? Let's say you feel like patting yourself on the back because you sat through a *shiur* today. Well, out of the hour-long class, how much were you paying attention? Could you have accomplished more if you'd learned with a *chavrusa* instead? Or conversely, do you find yourself chatting half the time when you're meant to be learning with your *chavrusa*, and perhaps attending a *shiur* would be a more productive use of your time?

Let's say that you went to shul to daven this morning like a good Jew. Did you daven at the right minyan for you? Or was it too fast? Too slow? Too soft? Too loud? Sure, you get Heavenly marks simply for davening with the minyan, but if you can't honestly demonstrate to yourself that the time was well spent, you're not achieving your full potential in life.

Or maybe, you're pushing your kid in a certain educational direction that you think is a good idea, but he's overwhelmed and almost drowning. You have to ask yourself whether you are truly helping him. Whether all the stress that you're causing him will truly pay off or whether he should consider an alternative path of action.

We have to think about cost-benefit with our institutions as well. Sometimes, we keep a shul or a school or another charity going just because we've invested so much into it. But most institutions have a use-by date. And a frequent cost-benefit analysis ensures that we're acting responsibly with communal funds. Let's say, for example, that a demographic shift has caused a depletion in the number of Jews living in the neighborhood. It's tempting to want to continue the struggle for a daily minyan and the satisfaction of knowing that we've kept the shul's doors open. But maybe the area no longer needs two shuls. Has it ever crossed your mind that your dedication to keeping both institutions alive is directing community funding away from more pressing needs?

While we all chuckle at the story of the fellow who was washed up on the desert island and built two shuls, unfortunately, it's no joke. It's something that happens all too often in our communities. Obviously, two shuls for one person makes no sense. But does it make sense to have two shuls for twenty people? Fifty people? A hundred people? Why? While we certainly have many more people to daven in the multiple shuls than our lone survivor, most of the time a single shul would probably suffice. Not only would it suffice, but it would thrive.

For a number of years, I served as the rabbi of Hampstead Garden Suburb Synagogue in London, a shul with over 1200 families. It's a real *kiddush Hashem* when so many diverse kinds of people can put aside their differences and daven under one roof. More pooled resources mean a greater wherewithal to offer excellent programs, afford top Rabbinic leadership and other staff-members, and maximize the youth energy in the building. Not to mention the fact that we are enjoined to daven with as many people as possible, because the larger the crowd, the more we glorify the Supreme King of Kings.

You wouldn't keep investing time and effort in a business venture that's not working. Cost-benefit analyses must be performed in every aspect of your life, including your spiritual life. May you merit maximizing your growth by constantly assessing everything that you do and investing in the behaviors that will bring the most positive energy into your life!

DAF 81

Careful What You Wish For

King Balak of Moav is terrified of the impending arrival of the Children of Israel into his territory. Realizing that past military approaches have been unsuccessful, he turns to the sorcerer Bilaam and asks him to curse the Israelites. After all, the only way to overpower a nation fueled by spirituality is to seek a spiritual power in response. The king sends a delegation to Bilaam requesting his services saying, "There is a people that came out of Egypt; it hides the earth from view, and it is settled next to me. Come then, put a curse upon this people for me, since they are too numerous for me; perhaps I can thus defeat them, and drive them out of the land. For I know that he whom you bless is blessed indeed, and he whom you curse is cursed."

The elders of Moav and Midyan deliver Balak's message to Bilaam, who replies, "Spend the night here, and I shall reply to you as Hashem shall instruct me." God appears to Bilaam and says, "What do these people want of you?" Bilaam replies, "Balak son of Tzippor, king of Moav, sent me this message: Here is a people that came out from Egypt and hides the earth from view. Come now and curse them for me; perhaps I can engage them in battle and drive them off." But God says to Bilaam, "Do not go with them. You must not curse that people, for they are blessed." Bilaam arises in the morning and says to Balak's dignitaries, "Go back to your own country, for Hashem will not let me go with you."

The Moabite dignitaries leave and return to Balak and tell him, "Bilaam refused to come with us." So Balak sends other dignitaries, more numerous and distinguished than the first. They come to Bilaam and say to him, "Thus says Balak son of Tzippor: Please do not refuse to come to me. I will reward you richly and I will do anything you ask of me. Only come and curse this people for me." Bilaam replies to Balak's officials, "Even if Balak were to give me his house full of silver and gold, I could not do anything, big or small, contrary to the command of Hashem, my God. Nevertheless, stay here overnight, and let me find out what else Hashem may say to me."

That night God came to Bilaam and said to him, "If these men have come to invite you, you may go with them. But whatever I command you, that shall you do."

> מֵתוּ בַּעֲלֵיהֶן עַד שֶׁלֹּא שָׁתוּ בֵּית שַׁמַּאי אוֹמְרִים נוֹטְלוֹת כְּתוּבָּה וְלֹא שׁוֹתוֹת וּבֵית הִלֵּל אוֹמְרִים אוֹ שׁוֹתוֹת אוֹ לֹא נוֹטְלוֹת כְּתוּבָּה. אוֹ שׁוֹתוֹת וְהֵבִיא הָאִישׁ אֶת אִשְׁתּוֹ אֶל הַכֹּהֵן אָמַר רַחֲמָנָא וְלֵיכָּא אֶלָּא מִתּוֹךְ שֶׁלֹּא שׁוֹתוֹת לֹא נוֹטְלוֹת כְּתוּבָּה.
>
> *If the husbands [of women suspected of being unfaithful] died before their wives drank [from the sotah waters], Beis Shammai say: They receive the ketubah entitlement and do not drink, and Beis Hillel say: Either they drink or they do not take the ketubah entitlement. Either they drink? But the Torah states: "Then the man shall bring his wife to the Kohen," and the husband is no longer present! Rather, just as they cannot drink, likewise they do not receive the ketubah entitlement.*

Concerning the *Sotah*, the Torah declares, "If a man's wife goes astray, and acts unfaithfully toward him, he shall bring his wife to the Kohen, and the Kohen shall have in his hand the water of bitterness." It's important to emphasize that the bitter waters are only administered when a husband cautions his wife not to seclude herself with another individual, and she defies his warning. If witnesses later testified that they saw her secluded with that fellow about whom she had been warned, she drinks the bitter waters to ascertain whether or not she acted unfaithfully.

In the case of this Mishnah, the husband accused his wife of defying his warning, but before he could bring her to the Kohen, he died. Imagine the stroke of luck this woman feels that she's just experienced. Whether or not she was unfaithful, she certainly crossed the line by secluding herself with another man, from whom her husband explicitly had warned her to stay away. Clearly, their marriage was far from perfect. And so, when she gets caught, undoubtedly she's praying for a way out of the public shaming that is about to take place. Lo and behold, before she's had a chance to stand trial publicly, her husband dies. Her first reaction is an overwhelming sense of relief.

But then she's overcome by guilt. "Maybe I killed him?" she says to herself. "Maybe I prayed so hard for the problem to disappear and for something awful to happen to my overly suspicious and anxious husband that I'm now responsible for this tragic situation?" The good news is that while you might be able to pray for someone else's good fortune, your thoughts and declaration can't really bring misfortune upon someone if he doesn't deserve to be harmed.[1]

Let's contrast that axiom with personal prayers about one's own life. When it comes to your own situation, you certainly need to be careful what you pray for, because praying for bad things to happen could cause those things to transpire.

But seriously, why would anyone pray for bad things to happen to him?

Unfortunately, it occurs all the time. Here's how it works: Sometimes, you pray for something and God answers your prayers. Other times, you pray and God appears unresponsive. So, you pray harder. And still no response. You then go into overdrive praying for something that the Almighty knows is a bad idea. Our Sages teach us something counterintuitive:[2] If you pray hard enough for something, sometimes, God will say, "Fine, if you insist. I'll grant you your prayer and let you learn the hard way why this is a bad idea." That's what happened to Bilaam when he repeatedly beseeched God for permission to go with King Balak's men. God told him not to go. But when he refused to take no for an answer,

1 *Rambam, Sefer Hamitzvos, Lavin* 317.

2 *Makkos* 10b.

God acquiesced to his request, knowing that his plans wouldn't come to pass anyway. All he would get would be aggravation from the king for failing to fulfill what he'd been hired to do.

We only see things in life through our mortal eyes in the here and now. God sees all possible outcomes and the big picture. Sure, He wants you to pray for your needs and wants. But if you don't get what you're asking for, don't stop believing in Him. He doesn't want you to get hurt. He knows what's best for you. Sometimes, you just have to accept His decision even if you don't understand it. When you start arguing with Him and think that you know what's best, He might just allow you to learn from your own mistakes. Don't go there! Instead, allow Him to decide whom you should marry and whom you shouldn't; for whom you should work and for whom you shouldn't; in which house you should live and in which you shouldn't.

Sometimes, we want something so badly that we pray for it to work out. But that's not the right prayer. The ideal prayer is that if it's the right path, then may it work out. And if it's the wrong path, may it fail as quickly as possible, so that the right doors can open. My blessing to a young couple who has begun dating is always, "If it's meant to be, may you both know as quickly as possible. And, if it's not meant to be, may you also both know as quickly as possible."

Be careful about what you pray for. The best prayer is the one where you place your complete trust in the Almighty to do what's best for you. May you maintain your faith in Heaven both on those occasions when He gives you what you asked for and on those occasions when He appears unresponsive!

DAF 82

Check Your Pockets Constantly

Nine plagues have struck Egypt, wreaking havoc and devastation throughout the land. It's now time for the tenth and final plague, the death of the firstborn. Moshe instructs the Children of Israel to smear their doorposts with the blood of the sacrificial lamb. God would then pass over the Hebrew homes and not allow the Angel of Death to touch their families.

From the Torah's narrative to the retelling of the story each year in the Haggadah, it is unclear, however, who carried out the task. Was it God Himself? Or was it an angel of destruction acting on His behalf?

> תַּנְיָא רַבִּי נָתָן אוֹמֵר מִנַּיִן לַנּוֹשֶׁה בַּחֲבֵירוֹ מָנֶה וַחֲבֵירוֹ בַּחֲבֵירוֹ מִנַּיִן שֶׁמּוֹצִיאִין מִזֶּה וְנוֹתְנִין לָזֶה תַּלְמוּד לוֹמַר וְנָתַן לַאֲשֶׁר אָשַׁם לוֹ.
>
> *Rabbi Nosson says: How do we know that if person A claims one hundred from person B, who in turn claims money from person C, that we may take the money from person C and give it directly to person A? The verse states: "And he shall give it to the one to whom he has sinned."*

The *Kaftor Vaferach* presents an extraordinary idea in his commentary on our Gemara:[1]

---

1 *Mesivta Oz V'Hadar* Gemara.

On Shabbos, we are forbidden from engaging in thirty-nine creative activities associated with the building of the Tabernacle in the wilderness. The 39th melachah is the prohibition against carrying in the public area. The Torah states that on Shabbos we may not transfer from the reshus ha'yachid, individual domain, to the reshus ha'rabim, the domain of the many. At first blush, the melachah seems rather insignificant and unrelated to creative activity. What could be so wrong with having a tissue in your pocket as you walk outside? After all, if it were so egregious, how do we resolve matters so easily by building an eiruv?

Rabbi Shlomo of Radomsk explains the deeper significance of the melachah.[2] *Have you ever noticed that it's not called "an" individual domain," but "the" individual domain? Who is the one and only Yachid in this universe? God. When we sin in any area of our service of Heaven, we make a transfer from the domain of "The Individual" to the domain of the many. "The many" refers to the forces of impurity—the many false "gods"—that try to distract us from our service of the One God.*

That's a very powerful thought that should deter us from any sin. Sometimes, we think that a sin we're about to commit is just an unimportant, tiny little misdeed. But when we realize that we're making a transfer from God's domain to the domain of the forces of evil, we think twice. After all, we wouldn't dream of carrying that tissue in our pockets, as insignificant as it might seem. Because a *melachah* is a *melachah*. And that's the same reaction that we should have to any improper transfer.

What exactly are we transferring? Citing the verse in our Gemara, "And he shall give it to the one to whom he has sinned," Rabbi Shlomo of Radomsk teaches that when we sin, we bring our entire selves along with us for the journey, including all the Torah and mitzvos that we've learned and performed. At that moment, we "give it to the one to

---

2 *Tiferes Shlomo, Mo'adim, L'Chag HaSukkos.*

whom we have sinned." The Satan has the ability to capture our Torah and mitzvos and transfer them over to the *sitra achra,* the other side, God forbid.

The good news, however, is that just like sin gives the Satan the opportunity to transfer our mitzvos over to the other side, *teshuvah* allows us to transfer back not only our mitzvos, but even certain sins. When a person engages in a true and complete form of *teshuvah*, Reish Lakish teaches that his iniquities are transformed into merits![3]

Let's return to the matter of transferring between domains. Next time you find yourself thinking, "It's not a big deal," think of the teaching of the *Tiferes Shlomo*: either you're in the *reshus ha'yachid*, God's domain, or you're not. That little tissue might not feel like a big deal, but it's exactly the same as schlepping three suitcases across the street. There's no bigger and smaller. Either you're in or you're out.

You know you want to be in, and now you have the key to staying in. It's the tissue in your pocket. As Shabbos is about to begin, we are obligated to check our pockets.[4] If, like most Shabbos-observant Jews, you live within an *eiruv*, you probably don't get the opportunity to fulfill this mitzvah very often. But the mitzvah is much bigger than simply a Shabbos directive. Every decision you make, every step in life that you take, you need to check your pockets for that tissue.

While the commentaries[5] offer different approaches to understanding the tenth plague in Egypt, one thing's for sure: Hashem has never left our side. He may have passed over our houses with the plague, but at the very same time, He was there with us at the inaugural Pesach Seder. After all, every family had offered the sacrifice to God! But upon which altar? The altar of our personal family dining rooms. The Pesach offering that year and in all future years was a meal shared with our Father in Heaven right there in the comfort of our own homes. While He passed over in one sense, He really never left our side at all. On that night, our homes became His home. Our domain is His domain.

---

3 *Yoma* 86b.

4 *Shabbos* 12a.

5 See *Targum Yonasan*, *Rashi*, and *Rasag*.

On that night, we realized what it means to stay on the right side of the threshold. As long as you're in Hashem's domain, you will always be safe and secure. May you forever remain in Hashem's domain!

DAF 83

Rabbi, I Miss My Wife's Strudel

Rabbinical conventions are filled primarily with opportunities for professional development, including advanced Torah seminars and training sessions from experts in pastoral fields, including management consultants and psychologists. Nevertheless, there's always time for networking and the sharing of ideas and experiences.

On one such occasion, I recall sitting with a few rabbis in the tearoom and discussing some of the more unusual funeral and *shivah* anecdotes. The topic turned to food and the common theme many rabbis encounter when they meet with a family in mourning.

"Rabbi, you have to mention mama's kugel. Shabbos just won't be the same without her kugel," one of my colleagues retold.

"That's nothing," recounted a seasoned colleague, "I was once conducting a funeral when the husband of the deceased began wailing, "*Oy*, the apple strudel, *Oy*, the apple strudel. I can't live without your apple strudel!" At one point, as we were lowering the coffin," continued the rabbi, "the man had to be held back physically. It looked like he was serious about being unable to go on with his life without his wife's apple strudel..."

The rabbis sitting there nodded in unison and agreed that it was difficult, but necessary, to impress upon the families in mourning that the important aspects to memorialize were the good *middos* of their dearly departed loved ones. The acts of kindness that they'd performed. The charity that they'd given. The lessons that they'd imparted to their family.

מתני׳ הַכּוֹתֵב לְאִשְׁתּוֹ דִּין וּדְבָרִים אֵין לִי בִּנְכָסַיִךְ הֲרֵי זֶה אוֹכֵל פֵּרוֹת בְּחַיֶּיהָ וְאִם מֵתָה יוֹרְשָׁהּ אִם כֵּן לָמָּה כָּתַב לָהּ דִּין וּדְבָרִים אֵין לִי בִּנְכָסַיִךְ שֶׁאִם מָכְרָה וְנָתְנָה קַיָּים: גמ׳ וְתֵימָא לֵיהּ מִכָּל מִילֵּי סַלֵּיקְתְּ נַפְשָׁךְ אָמַר אַבָּיֵי יַד בַּעַל הַשְּׁטָר עַל הַתַּחְתּוֹנָה וְאֵימָא מִפֵּירֵי אָמַר אַבָּיֵי בּוּצִינָא טָב מִקָּרָא.

Mishnah: *One who writes a prenuptial agreement stating: "I have no legal claim to your property," may still consume the produce of his wife's property during her lifetime. And when she dies, he is her inheritor. But if he still retains his rights, why would he write "I have no claim to your property"? The result of this statement is that if she sold or gave away her property, the transaction is binding.*

Gemara: *But why can the wife not say to him, "You removed your entire claim"? Abaye said: The holder of the claim-document always has the lower hand [and can therefore only make the narrowest claim]. Then why not say that the husband has merely withdrawn his rights from the produce [and retains the rights to sold property]? Abaye said: A cucumber [in the hand] is better than a gourd [in the bush].*

The Mishnah discusses a couple who wrote a prenuptial agreement whereby the groom relinquished all rights to his bride's assets. The effect of such an agreement is that he has no say if she decides to sell her property and no claim to the proceeds of the sale. Nevertheless, so long as the property—let's say a field—remains in her possession, he may benefit from the crops it produces. The Gemara asks why he retains a claim to that produce. Abaye answers that we interpret their prenuptial agreement in the narrowest terms possible. We cannot assume that the groom relinquished all his rights, but only certain rights. Therefore, we say that the relinquished rights concern the proceeds of a property sale, but not the crop that her property is producing.

The Gemara then asks why we don't make the opposite assumption. A sale of the entire land is a significant matter relative to the minor value of its produce. Why would he have given up his claim to the actual property? Abaye answers that a cucumber is better than a gourd, which is akin to the contemporary adage, "A bird in the hand is worth two in the bush." The husband's immediate access to the produce would concern him more than a potential future sale of the property.

In *Pirkei Avos* we learn that Rabbi Yaakov teaches, "One moment of bliss in the World to Come is greater than an entire lifetime in this world."[1] But if a cucumber is better than a gourd, who would want to wait until the World to Come to receive reward? Wouldn't it be better to receive reward right here, right now? The Kotzker Rebbe explains that the concept of the cucumber and the gourd is only true in this world of falsehood.[2] In Heaven, which is the World of Truth, it goes without saying that immediate pleasure is valueless next to eternal bliss.

Two of my favorite teachings about pleasure in this world are ideas expressed so beautifully by Rabbi Moshe Alshich and Rabbi Samson Raphael Hirsch. The *Alshich* explains Rivkah's insistence on Yaakov receiving the material blessings of earthly prosperity in terms of her belief that one who dedicates himself to Torah and mitzvos is entitled to blessing both in the next world *and* in this world. In our tradition, we don't repudiate the joys and pleasures of this Earth. God wants to reward us both in this world and in the World to Come. Similarly, Rav Hirsch would explain to his flock that to vacation in the Swiss Alps was a fulfillment of his Divine mission of appreciating all the wonders of the Creator. Judaism is not an ascetic, other-worldly religion. God gave us this world to enjoy. And He gets *nachas* when we're enjoying ourselves. After all, the nature of Goodness is to bestow goodness.

From these two great rabbis it's clear that pleasure in this world is not something that we simply ignore while we save up for the World to Come. And so, the question becomes: What should be our approach to enjoyment in this world? While we're not ascetic, we're certainly not hedonistic either. It's not all about pleasure-seeking. Nor is it all about pleasure-denial. Like most things in Judaism, it's about finding the golden path down the middle. Enjoyment in moderation.

What's most extraordinary about the teaching of the Kotzker is that he doesn't say that we should strive to place the gourd before the

---

1 Ch. 4.

2 *Ohel Torah.*

cucumber throughout our lives. His contrast between this world and the next appears to acknowledge that in this world it's OK to enjoy our cucumbers. Not all the time, because we're not hedonistic. But constant denial of the cucumber is also not a Jewish value.

That's why we have a mitzvah of *Oneg Shabbos*. Every week, we are enjoined to enjoy ourselves, with "meat, fish, and all manner of delicacy."[3] And on Yom Tov, we are instructed to step it up and provide even greater delicacies in order to amplify and elevate our level of joy.

But it's an important message for our lives in general. Too many people work and work and believe in postponing their pleasure until some occasion in the future when they'll have time and money to retire and enjoy life. Meanwhile, they're so busy that they miss out on all the joyous moments in the present. Their child's siddur presentation. The Chanukah concert. The little-league baseball game.

And sadly, so much more. I cry when I think about the people whom I have known over the years who postponed everything till later, and then sadly, Heaven decreed that there would be no later. The message of the cucumber is that Hashem wants us to enjoy His world today. In fact, retirement is a secular social construct. Judaism has no such concept. Hashem wants you to work for as long as you physically can. And He wants you to allocate time to enjoying His world along the way.

While the stories of the kugel and apple strudel might have sounded a little inane to certain of my colleagues, I believe that they are no less important than the stories of their charitable pursuits. Hashem wants us to enjoy this world. And if the strudel enhanced the family's Shabbos experience, then it deserves a mention in the eulogy because the deceased achieved exactly what our Father in Heaven desires most: that we have pleasure. What better way to eulogize a loved one than to extol his unique ability to fulfill Hashem's ultimate plan? May you enjoy this world in just the right amount for every stage of your life!

---

3 *Shabbos Zemiros, "Mah Yedidus."*

DAF 84

We Are Weak, but Hashem Is Merciful

The Children of Israel have just committed the heinous sin of the Golden Calf. God is ready to destroy them, but Moshe beseeches Him for mercy, and He acquiesces to Moshe's prayers.

"And Hashem passed before him and proclaimed: 'Hashem, Hashem, God, Merciful, Gracious, Slow to anger, Abundant in loving-kindness, and Truthful, Extender of kindness to the thousandth generation, Bearer of Iniquity, and Transgression, and Sin, and Cleanser.'"[1]

Rabbi Yochanan said: Were it not explicitly written in the verse, it would be impossible to say this, as it would be insulting to God's honor. The verse teaches that the Holy One, blessed be He, wrapped Himself in a tallis like a *chazzan* and showed Moshe the structure of the order of the prayer.

He said to him, "Whenever the Jewish people sin, let them act before Me in accordance with this order. Let the *chazzan* (leader) wrap himself in a tallis and publicly recite the thirteen attributes of mercy, and I shall forgive them."

1 *Shemos* 34:6.

מַתְנִי׳ מִי שֶׁמֵּת וְהִנִּיחַ אִשָּׁה וּבַעַל חוֹב וְיוֹרְשִׁין וְהָיָה לוֹ פִּקָּדוֹן אוֹ מִלְוָה בְּיַד אֲחֵרִים רַבִּי טַרְפוֹן אוֹמֵר יִנָּתְנוּ לַכּוֹשֵׁל שֶׁבָּהֶן רַבִּי עֲקִיבָא אוֹמֵר אֵין מְרַחֲמִין בַּדִּין אֶלָּא יִנָּתְנוּ לַיּוֹרְשִׁין.

Mishnah: *One who died and left behind a wife, a creditor, and heirs [all of whom claim payment from his property], and he had a deposit or a loan in the possession of others, Rabbi Tarfon says: The money should be given to the weakest [koshel] of them [whoever is in greatest need]. Rabbi Akiva says: We do not show mercy in judgment. Rather, the money will be given to the heirs.*

When a mortal court shows mercy in a civil case, favoring the weaker party, they, in effect, become Robin Hoods, stealing from the rich and giving to the poor. As much as the judge's heart may be bleeding for this poor widow, he has no right to take money away from the heirs, money that rightfully belongs to them.

While that's true for a mortal court, the good news is that the Heavenly court may indeed show mercy in judgment. Why? Because God has more than enough to go around. He has an unlimited supply of abundant prosperity, health, and success for all His children. When He gives of His bounty to one child, He has not depleted His supply. He still has loads more to give His other children!

If God were to employ His attribute of justice in our lives, most of us would not fare very well. Instead, He takes His attribute of mercy and allows it to overpower the attribute of justice and be gracious toward us, treating us all with abundant loving-kindness. That doesn't mean we should take advantage of His graciousness and act disdainfully toward Heaven. Rather, it means you can count on Hashem to show you mercy and compassion for your mistakes in life.

The prophet Hoshea declared, "Return O Israel to Hashem, your God, for you have stumbled [*koshalta*] with your sin."[2] The *Divrei Yoel* points out that the verse employs the same word as our Mishnah.[3] In our

---

2 *Hoshea* 14:2.

3 *Shabbos Shuvah*.

case the word means "weak." And so, it stands to reason that the same connotation may be applied to the verse. He explains that when we return to our Father in Heaven, He understands that we sinned because we were weak. Back in the days of yore, continues the *Divrei Yoel*, people had the strength to do *teshuvah* on their own. Nowadays, we've fallen so low and so far from our holy Source that we cannot do it alone. We need Hashem's assistance to get back up. All we need to do is turn to Him and He will reach out His Hand and help us up.

In fact, the Almighty doesn't just have one type of mercy for His children. As we all chant repeatedly over the Yamim Nora'im, God has thirteen attributes of mercy! How many of us say them over and over again with little thought as to what they mean? While the commentators have written volumes explaining their secrets, let's take a moment for a brief overview:[4]

1. *Hashem*—God has mercy upon us, even though He sees the future and knows that we will sin. He judges us based on who we are today.
2. *Hashem*—Even after we sin, God still takes care of us, despite the fact that we are undeserving.
3. *Kel* (God)—The *Maharal* equates this attribute with God's over-abundant giving. Not only does He give us what we don't deserve, He gives us way more than we ever anticipated.
4. *Rachum* (Merciful)—God gives us because He is our Father. A parent gives his child with no strings attached.
5. *Chanun* (Gracious)—The *Gra* relates this attribute to the word *chinam*, meaning "free." God provides for us on a silver platter, without expectation of receiving anything in return.
6. *Erech Apayim* (Slow to anger)—God does not punish us immediately for any wrongdoing. He gives us ample time to fix our mistakes.
7. *Rav Chessed* (Abundant in loving-kindness)—Despite the fact that too much giving is not always a good thing (think about the

---

4 Compiled from *Rosh Hashanah* 17b; *Sefer Chaneinu V'Aninu*, Y. Rappoport.

parent who never disciplines his child), when we beseech God, He nonetheless gives us more than we really need.

8. *Emes* (Truthful)—God promised to provide for us. That's the truth. And nothing that we can do can change that truth.
9. *Notzer Chessed La'alaphim* (Extender of kindness to the thousandth generation)—Even if we're not worthy, God will provide for us because our forebears served God faithfully.
10. *Nosei Avon* (Bearer of Iniquity)—He simply forgives us and treats our sins as accidents.
11. *Va'fesha*—(and Transgression)—According to *Rashi*, this attribute means that even if we committed a sin to spite God (*l'hach'is*), He still bears it.
12. *V'chataah* (and Sin)—The *Shelah* explains that this refers to God's mercy when we sin *l'tei'avon*, simply because we can't resist the temptation.
13. *V'nakeh* (and Cleanser)—And finally, God not only forgives our iniquities, but in His great mercy, He completely wipes the slate clean, considering it as if we'd never sinned at all.

Our Father in Heaven loves us more than any mortal parent. He might be the Judge, but He still treats us with unparalleled mercy. May you always turn to Him knowing that He will pardon you immediately and cannot wait to bestow His abundant loving-kindness upon you!

DAF 85

First-Name Basis

A fellow once deposited seven pearls tied up in a sheet in the house of Rabbi Meyasha the grandson of Rabbi Yehoshua ben Levi. Rabbi Meyasha passed away without instructing the members of his household on his deathbed to whom the gems belonged. Rabbi Meyasha's family and the depositor came before Rabbi Ami to discuss the ownership of the gems. He said to them: They belong to the claimant. First, I know that Rabbi Meyasha was not wealthy enough to be able to afford such gems. And furthermore, the depositor has provided a distinguishing mark that proves that he is the owner.

Likewise, on another occasion, a fellow deposited a silver goblet in the house of the Sage Ḥasa. Ḥasa passed away without instructions about the goblet. They came before Rav Nachman to discuss the ownership of the goblet. He said to them: I know that Ḥasa was not wealthy, and this goblet would not have belonged to him. And, furthermore, the depositor has provided a distinguishing mark.

And finally, there was once a fellow who deposited silk in the house of Rav Dimi, brother of Rav Safra. Rav Dimi passed away without instructing anyone about the silk. They came before Rabbi Abba to discuss the ownership of the silk. He said to them: It belongs to the claimant. First, I know that Rav Dimi was not wealthy. And second, because he has provided a distinguishing mark.[1]

---

1 *Kesubos* 85b.

הָהוּא דַּאֲמַר לְהוּ נִכְסַיי לְטוֹבִיָּה שָׁכֵיב אֲתָא טוֹבִיָּה אָמַר רַבִּי יוֹחָנָן הֲרֵי בָּא טוֹבִיָּה אֲמַר טוֹבִיָּה וַאֲתָא רַב טוֹבִיָּה לְטוֹבִיָּה אֲמַר לְרַב טוֹבִיָּה לָא אֲמַר וְאִי אִינִישׁ דְּגִיס בֵּיהּ הָא גִּיס בֵּיהּ.

A fellow once said to those present at his deathbed: My property should go to Tuviyah. He passed away, and Tuviyah came to claim his possessions. Rabbi Yochanan said: Tuviyah has arrived [and there is no need to be concerned that he might have meant a different Tuviyah]. But if the deceased had said: My property should go to Tuviyah, and Rav Tuviyah came forward [it is assumed that this is not the person whom the deceased had in mind], for he said: Tuviyah. He did not say: Rav Tuviyah. But if the deceased was haughty with him [on a first-name basis], he was haughty with him [and the title is irrelevant.

This *daf* has a series of stories about property exchanges as a person passes on. In the first three stories, an individual comes forward after the person died claiming certain property in his care. In the fourth story, the dying man requests that his property be given to Tuviyah. If someone calls Tuviyah shows up, we assume that's the person whom the deceased meant. Unless, he was mostly known as Rabbi Tuviyah. Because then he should have called him Rabbi Tuviyah. But then again, some people are a little haughty.

This Gemara might raise some eyebrows, but believe it or not, there was a time when it wasn't normal to call your rabbi by his first name. Sadly, we live in an age when respect has plummeted. Children call their parents by their first names. Students call their teachers by their first names. The younger generation lacks respect for their elders. Instead of seeking their wisdom, they think they know better.

Unfortunately, our generation's problem of disrespect has reached so deep, that our authority figures often even encourage people to be disrespectful. It's the teachers themselves that are telling their students to call them by their first names. It's the parents themselves that are telling their children to call them by their first names. And despite the haughtiness, as the Talmud calls it, we live in an age where many rabbis are asking people to call them by their first names.

But let's be honest. Does anyone call the queen "Elizabeth"? Would you walk into the president's office and say, "Hi Joe"? Would you address a judge in court by her first name? Of course not. We still have some shred of respect left. When rabbis, teachers, or parents offer their first name to be used, their motivation is misguided. In their minds, they want to remove barriers and forge a closer relationship with those in their care. But they've forgotten what they represent. When you show respect for your teacher, you are showing respect for the institution of education. That's what teachers embody. When you show respect for your rabbi, you are showing respect for the Torah. And when you show respect for parents, you are showing respect for Hashem. Parents are His partners in giving you life.

Just like the night is darkest before the dawn, our Sages tell us that in the era before the coming of Mashiach, chutzpah will abound. "Rabbi Nehorai says: Youth will humiliate elders and elders will stand before youth; a daughter will rebel against her mother, and a bride against her mother-in-law. The face of the generation will be like the face of a dog, and a son will not be ashamed before his father. Rabbi Nechemiah says: During the generation that the son of David comes, arrogance will proliferate."[2]

It's time that we started teaching our kids respect. When you show the right respect, you appreciate your values and the importance of where you've come from. May you merit showing, earning, and receiving respect, and may Mashiach speedily come despite our good manners!

---

2 *Sanhedrin* 97a.

DAF 86

Signs of a Controlling Spouse

It was the day after Yom Kippur.[1] Moshe gathered the Children of Israel and instructed them to build the Tabernacle, the very first synagogue, a place where they could worship together. But it wasn't just about worshipping together. The entire project was about uniting the people:

"Take from among you gifts to Hashem. Everyone whose heart so moves him shall bring gold, silver, and copper," he instructed them. "And those among you who are skilled should come forth and make all that Hashem has commanded."

Why did Moshe choose the day after Yom Kippur to gather the people together?

מַתְנִי׳ הַמּוֹשִׁיב אֶת אִשְׁתּוֹ חֶנְוָנִית אוֹ שֶׁמִּינָּהּ אַפּוֹטְרוֹפְּיָא הֲרֵי זֶה מַשְׁבִּיעָהּ כָּל זְמַן שֶׁיִּרְצֶה רַבִּי אֱלִיעֶזֶר אוֹמֵר אֲפִילּוּ עַל פִּילְכָּהּ וְעַל עִיסָּתָהּ: גְּמָ׳ אָמְרוּ לוֹ לְרַבִּי אֱלִיעֶזֶר אֵין אָדָם דָּר עִם נָחָשׁ בִּכְפִיפָה דְּאָמְרָה לֵיהּ כֵּיוָן דְּקָדֵייקַתְּ בָּתְרַאי כּוּלֵּי הַאי לָא מָצֵינָא דְּאֵידוּר בַּהֲדָךְ.

רש״י: הואיל וקא דייקת בתראי—אינך אוהב ומאמין אותי ולא מצינא דאידור בהדך.

Mishnah: *One who appoints his wife as a storekeeper, or if he installed her as a director, he may make her swear [that she did not misappropriate any goods] whenever he wants.*

---

1 *Shemos* 35:1, *Rashi*.

> *Rabbi Eliezer says: He may administer an oath even regarding her spindle and dough [household matters unrelated to her employment].*
>
> ***Gemara:*** *The Rabbis said to Rabbi Eliezer: A person does not reside in a basket with a snake. She may say to him: Since you are so exacting with me, I cannot live with you.*
>
> ***Rashi:*** *Since you are you so exacting with me—you do not love me and trust me, and I therefore cannot live with you.*

The Gemara discusses a husband who asks his wife to mind the shop. He then makes her swear that she hasn't stolen any of his goods or money. Rabbi Eliezer adds that while he's at it, the husband can throw into the oath a clause that says she's also not skimming off the top of any of their household goods, including the product of her own knitting or baking! The Rabbis tell Rabbi Eliezer that nobody wants to live in a basket with a snake. *Rashi* explains that without love and trust, a marriage is doomed to fail.

Successful relationships are built on trust. When there is no trust, there can be no relationship. And if there is no relationship, then there is certainly no love. As strange as this scenario sounds, such controlling spouses are more common than most of would like to believe. Thank God, the wife here has the good sense to realize that she's living with a "snake" and is prepared to walk away unless the situation improves. Tragically, too many spouses—mainly women—remain in abusive relationships living with psychological and emotional abuse on a daily basis.

The fact that the husband does not trust her with money matters is merely one symptom of controlling, abusive, narcissistic behavior. What are some other signs that a person is in an emotionally abusive relationship?

Isolation: Just like a cult-leader who cuts off his followers from family and all prior relationships, the narcissistic spouse will slowly but surely work to curtail his partner's contact with parents, siblings, and friends. Every visit, every phone-call, the abused party will find herself subjected to intense scrutiny. Time spent with others is treated as time that she's been "unfaithful" to her narcissistic partner. He will complain about how often the abused talks to her brother on the phone, or he will say that he doesn't like her best friend and doesn't think that she should spend time with her anymore. Such an abusive spouse tends to turn his partner against anyone whom she's used to relying on for support besides him. The goal is to strip her of her support network and make her totally dependent on him alone.

Criticism: The next defining mark of the abusive spouse is constant criticism. Sometimes, it will be overt. Other times it will be subtle. But the abuser is continually making her partner feel like he's just not good enough. Often it may be masqueraded as a desire to help him improve and become a better person. But generally, we're all familiar with the 80/20 praise-critique rule. Certainly, there are times when a spouse feels the need to say something to her partner to help him. But that's only acceptable when the vast majority of the time, she is showering him with praise and working to build up his self-esteem. When it's primarily criticism and put-downs, that's a sign of abuse.

Gaslighting: This term is based on the story of a husband who would gradually decrease the amount of gas in the lamps in the house. When the wife asked him what was happening, he made her feel like it was all in her head. What happens next is that he convinces her that the world is out to get her and that he's the only person whom she can trust. Of course, the gaslighter is the last person she should be trusting. Gaslighters will lie about things that the abused party knows to be true and then question the abused party's cognitive ability when she disagrees. They will project their own inadequacies onto their partner. And when their partner shares insecurities with them, they use the information against them.

If you find yourself experiencing these patterns of behavior from your spouse, the worst approach that you can take is to convince yourself that things will get better with time. Abusive personalities don't simply dissipate. The issues don't improve with time. They deteriorate with time. They need to be addressed. And the sooner the better. It's paramount to seek help from a reputable and licensed therapist, psychologist, or psychiatrist.

Sadly, the abusive partner will, more often than not, refuse to see a therapist with you. He will justify his refusal with excuses, such as not having the money for such "luxuries" or having insufficient time for therapy because he's working so hard to feed the family. Once again, the victim finds herself to blame for her "self-indulgence." As impossible as it may sound, when that happens, you need to be able to present an ultimatum. Just like the wife in the Gemara who tells her husband, "Since you are you so exacting with me—you do not love me and trust me, and I therefore cannot live with you," an abusive spouse must be made aware that there are only two choices here: either we seek help, or the marriage is over.

Why did Moshe choose the day after Yom Kippur to gather the Children of Israel and instruct them about the building of the Tabernacle? The *Kli Yakar* writes that a prerequisite for the task was national unity.[2] "A person does not reside in a basket with a snake," he explains. As long as there was conflict in the Israelite camp, it would be impossible to build. But on Yom Kippur, as part of the *teshuvah* process, we make amends with anyone we've had differences with. And so, once again reunited, the day after Yom Kippur was the perfect day to begin building the Tabernacle.

You are a child of the Supreme King of Kings, the Holy One blessed be He. You are a prince. You are a princess. You both deserve to be treated as such. Just as you are dedicated to making your spouse feel like the most important, special, and cherished person in the universe, that's how your spouse should be making you feel. Trust and unity are prerequisites to making your home into a Tabernacle. May you forever feel loved, cherished, trusted, and made to feel amazing by your spouse!

---

2 *Shemos* 35:1.

DAF 87

Short Appreciation Span

During World War II, Rabbi Nachum Zev Dessler, son of the famed Rav Eliyahu Dessler, managed to escape the horrors of the Shoah and made his way to America. A few years later, as the war was subsiding, Rav Dessler journeyed from the UK to the US to visit his dear son, whom he hadn't seen for so long.

In the midst of the conversation, Rav Nachum recounted to his father the warm hospitality and refuge that he experienced in the home of Rabbi Eliezer Silver of Cincinnati. Upon hearing the story, Rav Dessler jumped up and said, "I need to thank him."

"OK," replied the son, "let me just find his phone number." And he proceeded to open up his personal phonebook and leaf through it, looking for the contact details. But Rav Dessler shook his head. He didn't want to call Rabbi Silver to thank him. He wanted to offer his thanks in person. Rav Nachum tried to dissuade his father from the idea, thinking it unwise for a man of such senior years to set out on the long journey to Ohio, but Rav Dessler had made up his mind.

And so, nine hours of train-ride later, they arrived in Cincinnati. They went straight to shul to daven *Shacharis,* following which Rabbi Silver invited them back to his home for breakfast. After they'd eaten and chatted generally, Rabbi Silver turned to his guests and asked, "And so, what brings you to Cincinnati?" He was sure that they'd come seeking his assistance in some way, shape, or form. After all, Rabbi Silver was known across the globe for his generosity and ability to solve major problems.

"I'm here," Rav Dessler replied, "to express my deep appreciation for all the kindness that you showed my son." Rabbi Silver, however, was not buying it. A few minutes later, he posed the question once again, "*Nu*, really, what brought you here?" And Rav Dessler responded the same way to his host's great surprise, "I have no ulterior motive for being here. I had one goal and one goal alone to come here. I wanted to express my gratitude personally."

It was only after the third time that Rabbi Silver tried to press Rav Dessler on his true intentions and received the same response, that he smiled and exclaimed, "Now I understand how important gratitude really is."[1]

מַתְנִי׳ הַפּוֹגֶמֶת כְּתוּבָּתָהּ לֹא תִּפָּרַע אֶלָּא בִּשְׁבוּעָה כֵּיצַד הָיְתָה כְּתוּבָּתָהּ אֶלֶף זוּז וְאָמַר לָהּ הִתְקַבַּלְתְּ כְּתוּבָּתֵיךְ וְהִיא אוֹמֶרֶת לֹא הִתְקַבַּלְתִּי אֶלָּא מָנֶה לֹא תִּפָּרַע אֶלָּא בִּשְׁבוּעָה: גְּמָ׳ אָמַר רָבָא מִדְּרַבָּנַן דְּפָרַע דָּיֵיק דְּמִיפְּרַע לָא דָּיֵיק.

Mishnah: *If a woman weakens her ketubah [by acknowledging that she has received partial payment], she can collect the remainder only by means of an oath. How so? If her ketubah was worth a thousand zuz, and her husband said to her, "You already received your ketubah payout," and she says, "I received only one hundred," she [has made a partial admission and] can collect the remainder only by means of an oath.*

Gemara: *Rava taught: This oath is a Rabbinic enactment. The one who is paying always pays attention. The one who is getting paid, does not always pay attention.*

"The one who is paying always pays attention. The one who is getting paid, does not always pay attention." What a powerful idea! True not only when it comes to financial transactions, but even in the realm of *chessed* and voluntary contributions. When you "pay" someone a favor or do him a kindness, you are keenly aware of how much effort you've made. The likelihood is that you won't forget the "transaction" anytime

---

1 Horowitz, *Otzar Sippurim L'Mechanchim* #346.

soon. All too often, however, the recipient will acknowledge your kindness at the time, but it doesn't take them long to forget how you helped him.

A good friend of mine was an incredible pulpit rabbi who was dedicated to being there and helping his congregants 24/7. There was one congregant for whom he felt that he had always gone the extra mile—he even traveled overseas to pay the congregant a *shivah* visit. Then the day arrived for his contract renewal a few years later. This gentleman for whom he'd always been there was the deciding vote on the board: the rabbi's contract would not be renewed. He was devastated—he'd dropped everything for this person; he'd spent thousands of dollars out of his own pocket and suddenly, he just wasn't "dynamic" enough for the congregation! Thank God, today he's a successful businessman, but sadly, his departure from the rabbinate was a huge loss to Klal Yisrael.

Politicians running for reelection are acutely aware of this sad side of human nature. One politician friend who brought substantial grant money into his community to build a new park went door knocking on the campaign trail. "Yes, I know you helped fund the park a couple of years back," came one response at the town-hall meeting, "but what have you done lately for us?" Unfortunately, some recipients of kindness have terribly short memories and appreciation spans.

Never forget those who have been kind to you in life. Keep a constant mental log, or even a written log, of all the wonderful things that people have done for you in life on a day-to-day basis. And more particularly, the big kindnesses that have brought you to this point in your life and made you who you are! Call them out of the blue and thank them. Update them on how things have played out in your life. They've played a major or minor role; don't ever forget your eternal gratitude!

It's easy for the payee to forget how much he's been paid. Just like the oath the Rabbis administered, make a commitment to yourself to pay attention to remembering those who have been good to you. May you never forget the people who have made you who you are today and maintain everlasting gratitude!

DAF 88

The Eternal Truth

In one of the narrow lanes of the Beis Yisrael neighborhood in Jerusalem stands a large, handsomely built synagogue. For a hundred years, a marble plaque affixed to its north wall has borne the legend:

"For everlasting remembrance in the House of God. This synagogue has been erected by the generosity of a donor, whose name shall remain hidden and concealed, who contributed a sum of 110 napoleons of gold."

For many years it was presumed that the funds were provided by one of the wealthy citizens of Jerusalem who wished to preserve his charity from the taint of pride by remaining anonymous. Few knew the true identity of the donor and the story behind his donation.

Rabbi Shlomo Zalman Porush was a man of modest means, though large sums of money passed through his hands. He was the secretary of one of the *kollel* societies which supported the poor Jews of Jerusalem with funds collected for that purpose throughout the Diaspora. Rabbi Shlomo Zalman was responsible for the sustenance of several hundred families whose support had been pledged by the Jewish community of Minsk and its environs in White Russia.

One year, as Pesach approached, the arrival of funds was delayed. Rabbi Shlomo knew that the money would be forthcoming, but in the meantime, the families for whom he was responsible had to be provided with matzos, wine, and other festival needs. He therefore turned to a neighbor of his, Reb Faivish Stoller, a carpenter who had worked hard all his life and had managed to put aside a considerable sum.

Faivish agreed to lend him his life savings—two hundred napoleons of gold—until the money would arrive from abroad.

Shortly after Passover, the long-awaited messenger arrived from Minsk. The purse that he brought contained only 110 napoleons, but an accompanying letter promised that the remainder was on the way. Rabbi Shlomo lost no time in bringing the money to his neighbor.

Several weeks later, the rest of the money arrived. But when Rabbi Shlomo brought the ninety gold coins to Reb Faivish, a most unpleasant surprise awaited him. The elderly carpenter, whose memory had begun to fail him, had lost all recollection of the first payment, and was adamant in his insistence that he had received nothing of the two hundred napoleons owed.

No written contract recorded the loan or the payment, for the two men had had absolute trust in each other. Now they had no recourse but to present their case before the *beis din* of the venerated chief rabbi of Jerusalem, Rabbi Shmuel Salant.

From a halachic standpoint, this was a textbook case: the borrower admits the loan, but claims that a partial payment has been made, which the lender denies. This is a classic example of *modeh b'miktzas* ("one who partially admits" an otherwise unsupportable claim); in such a case, the burden of proof rests with the lender, but the borrower must take a "Biblical oath" in affirmation of his argument.

Upon hearing the verdict of the *beis din*, Rabbi Shlomo Zalman turned pale. Never in his life did he imagine that he would be required to take an oath in court, never mind a "Biblical oath" performed upon a Torah scroll! He begged to be given several days to think over the matter.

When the *beis din* reconvened, Rabbi Shlomo Zalman announced that he was prepared to pay the disputed 110 napoleons out of his own pocket rather than take an oath. He only asked that he be given a few weeks to raise the money. Faivish Stoller agreed, and it appeared that the matter had been settled. But Rabbi Shmuel Salant would not allow this arrangement. "I'm sorry," he said to Rabbi Shlomo Zalman, "but this is not a private matter that can be settled between the litigants. It involves communal funds. As one who is entrusted with charity monies, your honesty must be beyond reproach. Unless it is decisively established that the money was paid as you claim, people will talk. I therefore insist that you take the oath."

Again, Rabbi Shlomo Zalman requested, and was granted, a short respite. For three days he fasted, wept, and recited Psalms. On the fourth day, he came before the *beis din* and swore that he had paid 110 napoleons to Faivish Stoller.

Shortly thereafter, Rabbi Shlomo Zalman put up his modest home for sale. To his family he explained that he had intended to sell the house in order to avoid taking the oath, and now he did not want to benefit from money that he had "saved" by swearing on a Torah scroll. To the proceeds of the sale, he added almost all of his savings to make the sum of 110 napoleons, which he presented to a committee that was raising money to build a new synagogue. His only stipulation was that no mention should be made of the source of the money.

Several months later, Faivish Stoller appeared in the small apartment to which Rabbi Shlomo had moved after the sale of his home. Without a word, he placed on Rabbi Shlomo Zalman's table a purse containing 110 napoleons of gold, which he had uncovered in a drawer in his workshop.[1]

מַתְנִי׳ עֵד אֶחָד מְעִידָהּ שֶׁהִיא פְּרוּעָה לֹא תִפָּרַע אֶלָּא בִשְׁבוּעָה: **גמ׳** אָמַר רָבָא מִדְּרַבָּנַן כְּדֵי לְהָפִיס דַּעְתּוֹ שֶׁל בַּעַל. אָמַר רַב פָּפָּא אִי פִּיקֵּחַ הוּא מַיְיתֵי לַהּ לִידֵי שְׁבוּעָה דְּאוֹרָיְיתָא יָהֵיב לַהּ כְּתוּבְּתַהּ בְּאַפֵּי חַד סָהֲדָא וְסָמֵיךְ סָהֲדָא קַמָּא אַסָּהֲדָא בָּתְרָא וּמוֹקֵים לְהוּ לְהָנָךְ קַמָּאֵי בְּמִלְוֶה.

רש״י: לידי שבועה דאורייתא—שהיא בשם או בכנוי ואוחז ספר בידו כדאמרינן בשבועות וחמורה היא מאד אבל שבועה דרבנן קללה בעלמא כעין שלנו.

Mishnah: *If a single witness testifies that the ketubah money has already been paid, the woman can only claim payment if she takes an oath [swearing that she has not been paid].*

Gemara: *Rava taught: This oath is a Rabbinic enactment in order to put the husband's mind at ease. Rav Pappa says: If he is astute, he could cause her to take a Biblical oath, as follows:*

---

1 Story told by Rabbi Zalman Ruderman.

He now gives her the payment of her entire ketubah sum in the presence of one witness, and joins the first witness to the last witness [so that there are now two witnesses to the payment]. And then, he transforms the original payment into a loan [and claims payment of that sum from her, supported by the testimony of the first witness].

Rashi: *For a Biblical oath, one must use God's name or epithet and hold the Torah in his hand, and it is very serious. Whereas for a Rabbinic oath, it is merely an oath with the penalty of a curse attached to it.*

Why do we make an individual swear on a Torah before the court? If he's a criminal, why would we expect him to tell the truth? If someone has no problem stealing, why would we presume that he would think twice about lying? But even in secular courts in western countries, it has become the accepted norm to swear on a Bible. This bothers many atheists who refuse to take the Bible and insist on making an affirmation of truth. But what are these atheists afraid of? If they don't believe in the Divinity of the Bible, making an oath while placing their hand upon the Bible should not concern them whatsoever. And yet, many are so concerned that they flatly refuse to do it!

What difference does the oath make? What is the extraordinary power that swearing on the Torah exhibits?

Clearly, there's something about swearing in God's name upon His written word that makes a profound and indelible impression upon even those completely removed from the realm of the Divine. Every human being was created in the image of God, regardless of whether or not he's willing to acknowledge his *tzelem Elokim*. And so, from the most hardened crook to the most stubborn atheist, there is something terrifying about taking a false oath in God's name. The crook might be willing to swindle his neighbor. But he would never defy God. In fact, our Sages tell us that even a thief prays before setting out on his mission of crime![2] Likewise the repudiation of the Bible by the atheist

---

2 *Berachos* 63a.

signifies not a disbelief, but a sense of trepidation. Many "atheists" remove God from their lives because they are not willing to deal with the tough questions of life's purpose and their spiritual responsibility. Their rejection of the Bible is yet another example of their innermost repressed struggles with themselves and their spark of the Divine.

Certainly, swearing by God's name over the Torah or a Bible makes the most sense to people who claim to live according to God's word in the Torah. In the western world, until the time of the Enlightenment, most Jews and Christians believed that the Bible is a document of eternal truth, the literal word of God. And so, to deviate from the truth under an oath of the Bible would have been unfathomable.

The Enlightenment, however, introduced new ideas to western thought. People began to question and demystify every aspect of their lives, including religion. Biblical criticism grew in popularity, and many Jews and Christians adopted the documentary hypothesis theory and ceased to believe in the truth of the Torah. It wasn't that they no longer believed in God. After all, they still considered themselves religious individuals. Rather, they stopped believing in the Divine authorship and eternal truth of the Torah. They believed that the Bible was written by various authors and inspired by ancient ways of thinking. Consequently, many elements of the Torah that did not accord with their modern sensibilities, they treated as no longer binding or merely allegorical.

But now, they walk into court and here's the problem. How can anyone who believes the Bible is the handiwork of mortal men—and open to change—take an oath over it? If the Bible's truth can change and be reinterpreted, what use is it as a moral compass? If the truth of the Bible is malleable and open to interpretation, then what's the use of swearing over it to tell the truth, the whole truth, and nothing but the truth. Whose truth are we talking about?

A number of years ago, Rabbanit Batya and I were honored to attend the swearing-in of Judge Daniel Zalmanowitz as he became the fourth ever Orthodox Jewish judge in Edmonton, Alberta, Canada. What impressed us most about the ceremony was that when it came time to swear, Judge Zalmanowitz put his yarmulke on his head, placed his hand upon his Artscroll Tanach, and took the oath. It was clearly a moment that he took with the utmost seriousness, understanding that an oath on the Bible was a religious act, a moment when he was advancing his Divine mission here on Earth. A moment of truth.

The Torah is sacred. It is the ultimate source of truth. If you start to question the truth of the Bible, you will find that the entire foundation of your value-system and indeed, western civilization itself, will be called into question. May you forever accept, embrace, and affirm by the eternal never-changing truth!

DAF 89

You Are the Witness

Professor Deborah Lipstadt is the most prominent scholar on the terrible phenomenon of Holocaust denial. After publishing her monumental work *Denying the Holocaust,* she was sued by UK activist David Irving for libel for condemning many of his writings and public statements as Holocaust denial.

English libel law places the burden of proof on the defendant rather than the plaintiff. Lipstadt and her publisher Penguin won the case by demonstrating that her accusations against Irving were substantially true and therefore not libelous. The presiding judge produced a written judgment 349 pages long detailing Irving's systematic distortion of the historical record of the Shoah. In reporting the events, *The Times* declared, "History has had its day in court and scored a crushing victory."

The Germans initially kept detailed records of their heinous crimes. But as it became increasingly clear that the Allied powers were closing in, they systematically destroyed all the documentation and physical evidence of their genocidal activities. Following the Shoah, the surest evidence of the Nazi massacre was the testimony of the survivors who had personally witnessed the carnage.

With each passing year, however, we see fewer and fewer Holocaust survivors at Yom HaShoah commemorations. Before long, all the survivors will have passed on. When that happens, who will bear witness to the horrors of the Shoah?

מַתְנִי׳ הוֹצִיאָה גֵט וְאֵין עִמּוֹ כְּתוּבָּה גּוֹבָה כְּתוּבָּתָהּ כְּתוּבָּה וְאֵין עִמָּהּ גֵּט הִיא אוֹמֶרֶת אָבַד גִּיטִּי וְהוּא אוֹמֵר אָבַד שׁוֹבְרִי וְכֵן בַּעַל חוֹב שֶׁהוֹצִיא שְׁטַר חוֹב וְאֵין עִמּוֹ פְּרוֹזְבּוּל הֲרֵי אֵלּוּ לֹא יִפָּרְעוּ רַבָּן שִׁמְעוֹן בֶּן גַּמְלִיאֵל אוֹמֵר מִן הַסַּכָּנָה וְאֵילָךְ אִשָּׁה גּוֹבָה כְּתוּבָּתָהּ שֶׁלֹּא בְּגֵט וּבַעַל חוֹב גּוֹבֶה שֶׁלֹּא בִּפְרוֹזְבּוּל.

רש״י: מן הסכנה—שגזרו עובדי כוכבים על המצות והיו יראים לשמור גיטיהן ומשקיבלתו שורפתו וכן פרוזבוליהן.

Mishnah: *If a woman produced a get and it was unaccompanied by a ketubah [asking for her divorce payout, it is sufficient and], she collects payment of her ketubah sum. If she produced the ketubah but had no accompanying get, and she says: "I lost my get," and he says: "I lost my receipt"; and likewise, in a case of a creditor who produced a promissory note after the Sabbatical Year, unaccompanied by a pruzbul document [preventing the annulment of the debt], these debts may not be collected. Rabban Shimon ben Gamliel says: From the time of danger and onward, a woman may collect payment of her ketubah sum without the get, and a creditor may collect debts without a pruzbul.*

Rashi: *The gentile rulers made decrees against the performance of mitzvos and they were scared to hold on to their get documents. As soon as they received them, they would burn them. And similarly, their pruzbuls.*

When a married couple gets divorced, the husband must pay the wife a sum of money agreed to when they were originally married and recorded in the *ketubah* on the wedding day. The Mishnah discusses a case where a woman claims that the divorce proceedings have taken place, but she has not yet been paid the sum owed to her. Without a *get* in hand, she is unable to collect payment. Rabban Shimon ben Gamliel says that there were times in history when it just wasn't possible to produce the *get*. When evil rulers decreed against the performance of mitzvos, it was dangerous to hold on to any ritual items, including the *get* document. Thus, as soon as such documents were written, as the halachah prescribes, they would immediately destroy them. How then could the ex-wife collect her debt in such a situation?

All she needed to do was present witnesses who could testify that the divorce took place.

We see from here that human testimony is more powerful than any physical documentation. Documents may be destroyed, but witnesses are able to testify that they saw the event take place. As long as the witnesses remain present, the evidence of their testimony is much stronger than a piece of paper. Undoubtedly, they could bear false witness, but a document may also be forged. The advantage of human over physical evidence is twofold. First, as we see here in the Mishnah, it is easier to destroy physical evidence than human witnesses. And second, physical evidence often only exists in the form of one or two documents. After all, how many copies are needed when a transaction happens? And even when multiple copies of the document are presented, it doesn't serve as any stronger evidence. They are simply copies of the same original document.

In contrast, human testimony often consists of multiple witnesses. By its very nature, the existence of multiple human accounts strengthens the evidence as the facts are corroborated when the various witnesses agree. Human perception and memory are frail and open to distortion. And so, when multiple witnesses all attest to the same facts having taken place, the evidence becomes unassailable.

But nobody lives forever. What happens to the evidence when the witnesses eventually die? They can transfer their testimony to other human beings. If they present the facts to other witnesses, the new witnesses may testify to the facts that they heard from the first witnesses. Once again, if multiple witnesses corroborate the same set of heard facts, and there is no conflicting evidence, then their testimony becomes irrefutable evidence.

When countless Shoah survivors all tell the same story of the Nazi genocide, the evidence is irrefutable. Sadly, over the next few years, we will lose the last of the Shoah survivors. But their passing doesn't mean the demise of human testimony. Those who have heard the testimony then become witnesses with a responsibility to convey the testimony of the Shoah to the world at large and to the next generation, who will in turn become witnesses. As long as we tell the stories precisely as we have heard them, the evidence will remain unassailable.

That's how our *mesorah* has operated for three millennia. Our ancestors witnessed the miracles of Yetzias Mitzrayim and the Giving of the Torah at Sinai. They conveyed their testimony to their children, who in turn, passed on the evidence to their children. For three thousand years, we've been telling the same story, corroborated by Jews around the world who all sit at the annual Seder table on Pesach and bear witness to the testimony of their parents. We then pledge to convey the evidence precisely to our children and grandchildren.

Even when the Reform movement began in the nineteenth century, its founders didn't arise and claim that they'd heard a different story from their parents. No, the story was the same. They just felt it was time for Judaism to modernize. But all Jews agree about the basic facts of the story. To deny the truth of the Exodus means effectively accusing one's own parents or grandparents of fabricating evidence and bearing false witness.

You are a witness to history. You have a personal responsibility to convey to the next generation the stories that you have heard from your parents and from Shoah survivors. Make sure you listen closely and attentively. Your testimony must be as precise as possible. May you forever be a true and faithful witness to every detail of the colossal events of our nation's greatest and most tragic moments!

DAF 90

Pay Yourself First

A wealthy individual had lent a significant sum of money to a needy individual. The day for repayment arrived, but the borrower was nowhere to be seen. A few days later, they crossed paths in shul.

"I'm terribly sorry I didn't make it around the other day," said the debtor, "I'll pay you back shortly."

But as time wore on, the lender began to wonder whether he would ever see his money again. He wasn't about to take the fellow to *beis din* over the loan. After all, what was the point if he didn't have the money to pay him back? But he did have an idea that he took to Rabbi Meir of Rothenburg for halachic advice.

"Rebbi, look, I know this man really needs the money. Can I just deduct it from my *maaser* obligation and consider it a charitable gift?"

תַּנְיָא מֵתוּ אַחַת בְּחַיָּיו וְאַחַת בְּמוֹתוֹ בֶּן נַנָּס אוֹמֵר יְכוֹלִין בְּנֵי הָרִאשׁוֹנָה לוֹמַר לִבְנֵי הַשְּׁנִיָּה בְּנֵי בַּעֲלַת חוֹב אַתֶּם טְלוּ כְּתוּבַּת אִמְּכֶם וּצְאוּ רַבִּי עֲקִיבָא אוֹמֵר כְּבָר קָפְצָה נַחֲלָה מִלִּפְנֵי בְּנֵי הָרִאשׁוֹנָה וְנָפְלָה לִפְנֵי בְּנֵי הַשְּׁנִיָּה מַאי לָאו בְּהָא קָא מִיפַּלְגִי דְּמָר סָבַר אַחַת בְּחַיָּיו וְאַחַת בְּמוֹתוֹ יֵשׁ לָהֶן כְּתוּבַּת בְּנִין דִּכְרִין וּמָר סָבַר אַחַת בְּחַיָּיו וְאַחַת בְּמוֹתוֹ אֵין לָהֶן כְּתוּבַּת בְּנִין דִּכְרִין אָמַר רַבָּה אַשְׁכַּחְתִּינְהוּ לְרַבָּנַן דְּבֵי רַב דְּיָתְבִי וְקָאָמְרִי דְּכוּלֵּי עָלְמָא אַחַת בְּחַיָּיו וְאַחַת בְּמוֹתוֹ יֵשׁ לָהֶן כְּתוּבַּת בְּנִין דִּכְרִין וְהָכָא בִּכְתוּבָּה נַעֲשֵׂית מוֹתָר לַחֲבֶרְתָּהּ וְהוּא הַדִּין לְבַעַל חוֹב קָמִיפַּלְגִי מָר סָבַר כְּתוּבָּה נַעֲשֵׂית מוֹתָר לַחֲבֶרְתָּהּ וְהוּא הַדִּין לְבַעַל חוֹב וּמָר סָבַר אֵין כְּתוּבָּה נַעֲשֵׂית מוֹתָר לַחֲבֶרְתָּהּ וְהוּא הַדִּין

לְבַעַל חוֹב וְאָמֵינָא לְהוּ אֲנָא בְּבַעַל חוֹב כּוּלֵּי עָלְמָא לָא פְּלִיגִי דְּהָוֵי מוֹתָר כִּי פְּלִיגִי בִּכְתוּבָּה.

רש״י: כי פליגי בכתובה—באחת בחייו ואחת במותו שהשניה חוב היא פליגי בן ננס סבר הרי זו כשאר חוב והוי מותר ור׳ עקיבא סבר לאו כשאר חוב דמי כיון דאינהו גופייהו קא שקלי והלכך הנך בני שניה מקבלין ולא פורעין נמצא שאין כאן נחלה דאורייתא ולא איתקן ירושת בנין דכרין דרבנן למיעקר נחלה דאורייתא.

If two co-wives died, one during the husband's lifetime and one following his death, Ben Nanas says: The sons of the first wife can say to the sons of the second wife: You are the children of a creditor, so collect your mother's ketubah payment and leave. Rabbi Akiva says: When the husband died, the inheritance already eluded the sons of the first wife and came into the possession of the sons of the second. Do they not disagree about the following? One Sage, Ben Nanas, holds that in a case where one wife died in his lifetime and one outlived him, the first wife's sons are entitled to collect the kesuvas b'nin dichrin. And the other Sage, Rabbi Akiva, holds that in a case where one wife died in his lifetime and one died following his death, the first wife's sons are not entitled to collect the kesuvas b'nin dichrin. Rabbah said: I found the Sages of the school of Rav sitting and saying: Everyone agrees that in a case where one wife died in his lifetime and one outlived him, the first wife's sons are entitled to collect the kesuvas b'nin dichrin. Here, however, they disagree with regard to the question of whether or not one marriage contract becomes surplus for the other. And the same is true with regard to payment made to a creditor. One Sage, Ben Nanas, holds that one marriage contract becomes surplus for the other, and the same is true with regard to payment made to a creditor, and one Sage, Rabbi Akiva, holds that one marriage contract does not become surplus for the other, and the same is true with regard to the debt owed to a creditor. And I [Rabbah] said to them: With regard to payment made to a creditor, everyone agrees that it is considered surplus. When do they disagree? With regard to the ketubah.

> ***Rashi:*** *They are arguing about a scenario where one wife died during his lifetime, and one outlived him. Is the ketubah payment to the second wife considered a debt? Ben Nanas says yes, and considers it to be taken from the surplus funds. But Rabbi Akiva says it cannot be considered like all other debts because they themselves are the ones taking the money. In other words, these children of the second wife are taking and not giving, meaning that there's no Biblical inheritance. And the Sages did not institute the b'nin dichrin inheritance where it would uproot the Biblical inheritance law.*

Generally, a wife's primary heir is her husband. But sometimes that can cause family issues to arise. Here's the how the principle of *b'nin dichrin* works. If a woman entered marriage with assets to her name and then she had children and later died, her husband inherits her property, as her primary heir. Now, let's say he remarries and has more children with the second wife. Strictly speaking, when he dies, all of his property would be divided amongst his children, per the Biblical laws of inheritance. Nevertheless, the Sages instituted the rule of *b'nin dichrin*, which entitles the children of the first wife to collect the sum stipulated to their mother in her *ketubah*, prior to the disbursement among the children of the estate according to the Biblical allocation.

Now, our Sages did not institute their enactment in order to uproot and replace Torah law. And so, they inserted a caveat that says that there must be sufficient funds in the estate for a portion to be distributed according to Biblical inheritance laws and, only then, can their enactment of *b'nin dichrin* take effect. If there is no money in the estate to execute according to the process of Biblical inheritance laws, then the Rabbinic enactment of *b'nin dichrin* does not take effect. The children of the first wife have no claim to preferential treatment. The estate is allocated equally (except for the firstborn who receives his traditional double portion) amongst the sons of both wives.

In our Gemara, Rabbah presents a case where the husband-father had an outstanding debt that must be paid prior to any inheritance claims. He explains that all would agree that the availability of such monies activates the Biblical process of estate execution, and therefore the first children may subsequently make their Rabbinically enacted inheritance claims. The debatable situation would be where there is no external creditor, but the sons from the first marriage are claiming to be creditors. After all, they contend, they have a claim on the estate of the money belonging to their mother. As explained by *Rashi*, Ben Nanas accepts their claim and treats them as any other creditor, thus satisfying the Biblical inheritance process requirement.

Rabbi Akiva says that makes no sense. A creditor is a person to whom you pay money that you owe. In this case, the children are effectively their own creditor. They are paying themselves! How does that satisfy the spirit of the Torah law of inheritance?

Let's return to the question of the wealthy individual who asked Rabbi Meir of Rothenburg whether it would be permissible to write off his loan and deduct it from his *maaser* account. The *Maharam* ruled that it was not halachically acceptable.[1] What was the source of his ruling? The *Gilyoni HaShas* points to our *Rashi* as the basis.[2] *Rashi* states that one cannot pay himself as we require a bona fide recipient. Likewise, in the case of the wealthy lender, he's not really giving the charity to the needy individual. He's giving himself the charity! Nevertheless, the bottom line is that, according to the *Rama*, it is halachically permissible to write off a loan to a needy person and deduct it from one's *maaser* account.[3]

While we're on the topic of paying oneself, let's take a moment to mention the application of the concept as employed by contemporary financial advisers. At first blush, it sounds funny to pay yourself. But we see that our Sages already discussed the idea many centuries ago. The concept as it is espoused in the realm of personal finance refers to the importance of saving money even when you're struggling to keep your head above water. There are bills to pay, from rent or mortgage to groceries to clothing, not to mention credit card bills and debt.

---

1 *Shu"t Maharam bar Baruch, siman* 753.

2 *Kiddushin* 15a, s.v. *lo*.

3 *Yoreh De'ah* 257:5.

What's the first payment to make each month when your paycheck arrives?

Your own savings account.

If you wait until you've paid everyone else, there will be nothing left for your own savings account. But if you pay yourself before paying anyone else, before long you'll have significant savings to your name. Whether those funds pay for kids' weddings, education, a home purchase, or retirement funds, "future you" will be incredibly grateful for the sacrifices "present you" is making today.

And returning to the tzedakah discussion, there are really two pots that must be paid before anyone else: your savings account and your charity account. When the paycheck appears in your bank account, the key to success in both of these realms is to pay your debts immediately. Ten percent to the tzedakah pot. And ten percent to the savings pot. Once you've made those payments you can figure out how to pay all the other bills, as difficult as it might sound to work out how to make ends meet with only eighty percent of your paycheck.

Today it may be a serious challenge. But in the long run, paying yourself and tzedakah first will reap incredible rewards. May Hashem open His Heavenly treasure chest and shower overflowing blessing upon you!

DAF 91

May His Memory Be a Blessing

There was once a fellow who had a creditor with a claim of one hundred *zuz* against him. He died and left a small tract of land worth fifty *zuz*. The creditor came and seized it. Hoping to keep the land in the family, the children of the deceased came forward and gave the creditor fifty *zuz* to buy back the property from him. But he wasn't appeased. He returned and seized it again in order to collect the remainder of the debt. Feeling squeezed, they appeared before Abaye's *beis din*.

הָהוּא גַּבְרָא דַּהֲווֹ מַסְּקִי בֵּיהּ מְאָה זוּזֵי שָׁכֵיב שְׁבַק קַטִּינָא דְּאַרְעָא דַּהֲוָה שָׁוְיָא חַמְשִׁין זוּזֵי אֲתָא בַּעַל חוֹב וְקָטָרֵיף לֵיהּ אֲזוּל יַתְמֵי יְהַבוּ לֵיהּ חַמְשִׁין זוּזֵי הֲדַר קָטָרֵיף לַהּ אֲתוֹ לְקַמֵּיהּ דְּאַבָּיֵי אָמַר לָהֶן מִצְוָה עַל הַיְתוֹמִים לִפְרוֹעַ חוֹב אֲבִיהֶן הָנֵי קַמָּאֵי מִצְוָה עֲבַדִיתוּ הַשְׁתָּא כִּי טָרֵיף בְּדִין קָטָרֵיף.

רש"י: מצוה על היתומים לפרוע חוב אביהן—משום כבוד אביהן אלא שאין לבית דין לכופן על כך דלאו מצות עשה מפורשת היא כסוכה וכלולב אלא מצוה בעלמא דרבנן.

Abaye said to them: It is a mitzvah for orphans to settle their father's debt. With the money you paid initially, you performed a mitzvah. [But the payment did not cancel the lien on the property.] And so, now when he has come to seize the land, he is repossessing it lawfully.

Rashi: *It is a mitzvah for orphans to settle their father's debt—Due to the honor of their father. However, the court*

> *cannot force them to do so, since it is not a clear positive mitzvah like sukkah or lulav, but a general Rabbinic mitzvah.*

If someone died with unpaid debts, must his children pay? *Rashi* says that it's a gesture of honor toward their father to settle his debts—it's a mitzvah—but not enforceable. What situation are we talking about? According to Rabbeinu Nissim, we're asking them to pay the debts from the estate.[1] The *Rashba*, however, maintains that if their father left an inheritance, then they must certainly repay his debts from the estate.[2] In what case would it be praiseworthy, but not obligatory? When he left insufficient funds to cover his debts. It would be an honorable mitzvah to repay their father's creditors out of their own accounts even though they are not obligated to do so.

Our Sages teach that we are required to honor our parents both while they are alive and even when they have passed on.[3] The example given by the Gemara is that when quoting something one has learned from a parent, he should mention that he heard the teaching from his parent, "*zichrono li'vrachah*"—of blessed memory. What does *zichrono li'vrachah* mean? It signifies that the memory of the deceased is a source of blessing to those in this world.

The blessing provided by a son who gives over a lesson in his father's name is clear. In our Gemara, the meaning is even starker. The reason it's a mitzvah for children to repay their deceased parents' debts is that we want the parents' mention to always be for a blessing. If they don't pay off the debts, think about how people will respond when the person's name comes up in conversation. "Oh, him? That scoundrel borrowed money from me and never paid me back! He took his debts with him to the grave." When the children take it upon themselves to repay their parents' debts out of their own pockets, it's a huge mitzvah. While they're not under any obligation, doing so protects and honors the memory of their late parents.

---

1 *Ran* 50a.

2 *Shu"t HaRashba* 4:152.

3 *Kiddushin* 31b.

Of course, one doesn't need to have debt-ridden parents to show them honor after they have passed. There are so many ways that one can honor his loved ones that ensure their memory is an eternal blessing. When we do mitzvos in their name, we honor their memory. That's why it's customary to sponsor Torah learning and *sefarim* in memory of our dear departed loved ones. Connecting their names to the mitzvah we're performing enhances the blessing of their memory in this world.

So next time you open up a *sefer* to learn, take a quick glance at the names on the dedication page. Their children have made the publication of the *sefer* possible. They've done the mitzvah so that their parents' memory would be for a blessing. Take a moment to have them in mind when learning from that *sefer*, that their *neshamah* should receive reward through your learning, and thank them for making the *sefer* available for you to learn from.

Why is the blessing of memory important? Rabbi Sacks writes:[4]

> *"There is a profound difference between history and memory. History is his story—an event that happened sometime else to someone else. Memory is my story—something that happened to me and is part of who I am. History is information. Memory, by contrast, is part of identity. I can study the history of other peoples, cultures, and civilizations. They deepen my knowledge and broaden my horizons. But they do not make a claim on me. They are the past as past. Memory is the past as present, as it lives on in me. Without memory there can be no identity."*

When you bless the memory of a *niftar*, someone who has passed on to the Next World, you manifest and eternalize his being in this world. When you learn Torah in his memory, his spirit is expressed through you. Your actions give him spiritual energy in Heaven, known as an *aliyah*. That's why it's so important to seek opportunities to bring blessing to the memory of your loved ones. May you honor your parents throughout their lives and beyond!

---

4 *Chief Rabbi's Haggadah*, p. 29.

DAF 92

Just Your Average Joe

During the time between Adam and Noach, humankind became increasingly degenerate. One of the individuals in the individuals in the generations between them was a figure called Chanoch. The Torah states about Chanoch:[1] "Chanoch walked with God, but then was no more, for God took him." While Chanoch's 365 years weren't negligible, he lived a considerably shorter life than his father and his son, who both lived well into their nine hundreds. Our Sages teach that "God took him" means that he died prematurely. What was the cause of his death?

The *Midrash Lekach Tov* writes that while he was righteous, he wasn't on the highest level of righteousness. We're told that the patriarchs "walked *before* Hashem."[2] But Chanoch only "walked *with* Hashem," which is a lower level. According to *Rashi*, he was on the verge of sin and God took him prematurely to avoid his spiritual fall. Was he a bad person? Not at all. He was clearly righteous. Nevertheless, he wasn't on the highest spiritual level possible. Compared to Avraham, Yitzchak, and Yaakov, he was relatively average. And in a world filled with moral corruption, his mediocrity wouldn't have been able to stand up to the

---

1 *Bereishis* 5:24.

2 *Bereishis* 48:15.

spiritual challenges that lay ahead. And so, Hashem saw no choice but to take him before his time.[3]

> אָמַר רַבָּה רְאוּבֵן שֶׁמָּכַר כָּל שְׂדוֹתָיו לְשִׁמְעוֹן וְחָזַר שִׁמְעוֹן וּמָכַר שָׂדֶה אַחַת לְלֵוִי וַאֲתָא בַּעַל חוֹב דִּרְאוּבֵן רָצָה מִזֶּה גּוֹבֶה רָצָה מִזֶּה גּוֹבֶה וְלָא אֲמַרַן אֶלָּא דִּזַבְנֵהּ בֵּינוֹנִית אֲבָל זַבְנֵהּ עִידִּית וְזִבּוּרִית מָצֵי אֲמַר לֵיהּ לְהָכִי טְרַחִי וּזְבַנִי אַרְעָא דְּלָא חַזְיָא לָךְ.
>
> *Rabbah said: Reuven sold all his fields to Shimon, and Shimon subsequently sold one of the fields to Levi. Reuven's creditor then came [to repossess one of the fields that was mortgaged to him]. If he desires, he can collect from this one [Shimon], and if he desires, he can collect from that one [Levi, since he has a lien that applies equally to all the properties that once belonged to Reuven]. And we said this only if Shimon sold Levi land of average quality, but if he sold him land of superior quality or inferior quality, Levi may say to the creditor: It was for this reason that I toiled to buy land that is not fit for you.*

We have four characters in this story: Creditor lends money to Reuven who buys some fields. Reuven then sells the fields to Shimon. Shimon sells a single field to Levi. Creditor wants his money back. Reuven has no money. Creditor then goes to Levi and threatens to repossess the field. Levi tells him he has no right to this particular field because it's of either superior or inferior quality. Only average quality fields may be repossessed, which is exactly why Levi bought the field, because he knew that it couldn't be repossessed. Creditor must instead claim one of the average quality fields from Shimon.

It makes sense that Creditor cannot repossess the superior field. A superior product is obviously better than an average product. But what makes the inferior field more valuable than the average field? The reason is as follows: When Levi buys an inferior piece of property, does he buy it with the intention of treating it like he would his superior

---

3 It should be noted that some commentators maintain that he was actually taken early because of his superior righteousness, and he ascended to Heaven alive like Eliyahu HaNavi (*Maseches Derech Eretz* 1:18).

property? Of course not. He buys it to fix it up and make a profit. Many successful people have made a fortune buying inferior properties, fixing them up, and flipping them for a much higher price than they paid and invested.

In contrast, an average field will produce averagely. On the one hand, it's not producing a superior crop, but on the other hand, it's not inferior enough to warrant investment to rebuild it and flip it. That's why Levi toiled to purchase either a superior or inferior piece of property, but knew that there's little to be gained from an average piece of land. That's the general problem with mediocrity and averageness.

In life, many people fall into lives of averageness and mediocrity. On the one hand, they're not reaching their potential, but on the other hand, they're not performing poorly enough to make the decision to pull their socks up. Any employer will attest to this idea—great employees are wonderful and bad employees can be terminated. The most challenging employees are the mediocre workers who are doing enough just to get by. They did nothing wrong, so you can't get rid of them, but they're not really doing a great job.

It's not just at work that mediocrity is a problem. Throughout life, being average is the worst place a person can be. Such a person gets stuck in a rut and doesn't feel compelled to make a change and become who he was destined to be. He coasts through school. He goes with the flow in his career. He's average when it comes to community volunteerism. He's an OK family member. He's an OK friend. There's just nothing spectacular about him. He never really pours his heart and soul into what he's doing, because getting by is often good enough.

But you know that your life is a superior product. You are a child of the Almighty. He has chosen you for greatness. You have unlimited potential and it's time to unleash your inner true self. You have the power to be an incredible contributor to the world. You have the power to be an incredible parent, spouse, child, friend, neighbor, and community member.

Stop settling for mediocrity. God wants you to be magnificent. May you merit pulling yourself out of mediocrity and becoming everything the Almighty destined you to be!

DAF 93

Untying the Knot

It was Count Hevelburg's sixtieth birthday. Family, friends, government officials, and VIPs had traveled in to celebrate from across Europe. Count Hevelburg was renowned for his leadership and philanthropic pursuits. And so, when in the middle of the party, a knock was heard upon the door, it came as no surprise to the butler to see an old beggar on the doorstep.

"It's cold outside," said the man, "do you have any old clothes to keep me warm on this winter's night?"

The members of the household knew that no needy person was ever to be turned away empty-handed, but this wasn't quite the night to bring the old man into the house for a hot cup of soup.

"If you just head up the stairs on the side of the house, you'll find your way into the attic," the butler instructed him. "There we keep the old clothes. Feel free to take whatever you and your family needs."

The old man nodded gratefully and headed up the stairs. Once he reached the attic, he couldn't believe his good fortune. Clothing was in abundance. And not just any clothing. The finest garments he'd ever laid his eyes upon. Feeling he'd struck gold, he began to collect one piece of clothing after another, already picturing his wife and children in these beautiful designer pieces.

Once he'd gathered all the clothes that excited him, he said to himself, "But how will I bring them all home?" Just then he saw a bundle of string. "Perfect," he thought, "that's obviously there for people like me to tie up our acquisitions." But as he picked up the string, he realized it was full of knots. He started trying to untangle the knots but quickly gave up when he saw a better solution. There in the corner of the room was a clean, knot-free, piece of string, stretching from the ceiling to the floor of the attic. "Great," he thought as he pulled out his pocketknife. "All I need is to cut a small piece of this string and I don't have to waste my time undoing any knots."

He begins to cut, when suddenly he hears a massive crash and the sound of breaking glass in the room below him, followed by a piercing shriek. "My prize chandelier! My gorgeous chandelier!" he hears the countess sobbing. "I inherited it from my great-grandmother. It's been in the family for generations and now the rope that was holding it up must have severed..."

> אָמַר אַבָּיֵי רְאוּבֵן שֶׁמָּכַר שָׂדֶה לְשִׁמְעוֹן שֶׁלֹּא בְּאַחְרָיוּת וְיָצְאוּ עָלָיו עֲסִיקִין עַד שֶׁלֹּא הֶחְזִיק בָּהּ יָכוֹל לַחֲזוֹר בּוֹ מִשֶּׁהֶחְזִיק בָּהּ אֵינוֹ יָכוֹל לַחֲזוֹר בּוֹ מִשּׁוּם דְּאָמַר לֵיהּ חַיְיתָא דְּקִיטְרֵי סְבַרְתְּ וְקַבֵּילְתְּ.
>
> *Abaye said: If Reuven sold a field to Shimon with no guarantee, and it emerged that it had disputants, as long as Shimon has not yet taken possession of it, he can renege on the deal. However, once he has taken possession, he cannot renege, because at that point, Reuven can say to him, "You agreed to a sack of knots and accepted it."*

Many people go through life just agreeing to a sack of knots and accepting it. They avoid making changes in their life because there are just too many knots in the bag. For some, it's an unhappy marriage. For others, it's a dead-end job. And for others it's an impractical university degree that won't get them anywhere useful in life. They've been at it for so long that it's reached a point where it would be too much of a hassle to untie all the knots and reopen the bag. And so, they go through life plodding along unhappily, but not willing to face up to their issues.

What's the solution? Not to untie all the knots in the bag all at once. And certainly not to slash the proverbial Gordian knot. In most cases, that would have disastrous consequences. The right approach is to loosen one knot at a time. And then to figure out if matters now feel less constricted and more relaxed. Or whether you might need to tie up those loose ends, but in a better fashion than the previous time.

Let's say you're feeling constrained in your marriage. You want out, but you feel that at this stage of your life, it would be too complicated because it's now a "sack full of knots." You have children together. You have shared bank accounts, a shared family home. It's just not worth it.

You're right. It would be disastrous simply to walk away from all those commitments. But that doesn't mean you need to remain in an unhappy marriage. The solution is to untie one knot at a time. The Hebrew word for knot, "*kesher*" contains the same letters as the word for falsehood, "*sheker*." Those feelings of knottiness in your marriage result from certain falsehoods that have entered. Marriage should be the ultimate bliss in this world. Instead of viewing your sack as full of knots, what you need to do is address each knot individually and ascertain how the *kesher* has become manifest with *sheker*.

When you examine each knot individually, you'll find that it's not a sack full of knots. Rather, it's a number of falsehoods that are making life knotty and unbearable. Once they can be addressed, you will, with God's help, attain a happy marriage. While each couple has its unique challenges, one of the key starting points is how we talk about that sack full of knots. That's the language of *always* and *never*.

"You never clean up after yourself."

"You always come home late."

If those statements are true, then indeed the marriage needs serious fixing. But more often than not, the statements are massive over-generalizations.

"What do you mean I *never* clean up? Just yesterday, I did!"

"What do you mean I *always* come home late? Many days, I'm here earlier than expected!"

The problem with thinking of life as a sack full of knots is that it probably isn't really full of knots. Most of the sack is filled with blessing! Yes, there are some knots there, but when we examine them one-by-one we realize that they're not all-encompassing, overwhelming, and unmanageable.

Likewise, when it comes to improving their spiritual lives, many people think of their lives as a sack full of knots. They might recognize the truth of Torah, but their lives are such a knotted sack that it would be too disruptive to untie all the knots and start fresh. Just the thought of turning your kitchen and diet around is scary. Just the thought of completely transforming one day a week into Shabbos is daunting. Just the thought of becoming "observant"—what would that mean for your social life and relationships?

When you think about it like that, it truly is overwhelming. But that's not the right way to think about spiritual change. God doesn't want you to suddenly let all the air out of the bag—you're right that it would leave you in a vacuum. No, He wants you to go about spiritual change one knot at a time. Now suddenly it doesn't feel so overwhelming and impossible.

When we see a sack full of knots, human nature is to walk away and find a short-cut solution. But that's not what Hashem wants. He wants us to set out on a gradual journey of resolution, one knot at a time. May you massage out the knots in your life, one by one, and never be afraid to confront and work at resolving the issues in your life!

DAF 94

The Shul President

It was a wonderful High Holy Day season and the president decides to treat the rabbi and cantor to a few days at his Caribbean island villa. They set out in his yacht. But en route, they are overrun by pirates. The pirates capture their boat and bring them aboard the pirate ship.

"Let's see how well you swim," they tell the vacationers. "It's time to walk the plank, but we'll allow you each one wish before we send you to your destiny."

They turn to the rabbi who tells them, "Look, I have one sermon that I was working on for months. It was going to be the half hour piece de resistance of Yom Kippur, but then, we were running out of time before the end of the fast. So, I just gave a quick *vort*. I'd like to deliver it now."

"That's fine," they respond, "you can give that sermon in just a moment. But mate," they continue turning to the cantor, "what's your final wish?"

"Funny you should ask," he replies, "I, too, prepared a masterpiece for *Neilah* that I didn't have the chance to present to the congregation. I would like to sing that now."

"OK, you can do that. But before you do, what is your final wish?" they ask the president.

"Gentlemen," exclaims the president, "PLEASE just let me walk the plank first!"

אָמַר רַב הוּנָא הָנֵי תְּרֵי אַחֵי וּתְרֵי שׁוּתָּפֵי דְּאִית לְהוּ דִּינָא בַּהֲדֵי חַד וַאֲזַל חַד מִינַּיְיהוּ בַּהֲדֵיהּ לְדִינָא לָא מָצֵי אִידָּךְ לְמֵימַר לֵיהּ אַתְּ לָאו בַּעַל דְּבָרִים דִּידִי

אַתְּ אֶלָּא שְׁלִיחוּתֵיהּ עֲבַד הָכָא אָמַר אִילּוּ אֲנָא הֲוַאי טָעֵינְנָא טְפֵי אִיתֵיהּ בְּמָתָא אִיבְּעִי לֵיהּ לְמֵיתֵי.

Rav Huna said: In a case of two brothers or two partners who have legal proceedings against another individual, and one of them went to attend to the legal proceedings against him and lost, the other brother or partner cannot say to the litigant: I am not bound by the legal decision. Rather, the brother or partner who appeared in court is considered to have acted as his agent. Here, [he cannot] say: Had I been there, I would have presented a more convincing claim. If he is in town, he must come to court to participate.

Probably the most thankless job in the world is that of the shul president. In shuls, everyone has an opinion, from the color of the carpet, to the flavor of the herring at the *kiddush*, to staffing issues, to who should be invited as scholar-in-residence. And so much more. Humbly keeping the shul together, getting precious little *kavod* or gratitude for the hours and hours of work each day, most people have no idea what goes into the ultimate volunteer position.

Whenever I read this Gemara, I think of the number of complaints the shul president and other dedicated volunteers get from congregants who don't like this or don't like that and would do it better. In my decades of communal life, I've worked with some incredible volunteers. They work tirelessly to make the shul the center of Jewish life with all the finest programs. But you can rest assured that no matter how hard they've worked, someone will arrive at the event and find something to criticize.

I'll never forget one year in shul when we staged Purim in the Land of Oz. Our volunteers were hammering and painting and decorating for weeks leading up to the event. Just prior to the kick-off, a shul member walks in and decides that the window on a wood house vaguely resembles a cross and that the sleep-deprived volunteers should remove it immediately. Believe it or not, the really nice folks just wanted everyone to feel special and without blinking, they accommodated and repainted the window. They really didn't need to do it. But they did. Because shul volunteers are very special people.

What made that individual think that he had the right to criticize? Along with all the other shul critics who know how to run the shul better than the president and the board?! Says the Gemara: If you want a say, then show up and make yourself available. Don't come afterwards and say you could have done a better job. There's no shortage of spots on most shul boards and committees. Every organization is aching for volunteers.

Unfortunately, too many shul members treat their shul as customers. If they don't get their way, then they'll just go elsewhere. But who do they think they're threatening? Other "customers." The difference is that the customers who are being criticized are the ones who have stepped up to take ownership of their shul. They're the ones who care. They're the ones who lose sleep at night when the expenses column of the budget sheet is greater than the income column.

Some people know how much stress and anxiety goes into communal work and swear they'll never go near it. But it's worth every moment. The Chafetz Chaim is said to have once taught: It's already been decreed on High how much stress and anxiety you will experience this year. If you decide to dedicate yourself to the needs of the community and have to deal with a ton of stress and anxiety in the process, that anxiety will be deducted from your pre-ordained account. And you'll now have less stress and anxiety to deal with in your family and professional life. Less stress from your teenagers. Less anxiety at work. Clients who pay up so that you can get home and be there for your spouse and kids and have time to deal with the communal issues.

Thank you to shul presidents for everything you do.

And to everyone else: It's time to stop criticizing. It's time to step up and be part of the solution. May you forever merit to serve the community faithfully!

DAF 95

I Am a Tzaddik

The Gemara in *Berachos* teaches:[1] The *tzaddik* is directed by his good inclination. The *rasha* is directed by his bad inclination. The *beinoni*—an average person—is directed by both. Rabbah comments, "Like us, we're *beinonim*!"

"How can you say that?" asks his disciple Abaye. "The master is not giving a chance for anyone else to survive! If the great Rabbah is only considered average, every other person in the world in comparison must be a *rasha*!"

What did Rabbah mean by his enigmatic comment?

> אָמַר אַבָּיֵי נְכָסַי לִיךְ וְאַחֲרַיִךְ לִפְלוֹנִי וְעָמְדָה וְנִיסֵּת בַּעַל לוֹקֵחַ הָוֵי וְאֵין לְאַחֲרֶיךָ בִּמְקוֹם בַּעַל כְּלוּם כְּמַאן כִּי הַאי תַּנָּא דְּתַנְיָא נְכָסַי לִיךְ וְאַחֲרַיִךְ לִפְלוֹנִי יָרַד הָרִאשׁוֹן וּמָכַר הַשֵּׁנִי מוֹצִיא מִיַּד הַלָּקוֹחוֹת דִּבְרֵי רַבִּי רַבָּן שִׁמְעוֹן בֶּן גַּמְלִיאֵל אוֹמֵר אֵין לַשֵּׁנִי אֶלָּא מַה שֶּׁשִּׁיֵּיר רִאשׁוֹן וּמִי אָמַר אַבָּיֵי הָכִי וְהָאָמַר אַבָּיֵי אֵיזֶהוּ רָשָׁע עָרוּם זֶה הַמַּשִּׂיא עֵצָה לִמְכּוֹר בִּנְכָסִים כְּרַבָּן שִׁמְעוֹן בֶּן גַּמְלִיאֵל מִי קָאָמַר תִּינָּשֵׂא נִשֵּׂאת קָאָמַר.
>
> *Abaye said: If a man said to an unmarried woman: My property is hereby bequeathed to you, and after you die, it will pass to so-and-so, and the woman went and married someone and then died, her husband takes possession of the property and is considered a purchaser. And the "after you" person receives*

1 61b.

nothing in a case where there is a husband. In accordance with whose opinion did Abaye rule? In accordance with the opinion of this Tanna, as it is taught: My property is hereby bequeathed to you, and after you die, it will pass to so-and-so, and the first beneficiary entered, i.e., took possession of the field, and sold it, the second beneficiary has the right to repossess that property from the purchasers. This is the statement of Rebbi. Rabban Shimon ben Gamliel says: The second beneficiary has a claim only to that which the first beneficiary left over. And did Abaye actually say so? Didn't Abaye say: Who is a cunningly wicked person [rasha arum]? One who gives his fellow advice to sell his property in accordance with the ruling of Rabban Shimon ben Gamliel [in order to prevent the second beneficiary from taking possession of the property]. Did he say that the woman should be advised to marry? He said his ruling with regard to a case where the woman did get married.

In various places in the Torah and Gemara, we find Abaye's term "*rasha arum,*" meaning "cunningly wicked." In *Sotah*, we learn that the *rasha arum* is responsible for destroying the world.[2] And in *Parashas Mishpatim*, the Torah states, "If a man shall sin against his fellow to murder him with cunning."[3]

Rabbeinu Bachya explains that murder necessitates cunning. The murderer must plot the perfect time and place to commit the crime. Where does this cunning originate? From the snake of the Garden of Eden that was "more cunning than any beast upon the face of the earth." The snake's wily ways brought Eve and Adam to sin and that led to the very first murder by Cain. Therefore, says Rabbeinu Bachya, any person who plans to sin is called cunningly wicked.[4]

Nobody is perfect. When we act contrary to the will of Hashem, at that very moment we are considered a *rasha*, and in order to restore

---

2 20b.

3 *Shemos* 21:14.

4 *Yeshayah* 3.

our righteous status, *teshuvah* is required.[5] And lest we think that those great individuals who never sin are not prone to it, Rabbah reminds us that his spiritual service was also a constant struggle between the voices inside his head pulling him in either direction.

But if we're all struggling, why was Abaye so concerned with his teacher's adoption of the *beinoni* title? Because such a declaration may lead to hopelessness on the part of the masses. If even the great Rabbah wasn't righteous, could anyone else ever expect to strive for righteousness?

Rabbi Shimon teaches, "Do not be wicked in your own estimation."[6] The *Rambam* explains that when a person thinks of himself as wicked, he loses his motivation to improve any deficiency that he may have. After all, if I was born a sinner and will forever remain a sinner, then why bother making any effort? Thus, the key to achieving righteousness is to think of yourself as righteous. What then happens is that you adopt the attitude of "*es past nisht*," which means "that's not appropriate."

If you believe that you're a righteous person, then you're going to constantly strive to lead a life that is morally and spiritually exceptional. It doesn't matter what anyone else is doing. You're righteous and you know what you need to do to maintain your elevated spiritual stature.

You are a *tzaddik*. It doesn't matter what's happened in the past. Our Sages tell us that if a man betroths a woman "on condition that I am a complete *tzaddik*," the marriage is effective. Even if we know he was a terrible sinner his whole life, we assume that at that moment, he resolved in his mind to do *teshuvah*. Just like that, in a mere instant, he has transformed his mindset.

But it's not enough to know that you're a *tzaddik*. You need to constantly remind yourself. You need to verbalize it. Your constant mantra should be: "I am a *tzaddik*." The more you tell yourself that you're a *tzaddik*, the more it will become ingrained in your very essence and dictate every aspect of your life.

You know that you're not wicked. After all, wickedness is equated with premeditated misbehavior. That's not you. You might not always get it

5 *Likutei Amarim*, ch. 1.

6 *Avos* 2.

right. But you're a *tzaddik* and you get it right nine times out of ten. In Hashem's eyes, He considers you a *tzaddik* as long as you're getting it right most of the time![7] May you always keep reminding yourself that you are a *tzaddik* and forever prosper spiritually!

---

7 *Rambam, Hilchos Teshuvah* 3:1.

DAF 96

The Rabbi's Friends

For sixteen years we lived in Edmonton, Alberta, Canada. During that period, I watched from afar as many of my colleagues aged out of small-community rabbinics. It just wasn't feasible anymore for them to live in places that didn't have satisfactory yeshiva day-school options for their children. And so most small communities end up with a new rabbi every couple of years as their rabbi and rebbetzin move on to big city life, and the shul, once again, seeks a young Rabbinic couple to lead them.

Thank God, we were able to stay in Edmonton for a decade and a half due to the generosity and philanthropy of one family: the Ghermezians, owners of North America's major malls, from West Edmonton Mall to Mall of America to American Dream. For many years, they were based in Edmonton, where their mall interests began. They realized that bringing up their children in Edmonton would require significant investment in Torah institutions, and so they created a *kollel* and a parallel school, Menorah Academy.

While Rabbanit Batya and I were associated with the major shul in town, we were very blessed with the resources the Ghermezian family brought to the community, especially Menorah. We had a formidable yeshiva day-school for our children—excelling in both Jewish and secular subjects—and our eldest, Millie, went all the way through twelfth grade and on to Michlalah Seminary and Yeshiva University.

Quite a number of the Rabbinic families that the Ghermezians brought out to Edmonton for the *kollel* and Menorah also stayed for many years because the Ghermezians know how to treat rabbis with love, care, and respect, tending to their every need. Any issue that arose, the Ghermezians made sure that the rabbis were assisted.

But why? Surely, the rabbis could change their own tires. Surely, the rabbis could shovel their own driveways. Why were the Ghermezians so intimately involved in the lives of their Rabbinic families?

אָמַר רַבִּי יְהוֹשֻׁעַ בֶּן לֵוִי כָּל מְלָאכוֹת שֶׁהָעֶבֶד עוֹשֶׂה לְרַבּוֹ תַּלְמִיד עוֹשֶׂה לְרַבּוֹ חוּץ מֵהַתָּרַת (לו) מִנְעָל אָמַר רָבָא לָא אֲמַרַן אֶלָּא בִּמְקוֹם שֶׁאֵין מַכִּירִין אוֹתוֹ אֲבָל בִּמְקוֹם שֶׁמַּכִּירִין אוֹתוֹ לֵית לַן בַּהּ אָמַר רַב אָשֵׁי וּבִמְקוֹם שֶׁאֵין מַכִּירִין אוֹתוֹ נָמֵי לָא אֲמַרַן אֶלָּא דְּלָא מַנַּח תְּפִלִּין אֲבָל מַנַּח תְּפִלִּין לֵית לַן בַּהּ אָמַר רַבִּי חִיָּיא בַּר אַבָּא אָמַר רַבִּי יוֹחָנָן כָּל הַמּוֹנֵעַ תַּלְמִידוֹ מִלְּשַׁמְּשׁוֹ כְּאִילּוּ מוֹנֵעַ מִמֶּנּוּ חֶסֶד שֶׁנֶּאֱמַר לַמָּס מֵרֵעֵהוּ חָסֶד רַב נַחְמָן בַּר יִצְחָק אוֹמֵר אַף פּוֹרֵק מִמֶּנּוּ יִרְאַת שָׁמַיִם שֶׁנֶּאֱמַר וְיִרְאַת שַׁ-דַּי יַעֲזוֹב.

Rabbi Yehoshua ben Levi said: All tasks that a servant performs for his master, a student should perform for his teacher, except for untying his shoes. Rava said: We said this only if the teacher and the student are in a place where people are not familiar with him [and he could be mistaken for a servant]. However, in a place where people are familiar with him, we have no problem with it. Rav Ashi said: And in a place where people are not familiar with him, we said this only if he is not donning tefillin, but if he is donning tefillin, we have no problem with it. Rabbi Chiya bar Abba quoted Rabbi Yochanan who said: Anyone who prevents his student from serving him, it is considered as though he is withholding from him kindness, as it is stated: "To him that is ready to faint, from his friend, kindness is due." Rav Nachman bar Yitzchak says: He even removes from the student the fear of Heaven, as it is stated: "Even to one who forsakes the fear of the Almighty."

The Torah commands us, "And to Him You shall cleave."[1] But how can we mortals cleave to Hashem? Our Sages explain that when we cleave

1 *Devarim* 13:5.

to Torah scholars, we fulfill this commandment, as they embody the wisdom and attributes of Heaven.[2] The *Zohar* teaches that by internalizing the Torah, Torah scholars unite with Hashem, since He and His wisdom are one.

The more one serves another person, the greater the bond that develops. When you serve your spouse, you develop a stronger attachment to him. When you serve your community, you become an integral part of the community.

What does serving Torah scholars look like? Certainly, an elderly *talmid chacham* might need help untying his shoelaces. But for the most part, that's an extreme example that makes us forget what the Gemara is asking of us practically.

The Ghermezians take care of their rabbis because they realize that if a rabbi needs to spend an hour on the phone with the insurance company, that's an hour away from Torah learning. Most laypeople wouldn't spend that hour any more spiritually productively. But for *talmidei chachamim*, whose entire being is dedicated to Torah value every moment, that extra hour wouldn't eventually end up in front of the television or internet, but it's an extra potential hour of Torah that won't be learned unless someone else takes care of those mundane matters.

That's why serving Torah scholars is essential. By seeing to their mundane and material needs—day-to-day matters with which every living human being inevitably deals—they have freed up their time to devote to Heavenly pursuits. When that happens, more Divine blessing flows into the world and the one who has been the cause of that supernal *chessed* flow benefits. And so, if a *talmid chacham* chooses humbly to forego his service, he withholds *chessed* from his disciples. That's not his choice to make.

There are certain individuals whom I have encountered over the years as a rabbi who have been extraordinary Rabbinic disciples. You know who you are. I am forever grateful to you for giving of your personal

---

2 *Kesubos* 111b.

time and resources to ensure that I have been able to devote my time and energy to serving Hashem and the community.

We have a tradition that the tribesmen of Zevulun would support the tribesmen of Yissachar, facilitating their full-time dedication to Torah. When Moshe offers them his parting blessing, he declares, "Zevulun shall rejoice with your going out and Yissachar in your tents."[3] *Rashi* comments that Zevulun is mentioned first because none of Yissachar's learning would have been possible without them. May you merit being called a rabbi's friend!

---

3 *Devarim* 33:18.

DAF 97

Unlimited Blessing

After more than two decades abroad, Yaakov is now ready to face the music. He had fled the wrath of his brother Eisav in Canaan to lay low in Charan for a while. While there, he had amassed a small fortune and been blessed with an ever-growing family. But now, it was crunch time.

Yaakov sent messengers ahead of him to his brother Eisav, to the land of Se'ir, the field of Edom. And he commanded them, saying, "So shall you say to my master to Eisav, 'Thus said your servant Yaakov: I have sojourned with Lavan, and I have tarried until now. And I have acquired oxen and donkeys, flocks, manservants, and maidservants, and I have sent to tell this to my master, to find favor in your eyes.'"

The messengers returned to Yaakov, saying, "We came to your brother, to Eisav, and he is also coming toward you, and four hundred men are with him." Yaakov became very frightened and was distressed; so, he divided the people who were with him and the flocks and the cattle and the camels into two camps. And he said, "If Eisav comes to one camp and strikes it down, the remaining camp will escape."

And Yaakov said, "O God of my father Avraham and God of my father Yitzchak, Hashem, Who said to me, 'Return to your land and to your birthplace, and I will do good to you.' I am unworthy of all the kindnesses and from all the truth that You have rendered Your servant, for with my staff I crossed this Jordan, and now I have become two camps. Now deliver me from the hand of my brother, from the hand of Eisav, for I am afraid of him, lest he come and strike me along with a mother and the children. And You said, 'I will surely do good with you, and I will make your seed [as numerous] as the sand of the sea, which cannot be counted because of multitude.'"

> בְּעוֹ מִינֵּיהּ מֵרַב שֵׁשֶׁת מוֹכֶרֶת לִמְזוֹנוֹת מַהוּ שֶׁתַּחֲזוֹר וְתִטְרוֹף לִכְתוּבָּה קָמִיבַּעְיָא לְהוּ בִּדְרַב יוֹסֵף דְּאָמַר רַב יוֹסֵף אַרְמַלְתָּא דְּזַבֵּין אַחְרָיוּת אַיַּתְמֵי וּבֵי דִינָא דְּזַבֵּין אַחְרָיוּת אַיַּתְמֵי מַאי כֵּיוָן דְּאַחְרָיוּת אַיַּתְמֵי טָרְפָא אוֹ דִלְמָא מָצֵי אָמְרִי לַהּ נְהִי דְּאַחְרָיוּת דְּעָלְמָא לָא קַבֵּילְתְּ עִילָּוָךְ אַחְרָיוּת דְּנַפְשָׁךְ מִי לָא קַבּוֹלֵי קַבֵּילְתְּ אֲמַר לֵיהּ תְּנֵיתוּהָ מוֹכֶרֶת וְהוֹלֶכֶת עַד כְּדֵי כְתוּבָּתָהּ וְסֶמֶךְ לָהּ שֶׁתִּגְבֶּה כְּתוּבָּתָהּ מִן הַשְּׁאָר שְׁמַע מִינַּהּ שַׁיְּירָא אִין לָא שַׁיְּירָא לָא.
>
> *They asked Rav Sheshes: If a widow sells property for her sustenance, can she return and repossess those very properties that she had sold as payment for her ketubah? They raised this dilemma in reference to a teaching of Rav Yosef, as Rav Yosef said: In the case of a widow who sold liened property to a third party, the property guarantee rests upon the orphans. And so too, in the case of a court that sold property belonging to the deceased, the property guarantee rests upon the orphans. What is the halachah in this case? Do we say that since the property guarantee rests on the orphans, she is able to seize the property? Or perhaps, they may say to her: "Granted, you did not accept upon yourself to guarantee the property for everyone else, but did you not accept a guarantee for your own actions?" Rav Sheshes responded: You learned: A widow sells the deceased's property for her sustenance, and she continues to do so until there is nothing left except the value of her ketubah, and she relies upon the fact that she will collect payment of her ketubah from the remainder. Learn from this that if she left sufficient assets, then yes, she may claim it as her ketubah payment; but if she did not leave sufficient assets, then no, she cannot collect her ketubah.*

Here's the background information we need for this piece of Gemara:

1. While the Torah instructs that when a man dies, the sons are the primary heirs, our Sages instituted various enactments to take

care of his other dependents. One such enactment is that the sons are responsible for the widow's sustenance from the estate.

2. In addition to her sustenance, she is entitled to collect her *ketubah* payment. That money is considered a debt that must be repaid from the estate and her claim is treated like those of other creditors.
3. If someone sells a piece of property with a lien on it, the creditor may seize the asset from the purchaser. In order to avoid this scenario, the property owner will often sell the asset with a guarantee that states he will reimburse the purchaser if the asset should ever be subject to repossession.

Our Gemara discusses a case where the widow kept selling property to sustain herself from the estate. Those properties had liens on them and so the creditors came to seize them. When that happened, the children were required to reimburse the purchasers because the assets were bought with guarantees. She finally sells all the property and there's one piece of property remaining that she sells. She then realizes that she hasn't made the claim for her *ketubah* payment. And she makes a creditor claim on that property and asks the children to reimburse her "lien" on the sold property. In other words, she's making a claim on the very asset that she herself sold! At that point, they tell her, "Granted, you did not accept upon yourself to guarantee the property for everyone else, but did you not accept a guarantee for your own actions?"

While the situation in the Gemara is specifically referring to the rights of a widow to be sustained from her husband's estate and that is entirely justifiable and perfectly acceptable, there is certainly something to be learned from the turn of events discussed. In life, sometimes people find themselves unable to break free from their dependence on others. They become so accustomed to falling back on the good graces and the largesse of other individuals that they just keep coming back until the account is depleted. At that point, says the Gemara, one must "accept a guarantee for your own actions." When there's nothing left in the coffers of munificence, one must take responsibility for his own actions.

We all have people whom we rely upon and lean on in life. But we need to constantly check ourselves that we haven't become dependent upon the other person to the extent that we cannot stand on our own two feet. We need to ask ourselves what the long-term plan is for independence because when we're dealing with mortal human men and physical accounts, every pot has its limits.

There is only One being to Whom we can always turn. Our account with our Father in Heaven never runs dry. No matter how many times you have turned to Hashem and asked Him to sustain you, He has unlimited blessing to shower upon you. While we all might know this to be true, how often do we worry that there won't be anything left in Hashem's coffers tomorrow?

That only happens when we fail to acknowledge how many times we've dipped into the limitless pot until this point in our lives. When we take a moment to think about how Hashem has provided for us, exceeding all our expectations, there's no question that He will continue to provide for us. The key is to focus on today and ask whether right now things are OK. If they are, then rest assured, things will continue to be OK tomorrow.

That was Yaakov's perspective as he turned to Hashem just prior to his encounter with Eisav. Picture yourself in his predicament. You've got this large family including a number of vulnerable little children. And your arch-nemesis, the individual who has vowed to destroy you, is approaching with an army of four hundred. What would be going through your mind? Most people would be thinking: It's all over.

But that wasn't Yaakov's attitude. Yaakov looks around at his family and belongings, turns to Hashem and says, "I'm not worthy of all your kindnesses." Instead of worrying what tomorrow will bring, he considers his blessings today. "Right here, right now," he thinks, "I can't believe how much bounty Hashem has bestowed upon me. I'm really not deserving of all this. Thank you Hashem for my amazing life!" And with that thought in mind, He knows that just like Hashem has not let him down yet, He will never forsake him. There will always be largesse in Hashem's limitless coffers.

That's the attitude for which we must all strive. Instead of worrying what will happen tomorrow, ask yourself: Right here, right now, are you OK? Has Hashem provided for you? Is He taking care of you? If the answer is yes, then why are you worried that tomorrow His blessing will run dry? He has limitless coffers. Just like He has provided for you until now, His miracles are endless, and He will provide for you tomorrow.

Lean on Hashem. Place your entire weight upon Him because He will always be there to provide for you. His coffers never run dry. May you forever think about today's blessings and have faith in Hashem's unlimited bounty!

DAF 98

Lifetime Mileage Elite Status

As a top executive in his company, Shimmy spends a lot of time traveling around the world attending high level meetings. Over the years, he's amassed quite a few miles. Entry into the airport lounge is a nice perk of the job, and he very often gets a free upgrade as well.

Glancing at his mileage account, he starts thinking about the amazing family vacation that he can take. There's more than enough in the account to cover everyone's flights and hotels. "Sweet!" he thinks. But then he hesitates. Maybe the miles aren't his? After all, miles are a bonus that the airlines provide to attract business. However, it wasn't his business that they gained. It was the company's! Perhaps, the miles belong to the company, and it is their decision as to how to use them. What gives him the right to "steal" those miles? He didn't pay for them, the company did!

Is Shimmy permitted to use those miles for his own personal benefit?

מַתְנִי׳ אַלְמָנָה שֶׁהָיְתָה כְּתוּבָּתָהּ מָאתַיִם וּמָכְרָה שָׁוֶה מָנֶה בְּמָאתַיִם אוֹ שָׁוֶה מָאתַיִם בְּמָנֶה נִתְקַבְּלָה כְּתוּבָּתָהּ: גְּמָ׳ מַאי שְׁנָא שָׁוֶה מָאתַיִם בְּמָנֶה דְּאָמְרִי לַהּ אַתְּ אַפְסֵדְתְּ שָׁוֶה מָנֶה בְּמָאתַיִם נָמֵי תֵּימָא אֲנָא אַרְוַוחְנָא אָמַר רַב נַחְמָן אָמַר רַבָּה בַּר אֲבוּהּ כָּאן שָׁנָה רַבִּי הַכֹּל לְבַעַל הַמָּעוֹת.

רש״י: הכל לבעל המעות—השולח שלוחו לשוק לסחורה ולקח בזול הכל לבעל המעות ולא מצי למימר אנא ארווחי.

> ***Mishnah:*** *In the case of a widow whose ketubah was worth two hundred and she sold property from the estate that was worth one hundred for two hundred, or if she sold property worth two hundred for one hundred, she has received complete payment of her ketubah.*
>
> ***Gemara:*** *What's the difference between the case of her selling two hundred's worth for a hundred, whereby we effectively say to her, "your loss," and the case of her selling one hundred's worth for two hundred? Let her similarly say, "I made the profit and I'm entitled to a further hundred from the estate!" Rav Nachman quoted Rabbah bar Avuha: Here Rebbi is teaching that everything belongs to the owner of the money.*
>
> ***Rashi:*** *One who sends a messenger to the grocery store, and he finds the product cheaper, the owner keeps the profit. The messenger cannot say, "I made the profit."*

Based on this Gemara, Rav Wosner addresses the mileage question and suggests that Shimmy is merely a messenger when he receives free tickets resulting from his company's purchases.[1] As Rebbi maintains, "everything belongs to the owner of the money." The "profit" is not Shimmy's to claim.

Nevertheless, he clarifies that if some airlines offer incentives while others don't, and Shimmy's company doesn't care which carrier he chooses, there may be an argument that he is entitled to the miles that he has accrued. In other words, if the company specifically mandated that he choose an airline with a good mileage program and insisted that he sign up for the program, then they own the rights to the miles. But if there's no such stipulation, then there is room to suggest that the miles are his personal bonus.

Let's now expand and deepen the meaning of the Gemara. While the simple meaning is that the heirs to the estate are the owners of the money and so any profit accrues to them, on an allegorical level, the

1 *Shevet Halevi* 9:305.

Gemara reminds us that when we imagine "I made the profit," we should know that "everything belongs to the Owner of the money." There's only one true Owner of our wealth—the Holy One, blessed be He. Any profit that you have accrued is on account of His blessing. You must be ever grateful to the Almighty for all the bounty that He has bestowed upon you. Yes, you must work, but your efforts are merely a vessel for God's blessing. Ultimately, only He is the true Provider.

You are His messenger, flying on His personal carrier. You are here in this world as an ambassador of Heaven. As an ambassador, you always get to fly first class, without needing an upgrade. As long as you always remember that you're here on a mission, you automatically fly in first. What's more, you get to keep all the points to use for your own benefit in this world and the next!

Right now, our Father in Heaven is offering double miles on all purchases along with a host of other perks for His platinum members. You are a platinum member for life. Never lose sight of your mission and you will be showered with limitless member-only benefits. May you forever acknowledge the Owner of everything in this world and enjoy your lifetime elite status!

DAF 99

Partner with God

Naaman, the great Aramean general, was stricken with leprosy. At the urging of his wife, he goes off to see the prophet Elisha, who cures him of his malady, having him dip seven times in the Jordan River. He is supremely grateful to Elisha and wants to shower him with gifts of gold and silver, but the prophet will have nothing of it, noting that healing comes from God alone. With that, Naaman departs.

Watching the miracle and pursuant conversation unfold, Elisha's attendant Gechazi is astounded that his teacher has refused anything in return for his assistance. Running after Naaman, he pretends that he has been sent on a mission by his teacher Elisha to collect money and clothing for some poor *bachurim*. Naaman gives generously and Gechazi returns home and deposits the goods in his own tent. Upon encountering Elisha, however, the prophet knows what Gechazi has done and curses him and his progeny with the leprosy that was removed from Naaman.

> מַתְנִי׳ הָיְתָה כְּתוּבָּתָהּ אַרְבַּע מֵאוֹת זוּז וּמָכְרָה לָזֶה בְּמָנֶה וְלָזֶה בְּמָנֶה וְלָאַחֲרוֹן יָפֶה מָנֶה וְדִינָר בְּמָנֶה שֶׁל אַחֲרוֹן בָּטֵל וְשֶׁל כּוּלָּן מִכְרָן קַיָּים שׁוּם הַדַּיָּינִין שֶׁפִּיחֲתוּ שְׁתוּת אוֹ הוֹסִיפוּ שְׁתוּת מִכְרָן בָּטֵל: גְּמָ׳ אִיבַּעְיָא לְהוּ שָׁלִיחַ כְּמַאן רָבָא אָמַר רַב נַחְמָן שָׁלִיחַ כְּדַיָּינִין רַב שְׁמוּאֵל בַּר בִּיסְנָא אָמַר רַב נַחְמָן כְּאַלְמָנָה רָבָא אָמַר רַב נַחְמָן שָׁלִיחַ כְּדַיָּינִין מָה דַּיָּינִין לָאו לְדִידְהוּ אַף שָׁלִיחַ נָמֵי לָאו לְדִידֵיהּ.

Mishnah: *If a widow's ketubah was worth four hundred zuz, and she sold property to one purchaser for one hundred, and she sold property to another one for one hundred [and again to a third one], and she then sold property worth one hundred and one dinars to a final purchaser for only one hundred, the sale of the last property is void. But all the other sales are valid. With regard to the assessment of judges of the value of a piece of property, if they decreased the price by more than one-sixth of its market value or added one-sixth to its market value, their sale is void.*

Gemara: *They asked: Who is a messenger like? [Is he comparable to a judge, whose sale is effective if he did not err by more than one-sixth of the market price, or is he comparable to a widow, whose sale is void if she sold for anything less than the market price?] Rava quoted Rav Nachman: A messenger is like judges. Rav Shmuel bar Bisna quoted Rav Nachman: He is like a widow. Rava quoted Rav Nachman: A messenger is like judges. Just as judges do not act for their own benefit, so too, the messenger also does not act for his own benefit.*

Our Sages tell us that a judge who judges properly becomes a partner in Creation. The *Tur* elaborates:[1] God created the world to exist. The wicked who steal and commit acts of violence destroy the world via their actions. When a judge breaks the powerful arm of the wicked, he sustains the world and completes the will of the Creator, thereby becoming a partner with Him.

You are here in this world on a Divine mission. The Almighty sent you down here as His messenger from Heaven. Our Gemara states that a messenger is akin to a judge. Why? Because when you carry out the mission for which you were sent to Earth to fulfill, you too become a partner with Hashem in making this world a better, spiritually stronger, and more enduring place.

---

1 *Choshen Mishpat* 1.

As soon as a baby boy is born, he is reminded of his mission to perfect this world. If Hashem wanted us to be circumcised, why didn't He make us that way? The answer is that He wants our very first religious experience to be one where we acknowledge the imperfection of this world. We were sent down here to make things better. God created a world requiring human intervention to perfect it. Our job in the world is to teach and maintain a moral code that ultimately draws down Godliness into the world. When justice is carried out properly and when we are living examples of the Divine message, God's creation of the world is advanced.

According to the Gemara, what is the defining factor of a judge? He does not act for his own benefit. He faithfully carries out his duties for the sake of society and humanity. Sometimes it comes at great cost and risk to his own personal security. But he forges ahead, knowing Who his partner is. Likewise, every messenger who fulfills his Divine mission becomes like a judge. The less you act for your own benefit, and prioritize the Divine mission, the more you become a partner with the Almighty in the perfection of the world.

Don't be a Gechazi and let your own will get in the way of the mission. You have been handpicked to come down into this world to be Hashem's messenger and partner. May you merit staying focused on your mission and exceeding your Sender's expectations!

DAF 100

Descent for the Sake of Ascent

Rav Kahana was holding on to some beer that belonged to Rav Mesharshia, an orphan. He delayed selling it until the festival. When asked why he wasn't selling the beer and giving the money to the orphan immediately, he replied, "Although it is possible that the beer may deteriorate and risk souring, it's worth waiting. During the Yom Tov season, there are so many people who want to buy schnapps that even the poor-quality product sells better."

אָמַר רַב יְהוּדָה אָמַר שְׁמוּאֵל מְטַלְטְלִין שֶׁל יְתוֹמִים שָׁמִין אוֹתָן וּמוֹכְרִין אוֹתָן לְאַלְתַּר רַב חִסְדָּא אָמַר אֲבִימִי מוֹכְרִין אוֹתָן לִשְׁוָוקִים וְלָא פְּלִיגִי הָא דְּמִיקָּרַב שׁוּקָא הָא דִּמְרַחַק שׁוּקָא רַב כָּהֲנָא הֲוָה בִּידֵיהּ שִׁכְרָא דְּרַב מְשַׁרְשְׁיָא בַּר חִילְקַאי יַתְמָא שַׁהְיֵיהּ עַד רִיגְלָא אָמַר אַף עַל גַּב דְּנָפֵל בֵּיהּ אִיצְצָתָא מַיְיתֵי זוּזָא חֲרִיפָא.

Rav Yehudah quoted Shmuel: Movable property that belongs to orphans is appraised and sold immediately [so that it does not deteriorate over time]. Rav Chisda quoted Avimi: The movable property is sold on a market day, when there are many potential buyers, and the items will sell for a proper price. And they do not disagree with each other. Rather, this opinion [that the items are sold on a market day] applies when the market day is approaching. That opinion [that the items are sold immediately] applies when the market day is far off. Rav Kahana was holding on to some beer...

We all experience moments in life when everything seems to be going sour. It can feel like there's no hope. Bur Rav Kahana reminds us that if we just hang on a little longer, life will turn festive. Just when we think it's all over and deteriorated beyond repair, that's when the Almighty turns everything around for the better. In fact, sometimes, it's the very waiting that brings about the ultimate salvation.

In Chassidic thought, this process is called *yeridah l'tzorech aliyah.* For various reasons, a descent may be necessary in order to achieve an even greater ascent. The greatest example of this phenomenon is the descent of the soul into this world. Why does a *neshamah* come down into this physical world? It was already up in Heaven! What's the point of leaving Heaven to occupy a body for seventy, eighty, 120 years, only to then return to Heaven? The answer is *yeridah l'tzorech aliyah.* The hope is that it will accomplish great things in this physical world and merit subsequently residing on an even higher plane in the supernal worlds.

Yeridah l'tzorech aliyah is also the purpose of *galus* (exile). Why was the Holy Temple destroyed, leading to the dispersion of our people? There are multiple levels of explanation. Generally, we have four basic approaches to understanding spiritual ideas and events, called *p'shat* (simple), *remez* (hint), *d'rush* (homiletical), and *sod* (esoteric). On a *p'shat* level, the Holy Temple was destroyed because the Romans were seeking to expand their imperial conquest. On a *remez* level, there was considerable intra-Jewish strife, leading our Sages to conclude that the Temple was destroyed due to baseless hatred.[1] On a *d'rush* level, the Temple was destroyed because people were living according to the letter of the law, but had forgotten the spirit of the law.[2]

On a *sod* level, the destruction of the first and second Temples were all part of the Divine plan for history. Our Sages teach that we were exiled in order to find converts.[3] But according to Kabbalah, this teaching is an allegory for the lost sparks that are scattered across the globe. When we do mitzvos in the far-flung corners of the Earth, we elevate all those

---

1 *Yoma* 9b.

2 *Bava Metzia* 30b.

3 *Pesachim* 87b.

sparks of holiness and return them to their Divine source. Thus, exile was a necessary part of our story. While exile meant a serious *descent* from the glory that we once enjoyed, our endeavors will lead to an even greater *ascent* in the messianic era, such that the third Holy Temple will endure forever.

Right now, you may be enduring a moment of *descent* and it feels like there's no end in sight. Your predicament seems hopeless, and the deterioration appears unstoppable. Each day, the situation is getting sourer and there's no light at the end of the tunnel. Maybe it's money and career issues with which you're struggling. It feels like you're drowning in debt with no way out of the swirling tide around you. Or, perhaps, you're dealing with a health crisis and life feels like it's falling apart.

Don't despair. Our Father in Heaven can and will send His deliverance in the blink of an eye. Very soon, you will experience the festive season. Life may feel bleak and unbearable today, but every descent leads to an even greater ascent. When the salvation arrives, you will see blessings that you cannot begin to imagine today. Know that Hashem is with you, carrying you through the storm. As our Sages teach, when we go into exile, the Divine presence is exiled alongside us.

As difficult as life may be to endure right at this moment, we must always maintain our faith in the One Above. Our lives are filled with challenges, but when we look up to our Father in Heaven, we are able to see the ladder that we will eventually climb for the ascent out of the pit. That ladder leads to a Yom Tov season. May you very soon be blessed with festivities and salvation that you never imagined would be possible!

DAF 101

Good Debt vs. Bad Debt

Elisha, the disciple of Eliyahu HaNavi, was a great prophet and miracle-worker. A certain woman, the wife of one of the disciples of the prophets, once cried out to Elisha: "Your servant my husband is dead, and you know how your servant revered Hashem. And now a creditor is coming to seize my two children as slaves."

Elisha said to her, "What can I do for you? Tell me, what have you in the house?"

She replied, "Your maidservant has nothing at all in the house, except a jug of oil."

"Go," he said, "and borrow vessels outside, from all your neighbors, empty vessels, as many as you can. Then go in and shut the door behind you and your children, and pour oil into all those vessels, removing each one as it is filled." She went away and shut the door behind her and her children. They kept bringing vessels to her and she kept pouring.

When the vessels were full, she said to her son, "Bring me another vessel."

He answered her, "There are no more vessels," and the oil stopped. She came and told Elisha what happened, and he said, "Go sell the oil and pay your debt, and you and your children can live off the surplus."[1]

---

1 *Melachim II* 4.

הַנּוֹשֵׂא אֶת הָאִשָּׁה וּפָסְקָה עִמּוֹ כְּדֵי שֶׁיָּזוּן אֶת בִּתָּהּ חָמֵשׁ שָׁנִים חַיָּיב לְזוּנָהּ חָמֵשׁ שָׁנִים נִיסֵּת לְאַחֵר וּפָסְקָה עִמּוֹ כְּדֵי שֶׁיָּזוּן אֶת בִּתָּהּ חָמֵשׁ שָׁנִים חַיָּיב לְזוּנָהּ חָמֵשׁ שָׁנִים לֹא יֹאמַר הָרִאשׁוֹן לִכְשֶׁתָּבֹא אֶצְלִי אֲזוּנָהּ אֶלָּא מוֹלִיךְ לָהּ מְזוֹנוֹתֶיהָ לַמָּקוֹם שֶׁאִמָּהּ וְכֵן לֹא יֹאמְרוּ שְׁנֵיהֶם הֲרֵי אָנוּ זָנִין אוֹתָהּ כְּאֶחָד אֶלָּא אֶחָד זָנָהּ וְאֶחָד נוֹתֵן לָהּ דְּמֵי מְזוֹנוֹת נִיסֵּת הַבַּעַל נוֹתֵן לָהּ מְזוֹנוֹת וְהֵן נוֹתְנִין לָהּ דְּמֵי מְזוֹנוֹת מֵתוּ בְּנוֹתֵיהֶן נִיזּוֹנוֹת מִנְּכָסִים בְּנֵי חוֹרִין וְהִיא נִיזּוֹנֶת מִנְּכָסִים מְשׁוּעְבָּדִים מִפְּנֵי שֶׁהִיא כְּבַעֲלַת חוֹב הַפִּקְחִים הָיוּ כּוֹתְבִים עַל מְנָת שֶׁאָזוּן אֶת בִּתֵּךְ חָמֵשׁ שָׁנִים כָּל זְמַן שֶׁאַתְּ עִמִּי.

One who marries a woman, and she stipulated with him that he would sustain her daughter [from a previous marriage] for five years, is obligated to sustain her for five years. If in the course of those five years, they were divorced and the woman was married to another man, and she stipulated with him that he would sustain her daughter for five years, he too is obligated to sustain her for five years. The first husband may not say: When she comes to me, I will sustain her. Rather, he brings her sustenance to her, to the place where her mother lives. And likewise, both of them may not jointly say, "We will sustain the girl as one in a partnership." Rather, one sustains her, providing her with food, while the other gives her the monetary value of the sustenance. The astute ones would write an explicit stipulation into the agreement: I agree to sustain your daughter for five years only as long as you are with me.

Question: When this groom promises to support his stepdaughter for five years, how much money has he pledged? Answer: How long is a piece of string?

There's obviously no way to estimate and put a dollar value on this pledge as food and clothing prices go up and down as the market moves. The ensuing five years may be years of plenty when the cost of fulfilling his pledge is relatively low. Or it could turn out to be a very expensive promise if the ensuing years are hit with a famine or drought. Effectively, he is making an unlimited pledge! If the amount that he has pledged is so indeterminate, then is his commitment effective and binding? This is the conundrum posed by the *Rambam*.[2]

No mortal human being has the wherewithal to make an unlimited commitment. Only Hashem has that power. Why? Because His blessings come from a place of unlimitedness. He has more than sufficient resources to provide for every one of His children. Just as He is not limited, His storage house has no limits. That's what Elisha demonstrated to the needy woman with the miracle of the oil jug. God's ability to supply is only limited by how many vessels we have prepared to accept His blessing.

What's interesting in the story is that Elisha doesn't tell the woman to ask her neighbors for food and provisions. Would that not have been simpler than asking them for their pots and pans? The answer, of course, is that you can't eat pots and pans. Had she borrowed food, she would have had to figure out how to return the food that she'd borrowed. But that wouldn't have been possible, because she and her children would have already eaten the food!

All she needed were vessels. Hashem is the provider of our sustenance. Once she had the vessels, she could accept Hashem's blessing. And His blessing is unlimited. As long as we provide the vessels, He can and will provide the blessing.

Do you know the difference between poor and rich borrowers? Poor people borrow food. Rich people borrow vessels. Food gets consumed, making it impossible to repay. Vessels don't get eaten; they're borrowed simply as a receptacle for Hashem's blessing. Practically speaking, that's the difference between bad and good debt. Bad debt is overspending on your credit card for things that you're going to consume. If you're still making the same salary next month, how will you ever pay back those debts? You've already eaten them!

Contrast that with the borrowing behavior of wealthy individuals. They also borrow. But they borrow, not in order to consume, but in order to invest. So, for example, they will ask the bank for a loan to

---

2 *Hilchos Mechirah* 11:16–17.

buy a rental property. The house is not being used for their personal consumption. It is a vessel for Hashem's blessing. Each month they will receive rental income. That's the unlimited oil of Elisha. The only limit to the blessing is the number of vessels that one can borrow. Vessels don't cost anything because, unlike perishable consumable goods, they don't get used up and may be returned to their owners exactly as they were borrowed.

When the Children of Israel left Egypt, Hashem instructed them to borrow from their neighbors "vessels of silver and vessels of gold." Why didn't He instruct them to ask for silver and gold? Because "Unto Me is the silver and unto Me is the gold, says Hashem."[3] God is the owner and provider of all the silver and gold. All we need to prepare are the vessels and Hashem will do the rest. May all your borrowing be good debt and may Hashem overflow your vessels with His unlimited blessing!

---

3 *Chaggai* 2:8.

DAF 102

Limited Responsibility

The Children of Israel had been enslaved for many years in Egypt. From a mere seventy souls who had descended to Egypt, they had multiplied exponentially. Desperate not to see the Israelites overthrow them due to sheer numbers, the Egyptians turned to genocide.

Pharaoh, King of Egypt, spoke to the Hebrew midwives, one of whom was named Shifrah and the other Puah, saying, "When you deliver the Hebrew women, look at the birth-stool: if it is a boy, kill him, if it is a girl, let her live." The midwives, fearing God, did not do as the king of Egypt had told them and they let the boys live.

So, the king of Egypt summoned the midwives and said to them, "Why have you done this thing, letting the boys live?"

The midwives said to Pharaoh, "Because the Hebrew women are not like the Egyptian women; they are vigorous. Before the midwife can come to them, they have given birth." And God dealt well with the midwives, and the people multiplied and increased greatly. And because the midwives feared God, He established dynasties for them. Then Pharaoh charged all his people, saying, "Every boy that is born you shall throw into the Nile, but let every girl live."[1]

---

1 *Shemos* 1.

The defiance of the Hebrew midwives was incredibly courageous and admirable. And yet, if Pharaoh ended up instructing all the Egyptians to pitch in with the annihilation of our people, did the efforts of the Hebrew midwives really achieve anything at all?

עָרֵב הַיּוֹצֵא אַחַר חִיתּוּם שְׁטָרוֹת גּוֹבֶה מִנְּכָסִים בְּנֵי חוֹרִין מַעֲשֶׂה בָּא לִפְנֵי רַבִּי יִשְׁמָעֵאל וְאָמַר גּוֹבֶה מִנְּכָסִים בְּנֵי חוֹרִין אָמַר לוֹ בֶּן נַנָּס אֵינוֹ גּוֹבֶה לֹא מִנְּכָסִים בְּנֵי חוֹרִין וְלֹא מִנְּכָסִים מְשׁוּעְבָּדִים אָמַר לוֹ לָמָּה אָמַר לוֹ הֲרֵי שֶׁהָיָה חוֹנֵק אֶת חֲבֵירוֹ בַּשּׁוּק וּמְצָאוֹ] חֲבֵירוֹ וְאָמַר לוֹ הַנַּח לוֹ וַאֲנִי אֶתֵּן לָךְ פָּטוּר שֶׁלֹּא עַל אֱמוּנָתוֹ הִלְוָהוּ.

If a guarantor appears after the signing of the contracts, the creditor may only collect from his unsold property. An incident came before Rabbi Yishmael, and he said: The creditor collects from unsold property. Ben Nanas said to him: The creditor can neither claim from his unsold property nor from his liened property that was sold. [The post-facto that the guarantor wrote has no legal liability.] Rabbi Yishmael said to him: Why? He said to him: If someone was strangling another in the marketplace [and demanding money owed to him], and a friend found him and said to the aggressor, "Leave him alone and I will give you what you are demanding," he is exempt from payment because the creditor did not lend the money based on his trust in the friend.

The Hebrew word for responsibility is *achrayus*. Rabbi Sacks explains that both in Hebrew and English, the word connotes how will we "respond" to the needs of the "*acher*," another human being?[2] All too often people are afraid to respond to the pain and suffering of another human being for fear that they will end up bearing responsibility, for which they did not sign up. Comes along Ben Nanas who teaches that if you encounter someone feeling strangled in the marketplace of life, you have an obligation to alleviate that individual's suffering. But that doesn't imply that you will forever be responsible for that person's

---

2 *To Heal a Fractured World: The Ethics of Responsibility.*

situation. After all, you never made a binding promise. You simply stepped in to help when you saw him in a dire predicament.

Sadly, there is no shortage of people feeling strangled in the marketplace. They may be literally debt-ridden or they're dealing with family conflict or other issues. Most people would rather just not get involved. They don't want to take sides, or they don't want to appear nosy. Or they say to themselves: If I start helping them, where will it end? Will I become wholly responsible for their recovery? That's an endless road that I just cannot embark upon. The task is simply too great. And so, we turn a blind eye to our neighbor's suffering. Not because we don't want to help. But because the thought of getting involved is too overwhelming to even begin.

There's a classic fable told of a man who would take a stroll along the beach every morning. Early one day, he was walking along the shore after a big storm had passed and found the vast beach littered with starfish as far as the eye could see, stretching in both directions. Off in the distance, the man noticed a small boy approaching. As the boy walked, he paused every so often and as he grew closer, the man could see that he was occasionally bending down to pick up an object and throw it into the sea. The boy came closer still and the man called out, "Good morning! May I ask what you are doing?"

The young boy paused, looked up, and replied, "Throwing starfish into the ocean. The tide has washed them up onto the beach and they can't return to the sea by themselves. When the sun gets high, they will die, unless I throw them back into the water."

The man replied, "But there must be tens of thousands of starfish on this beach. I'm afraid you won't really be able to make much of a difference."

The boy bent down, picked up yet another starfish and threw it as far as he could into the ocean. Then he turned, smiled, and said, "That may be true, but to that one it made a difference."

That is why the Torah tells us about Shifrah and Puah. Once Pharaoh decreed that all babies be thrown into the Nile, it's tempting to dismiss the efforts of the midwives as futile. But just because they didn't save *all* the babies, that didn't make their work meaningless. Every baby that they saved was the rescue of an entire world!

And that must be our attitude toward helping others. You might not be able to solve all the problems of the world. You might not even be able to solve your local problems. You might not even be able to solve your neighbor's problems. But that doesn't mean you can't lend a hand. Every little bit helps.

It might be a local teenager who needs life coaching. Don't tell yourself that you don't have time to meet with him every week for the next ten years, that you simply can't assume that kind of responsibility. Instead, just start with a cup of coffee today. A meeting or two might be all he needs to get his life back on track.

Or maybe, it's a junior colleague who is struggling at work. Becoming that person's mentor may sound daunting. Who has the time for that kind of responsibility? It sounds potentially never-ending! But that's not the right approach. One session today might be all that person needs to refocus and find his groove.

We are all responsible for the welfare of our fellow. But don't let the formidability of the task deter you from taking those first steps. May you forever remember that every starfish saved makes a world of difference!

DAF 103

Bringing Kids into a Bad World

When Rebbi fell ill, Rabbi Chiya entered to be with him and found him crying. He said to him, “My teacher, for what reason are you crying? Did we not learn the following teaching? If one dies while laughing, it is a good sign for him. If one dies while crying, it is a bad sign for him. If one dies with his face upward, it is a good sign for him. If one dies with his face downward, it is a bad sign for him.”

Rebbi replied, “I am crying for the Torah and the mitzvos that I will be unable to fulfill after I die!”

תָּנוּ רַבָּנַן בִּשְׁעַת פְּטִירָתוֹ שֶׁל רַבִּי אָמַר לְבָנַי אֲנִי צָרִיךְ נִכְנְסוּ בָּנָיו אֶצְלוֹ אָמַר לָהֶם הִזָּהֲרוּ בִּכְבוֹד אִמְּכֶם נֵר יְהֵא דָּלוּק בִּמְקוֹמוֹ שׁוּלְחָן יְהֵא עָרוּךְ בִּמְקוֹמוֹ מִטָּה תְּהֵא מוּצַּעַת בִּמְקוֹמָהּ יוֹסֵף חָפְנִי שִׁמְעוֹן אֶפְרָתִי הֵם שִׁמְּשׁוּנִי בְּחַיַּי וְהֵם יְשַׁמְּשׁוּנִי בְּמוֹתִי הִזָּהֲרוּ בִּכְבוֹד אִמְּכֶם דְּאוֹרָיְיתָא הִיא דִּכְתִיב כַּבֵּד אֶת אָבִיךָ וְאֶת אִמֶּךָ אֵשֶׁת אָב הֲוַאי אֵשֶׁת אָב נָמֵי דְּאוֹרָיְיתָא הִיא דְּתַנְיָא כַּבֵּד אֶת אָבִיךָ וְאֶת אִמֶּךָ אֶת אָבִיךָ זוֹ אֵשֶׁת אָבִיךָ וְאֶת אִמֶּךָ זוֹ בַּעַל אִמֶּךָ וָיו יְתֵירָה לְרַבּוֹת אֶת אָחִיךָ הַגָּדוֹל הָנֵי מִילֵּי מֵחַיִּים אֲבָל לְאַחַר מִיתָה לָא תַּנְיָא כְּשֶׁחָלָה רַבִּי נִכְנַס רַבִּי חִיָּיא אֶצְלוֹ וּמְצָאוֹ שֶׁהוּא בּוֹכֶה אָמַר לוֹ רַבִּי מִפְּנֵי מָה אַתָּה בּוֹכֶה וְהָתַנְיָא מֵת מִתּוֹךְ הַשְּׂחוֹק סִימָן יָפֶה לוֹ מִתּוֹךְ הַבֶּכִי סִימָן רַע לוֹ פָּנָיו לְמַעְלָה סִימָן יָפֶה לוֹ פָּנָיו לְמַטָּה סִימָן רַע לוֹ אֲמַר לֵיהּ אֲנָא אַתּוֹרָה וּמִצְוֹת קָא בָּכֵינָא.

At the time of the passing of Rebbi, he said: I need my children. His children entered his room. He said to them: Be careful with the honor of your mother. As well, my lamp should be lit in its place, my table should be set in its place, and the bed should be arranged in its place. Yosef Chafni and Shimon Efrati; they served me during my lifetime, and they will serve me in my death.

"Be careful with the honor of your mother": But this is required by Torah law, as it is written: "Honor your father and your mother"? However, she was their father's wife. But honoring a father's wife is also required by Torah law, as it is taught: Honor your father [es avicha] and your mother [v'es imecha]. "Es" your father; this adds your father's wife. And "es" your mother; this adds your mother's husband. And the extra letter vav comes to add your eldest brother. Nevertheless, this applies only during the step-parent's lifetime. Following the step-parent's death, the obligation to honor a step-parent is no longer in force [which is why Rebbi made a special appeal to his children].

Most of us don't really appreciate everything that our parents have done for us until we have kids of our own. Remember the first time it dawned on you? It's the middle of the night and you've gotten up to change the baby's diaper, your toddler wakes up wanting breakfast and next thing you know you're cleaning up his mess all over the table and floor. You reach for the phone and, feeling like you're allowed just one phone call, you call your parents to thank them for everything that they ever did for you!

And then, before you know it, they're teenagers and they're able to think for themselves and talk back. You've asked them to tidy their bedroom or do the dishes and it's like pulling teeth. And you think: Why don't they appreciate everything I do for them? Why won't they do their bit around the house? Where's the gratitude?

While honoring parents is considered one of the mitzvos we basically comprehend, it is not always entirely straightforward and simple. If honoring parents were axiomatic and unproblematic for all, the Torah wouldn't have to tell us to do it. At the very least, it wouldn't need to be one of the Ten Commandments! Clearly, it's not always so obvious. Why not? Because, as anyone with teenagers will tell you, the give-and-take relationship is not a two-way street. It's one thing not to expect your toddler to fold the laundry, but why can't you have expectations of your teenager after all you've done for them? Why don't they intuitively respond to your kindness with kindness of their own?

The answer of course is that you chose to have them. They didn't choose to have you. Once you made the decision to bring them into the world, it goes without saying that you need to take care of them. You are duty-bound to feed them, clothe them, and clean up after them. But for their part, from a point of view of nature, they don't really owe you anything at all.

That's why the Torah must state, "Honor your father and your mother." Because it's not obvious. Even though your parents chose this duty, nonetheless, Heaven demands that you honor them for everything that they've done and give back whenever possible. With that understanding, it's no longer as difficult to wrap one's head around the obligation to honor one's step-parent. It might not be natural; you might think, "I don't owe him anything." But it doesn't matter. You honor a step-parent because the Torah says so, whether you understand why or not.

But, indeed, if it is not obvious, why then does the Torah require us to honor our parents? After all, why should we honor them when they chose to be our parents, but we never chose to be their children? The *Sefer Hachinuch* explains that in addition to the gratitude you should have for everything that they've done for you, the primary reason for your gratitude is the mere fact that they brought you into this world.[1]

That assumes we understand the importance of being in this world to begin with. Why is this world so special that we must thank our parents purely for our creation? We opened today's learning with a distraught Rebbi: "I am crying for the Torah and the mitzvos that I will be unable to fulfill after I die!"

---

1 Ch. 33.

This world is special because by learning Torah and doing mitzvos, we can elevate our souls. "Rabbi Yaakov would say: This world is comparable to a hallway before the world to come. Prepare yourself in the hallway, so that you may enter the palace. He would further say: A single moment of repentance and good deeds in this world is greater than all of the world to come."[2] Rebbi cried because one's place in the palace is based on one's religious accomplishments on Earth. Once one has passed from this world, his Heavenly status is sealed.

Your parents gave you an unbelievable opportunity—to elevate your soul through the performance of mitzvos in this world. No matter how bad a parent you might think you have, no matter how difficult your childhood may have been, you owe an eternal debt of gratitude to your parents, simply for bringing you into this world and literally giving you the opportunity of a lifetime!

Honoring your parents is an easy mitzvah for some, but far more challenging for others.[3] If it's one of the harder mitzvos for you, remember the teaching of the Arizal:[4] the most difficult mitzvos are the ones for which we were sent down into this world in order to repair our souls. May you successfully honor your parents and step-parents both during their lifetimes and even after their passing!

---

2 *Avos* 4.

3 If it is unbearable to attend to the parents' needs, our Sages advise that one appoint an agent.

4 Rav Chaim Vital, *Shaar Hagilgulim*.

DAF 104

Praying for the Passing of a Loved One

The day that Rebbi died, the Sages decreed a fast, beseeching Heavenly mercy that he would not die. They declared, "May the one who says that Rebbi has died be pierced by the sword!"

Rebbi's caregiver ascended to the roof and announced, "The upper worlds are requesting the presence of Rebbi and the lower realm is requesting the presence of Rebbi. May it be Hashem's will that the lower realm should impose its will upon the upper worlds!"

Nevertheless, when she saw how frequently he would have to enter the bathroom, necessitating the painful removal of his tefillin, and subsequent re-donning of them as he experienced intense physical pain and suffering, she announced, "May it be Hashem's will that the upper worlds should impose their will upon the lower!"

What kind of prayer is that? Did she just pray for Rebbi's death?

הָהוּא יוֹמָא דְּנָח נַפְשֵׁיהּ דְּרַבִּי גְּזַרוּ רַבָּנַן תַּעֲנִיתָא וּבְעוֹ רַחֲמֵי וְאָמְרִי כׇּל מַאן דְּאָמַר נָח נַפְשֵׁיהּ דְּרַבִּי יִדָּקֵר בְּחֶרֶב סְלִיקָא אַמְתֵיהּ דְּרַבִּי לְאִיגָּרָא אָמְרָה עֶלְיוֹנִים מְבַקְּשִׁין אֶת רַבִּי וְהַתַּחְתּוֹנִים מְבַקְּשִׁין אֶת רַבִּי יְהִי רָצוֹן שֶׁיָּכוֹפוּ תַּחְתּוֹנִים אֶת הָעֶלְיוֹנִים כֵּיוָן דַּחֲזַאי כַּמָּה זִימְנֵי דְּעָיֵיל לְבֵית הַכִּסֵּא וְחָלַץ תְּפִילִּין וּמַנַּח לְהוּ וְקָמִצְטַעַר אֲמַרָה יְהִי רָצוֹן שֶׁיָּכוֹפוּ עֶלְיוֹנִים אֶת הַתַּחְתּוֹנִים וְלָא הֲווֹ שָׁתְקִי רַבָּנַן מִלְּמִיבְעֵי רַחֲמֵי שָׁקְלָה כּוּזָא שָׁדְיָיא מֵאִיגָּרָא [לְאַרְעָא] אִישְׁתִּיקוּ מֵרַחֲמֵי וְנָח נַפְשֵׁיהּ דְּרַבִּי.

Meanwhile, the Sages would not desist from beseeching Divine mercy [for Rebbi to remain with them]. So, the caregiver grabbed a jug and threw it from the roof to the ground. [Due to the commotion], the Sages were suddenly silent and refrained momentarily from beseeching mercy. And Rebbi passed away.

Every moment in this world is precious, and we generally pray for the complete recovery of an ill patient, both for his own sake and for the sake of his loved ones. If, however, a patient is in great agony and there is no chance of recovery, we are not required to prolong his life utilizing unessential medical intervention. Certainly, it is forbidden to actively remove any life-giving aids from the person, such as life-support machines. At the same time, however, we are not obligated to go out of our way to intervene if the person is on his death bed and suffering unnecessarily.

What's more, our Rabbis teach,[1] just like Rebbi's caregiver, once we realize that there's no hope of recovery and there's no point praying for a recovery that will not happen, we may shift our focus and beseech Heaven's mercy for a calm and peaceful death. Instead of praying that the person remain in his state of pain and anguish, we ask Hashem that he pass with as little suffering as possible.

That's not to say, God forbid, that we ever lose faith in Hashem's ability to perform miracles. I have personally witnessed a number of patients with whom we recited *viduy,* the end-of-life confessional, only to behold their miraculous recovery, against all odds and contrary to the predictions of the medical experts. Rather, our prayers should be for a complete recovery with the caveat that if that is not the Divine will, then may the person's passing be as painless as possible.

In fact, even when a patient is in immense pain and the doctors give him a choice of whether or not to engage in "excessive" intervention, Rav Moshe Feinstein writes that one should whisper into his ear that every moment in this world offers an extraordinary opportunity to serve Hashem. But if the patient simply cannot bear his present

---

1 *Ran, Nedarim* 40a.

suffering, we should not engage in certain risky interventions against his wishes. That does not imply, God forbid, that one may resort to anything that at all resembles "physician-assisted dying," which tragically has been legalized in too many countries today. It simply means that we should not force a patient who is in immense pain to submit himself to life-prolonging procedures if he is unwilling.

We all experience pain in this world. Nevertheless, our Father in Heaven doesn't want us to suffer unbearably. May you merit only good health for you and your loved ones!

DAF 105

Tough Rabbis

Shmuel was once crossing a river on a narrow ferry. A fellow came along and gave him a hand to help him out of the ferryboat. Shmuel said to him, "What brings you here?"

The man replied, "I have a court-case to present before you."

Shmuel said to him, "I am disqualified from presiding over your case, as you did me a favor."

Ameimar was once sitting and judging a case when a feather floated and landed on his head. A fellow came by and removed it from his head. Ameimar said to him, "What brings you here?"

The man replied, "I have a case to present before you."

Ameimar said to him, "I am disqualified from presiding over your case, due to the favor you just performed for me."

The sharecropper of Rabbi Yishmael son of Rabbi Yosi was accustomed to bringing him a basket full of fruits every Erev Shabbos. One day, he brought him the basket on a Thursday. Rabbi Yishmael asked him, "Why are you early this week?"

The sharecropper replied, "I have a case to present before you, and I said to myself that along my way, I will bring *rebbi* the basket of fruits, as in any case I am coming on Thursday, the day the courts are in session." Rabbi Yishmael did not accept the basket of fruits from him, and he said to him, "I am disqualified from presiding over your case." Rabbi Yishmael then seated a pair of Rabbinic scholars and they judged the sharecropper's case.

As Rabbi Yishmael watched, he thought, "If he wants, he could claim this, and if he wants, he could claim that." He then said to himself, "May the souls of those who accept bribes suffer agony! If I, who did not accept anything—and even if I had accepted it, it would have been my own property—am nevertheless in this frame of mind due to the proposed gift, imagine the bias of those who actually accept bribes!"[1]

תַּנְיָא וְשׁוֹחַד לֹא תִקָּח מָה תַּלְמוּד לוֹמַר אִם לְלַמֵּד שֶׁלֹּא לְזַכּוֹת אֶת הַחַיָּב וְשֶׁלֹּא לְחַיֵּיב אֶת הַזַּכַּאי הֲרֵי כְּבָר נֶאֱמַר לֹא תַטֶּה מִשְׁפָּט אֶלָּא אֲפִילּוּ לְזַכּוֹת אֶת הַזַּכַּאי וּלְחַיֵּיב אֶת הַחַיָּב אָמְרָה תּוֹרָה וְשׁוֹחַד לֹא תִקָּח אָמַר רַבִּי אֲבָהוּ בֹּא וּרְאֵה כַּמָּה סְמוּיוֹת עֵינֵיהֶן שֶׁל מְקַבְּלֵי שׁוֹחַד אָדָם חָשׁ בְּעֵינָיו נוֹתֵן מָמוֹן לָרוֹפֵא סָפֵק מִתְרַפֵּא סָפֵק אֵינוֹ מִתְרַפֵּא וְהֵן נוֹטְלִין שָׁוֶה פְּרוּטָה וּמְסַמִּין עֵינֵיהֶן שֶׁנֶּאֱמַר כִּי הַשּׁוֹחַד יְעַוֵּר פִּקְחִים כִּי אֲתָא רַב דִּימִי אֲמַר דָּרֵשׁ רַב נַחְמָן בַּר כֹּהֵן מַאי דִּכְתִיב מֶלֶךְ בְּמִשְׁפָּט יַעֲמִיד אָרֶץ וְאִישׁ תְּרוּמוֹת יֶהֶרְסֶנָּה אִם דּוֹמֶה דַּיָּין לְמֶלֶךְ שֶׁאֵינוֹ צָרִיךְ לִכְלוּם יַעֲמִיד אָרֶץ וְאִם דּוֹמֶה לְכֹהֵן שֶׁמְּחַזֵּר עַל הַגְּרָנוֹת יֶהֶרְסֶנָּה אָמַר רַבָּה בַּר רַב שֵׁילָא הַאי דַּיָּינָא דְּשָׁאֵיל שְׁאֵילְתָּא פָּסוּל לְמֵידַן דִּינָא וְלָא אֲמַרַן אֶלָּא דְּלֵית לֵיהּ לְאוֹשׁוֹלֵי אֲבָל אִית לֵיהּ לְאוֹשׁוֹלֵי לֵית לַן בַּהּ אִינִי וְהָא רָבָא שָׁאֵיל שְׁאֵילְתָּא מִדְּבֵי בַּר מָרִיוֹן אַף עַל גַּב דְּלָא שָׁיְילִי מִינֵּיהּ הָתָם לְאַחְשׁוֹבִינְהוּ הוּא דְּבָעֵי אָמַר רָבָא מַאי טַעְמָא דְּשׁוּחְדָּא כֵּיוָן דְּקַבֵּיל לֵיהּ שׁוּחְדָּא מִינֵּיהּ אִיקָּרְבָא לֵיהּ דַּעְתֵּיהּ לְגַבֵּיהּ וְהָוֵי כְּגוּפֵיהּ וְאֵין אָדָם רוֹאֶה חוֹבָה לְעַצְמוֹ מַאי שׁוֹחַד שֶׁהוּא חַד אָמַר רַב פָּפָּא לָא לֵידוּן אִינִישׁ דִּינָא לְמַאן דְּרָחֵים לֵיהּ וְלָא לְמַאן דְּסָנֵי לֵיהּ דְּרָחֵים לֵיהּ לָא חָזֵי לֵיהּ חוֹבָה דְּסָנֵי לֵיהּ לָא חָזֵי לֵיהּ זְכוּתָא אָמַר אַבָּיֵי הַאי צוּרְבָא מֵרַבָּנַן דִּמְרַחֲמִין לֵיהּ בְּנֵי מָתָא לָאו מִשּׁוּם דִּמְעַלֵּי טְפֵי אֶלָּא מִשּׁוּם דְּלָא מוֹכַח לְהוּ בְּמִילֵּי דִּשְׁמַיָּא אָמַר רָבָא מֵרֵישׁ הֲוָה אָמֵינָא הָנֵי בְּנֵי מָחוֹזָא כּוּלְּהוּ רָחֲמוּ לִי כֵּיוָן דַּהֲוַאי דַּיָּינָא אָמֵינָא מִינַּיְיהוּ סָנוּ לִי וּמִינַּיְיהוּ רָחֲמוּ לִי כֵּיוָן דַּחֲזַאי דְּמַאן דְּמִיחַיַּיב (לֵיהּ) הָאִידָּנָא קָא זָכֵי לְמָחַר אָמֵינָא אִם מְרַחֵם כּוּלְּהוּ רָחֲמוּ לִי אִי מִסְנוּ כּוּלְּהוּ סָנוּ לִי .

"And you shall take no bribe": What is the meaning of the verse? If it comes to teach that one should not acquit the guilty and one should not convict the innocent due to a bribe, it is already stated, "You shall not twist justice." Rather, it teaches that even if one were to acquit the innocent and convict the

1 *Kesubos* 105b.

guilty, the Torah nevertheless says: "And you shall take no bribe." Rabbi Avahu said: Come and see how blind are the eyes of those who accept bribes. If a person has pain in his eyes, he gives a doctor money, and even still, it is uncertain whether he will be healed or whether he will not be healed. And yet, those judges who take the value of a prutah and actively blind their eyes, as it is stated, "For a bribe blinds those who have sight." When Rav Dimi arrived, he said that Rav Nachman bar Kohen interpreted a verse homiletically as follows. What is the meaning of that which is written: "The king by justice sustains the earth, but he who exacts gifts destroys it"? If a judge is like a king, in that he does not need anything and is not dependent on anyone, he sustains the earth, but if he is like a priest, who seeks out his gifts from various granaries, he destroys the earth. Rabbah bar Rav Sheila said: A judge who borrows items from others is disqualified from rendering judgment. And we said this only in a case where he does not have articles to lend [but is constantly borrowing without lending objects in return]. However, if he has items to lend, we have no problem with it. Is that so? But Rava would borrow items from the house of bar Marion even though they would not borrow from him. There, he wanted to cause them to promote their social status. Rava said: What is the reason for the prohibition against taking a bribe? Once a judge accepts a bribe from one party, his thoughts draw closer to him and he becomes like his own self, and a person does not find fault with himself. What is the meaning of shochad, bribe? She'hu chad, that he is one with the litigant. Rav Pappa said: A person should not judge a case involving one whom he loves, nor involving one whom he hates. He should not judge one whom he loves, as he will not find any fault in him, nor with one whom he hates, as he will not find any merit in him. Abaye said: A Torah scholar who is beloved by the residents of his town, it is not because he is a superior sage than others; rather, it is because he does not reprove them in Heavenly matters. Rava said: At first, I used to say that all

> *these residents of Mechoza love me; however, once I became a judge, I said that some of them hate me and some of them love me. When I saw that the one whom I declared guilty today would be found innocent the following day, I said: If they all want to love me, then let them all love me, and if they all want to hate me, then let them all hate me.*

A rabbi wears many different hats. There are two basic types of contemporary *semichah*. Basic ordination is called "*yoreh yoreh*," which means that "he shall surely guide." Advanced ordination is called "*yadin yadin*," meaning "he shall surely judge." Primarily, the rabbi's job is to show the way of our guidebook for life, the Torah (related to the word *yoreh*). Acting in that capacity, the rabbi must be as kind and gracious as possible, reaching out to his brethren in embodying the dictum that the Torah's "ways are pleasant ways and all her paths are peaceful."[2]

But there are times that a rabbi is required to act as a *dayan*, judge, adjudicating matters of halachah, and making tough, unpopular decisions. Do you think he enjoys being the proverbial bad guy? Of course not. It would be much easier to let things go and never have to lay down the law. But that's like giving candy to a whining child. Sure, it makes us feel better when the child stops crying. But is it good for the child? Not in the long run.

That's the feeling Rava experienced when he became a judge in Mechoza. Until then, as the community rabbi, everyone loved him. But then it came time to step up and become the community *posek*. Now he wasn't as popular. Because being the lawmaker means making tough decisions for the community. It means adjudicating court-cases where there are winners and losers. Placed in such a situation, it's not only impossible to please everyone, but it would be wrong to do so.

And the truth is, it doesn't take appointment to a *beis din* for a rabbi to become an adjudicator of Jewish law. Every rabbi should be guiding his flock in such a way that he strives to raise the level of their religious commitment. As well, he must never be afraid to issue a halachic

---

2 *Mishlei* 3:17.

ruling that he believes to be right, as unpopular as that might make him. That's part and parcel of the responsibility of the position. That's why community rabbis traditionally have a fixed-term contract or even *chazakah*, tenure. If the rabbi lived with the constant fear of having the board terminate his employment, he would never be able to issue unpopular halachic rulings. Like a politician, he would endeavor constantly to please the electorate. And there's nothing morally compelling about that mode of governance.

Rav Yisrael Salanter used to say that a rabbi who pleases nobody any of the time is obviously a bad rabbi. But a rabbi who pleases all the people all the time is even worse. May you find a rabbi who can guide you in the Torah's pleasant and peaceful ways and who, at the same time, is never afraid to stand up for what is right!

DAF 106

An Abundant Mindset

During the time of King Yehoram, there was a great famine in the land of Judah. The king sent messengers appealing to the prophet Elisha who responded that the following day, food would be found in such abundance that "a *se'ah* of choice flour shall sell for a *shekel* at the gate of Samaria, and two *se'ahs* of barley for a *shekel*."

The king's aide scoffed in response, "Even if Hashem was to make windows in the sky, could this come to pass?"

Elisha replied, "You shall see it with your own eyes, but you shall not eat from it."

Meanwhile, there were four lepers dwelling outside the city. They said to one another, "Why should we sit here waiting for our deaths? If we decide to go into the town where there is a famine, we shall die there. And if we just sit here, still we shall die. Come, let us desert to the Aramean camp. If they sustain us, we shall live; and if they put us to death, we would have died anyway."

They set out at twilight for the Aramean camp, but when they came to the edge of the Aramean camp, there was no one there. For Hashem had caused the Aramean camp to hear a sound of chariots, a sound of horses—the din of a huge army. They said to one another, "The king of Israel must have hired the kings of the Hittites and the kings of Mitzrayim to attack us!" And they fled headlong in the twilight, abandoning their tents and horses and donkeys, the entire camp just as it was, as they fled for their lives.

When the lepers came to the edge of the camp, they went into one of the tents and ate and drank; then they carried off silver and gold and clothing from there and buried it. They came back and went into another tent, and they carried off what was there and buried it. Then they said to one another, "We are not doing right. This is a day of good news, and we are keeping silent! If we wait until the light of morning, we shall incur guilt. Come, let us go and inform the king's palace."

Off they went and called out to the gatekeepers of the city and told them, "We have been to the Aramean camp. There is not a soul there, nor any human sound, but the horses are tethered, and the donkeys are tethered, and the tents are undisturbed." The gatekeepers called out, and the news was passed on into the king's palace.

The king rose in the night and said to his courtiers, "I will tell you what the Arameans have done to us. They know that we are starving, so they have gone out of camp and hidden in the fields, thinking: When they come out of the town, we will take them alive and get into the town."

But one of the courtiers spoke up, "Let a few of the remaining horses that are still here be taken and let us send and find out." They took two teams of horses and the king sent them after the Aramean army, saying, "Go and find out." They followed them as far as the Jordan and found the entire road full of clothing and gear which the Arameans had thrown away in their haste; and the messengers returned and told the king. The people then went out and plundered the Aramean camp. Thus, a *se'ah* of choice flour sold for a *shekel*, and two *se'ahs* of barley for a *shekel*, just as Hashem had spoken. Just then the skeptical king's aide was in charge of the gate. As the people ran out to gather the food he was trampled to death, just as Elisha foretold.[1]

תְּנַן מוֹתַר שְׁיָרֵי לִשְׁכָּה מָה הָיוּ עוֹשִׂין בָּהֶן לוֹקְחִין בָּהֶן יֵינוֹת שְׁמָנִים וּסְלָתוֹת וְהַשָּׂכָר לַהֶקְדֵּשׁ דִּבְרֵי רַבִּי יִשְׁמָעֵאל רַבִּי עֲקִיבָא אוֹמֵר אֵין מִשְׂתַּכְּרִין בְּשֶׁל הֶקְדֵּשׁ אַף לֹא בְּשֶׁל עֲנִיִּים בְּשֶׁל הֶקְדֵּשׁ מַאי טַעְמָא לָא אֵין עֲנִיּוּת בִּמְקוֹם עֲשִׁירוּת בְּשֶׁל עֲנִיִּים מַאי טַעְמָא לָא דִּלְמָא מִתְרְמֵי לְהוּ עַנְיָא וְלֵיכָּא לְמִיתְבָא לֵיהּ.

1 *Melachim II* 7.

> *What would they do with the surplus funds of the Holy Temple chamber? They would purchase wine, oil, and fine flour [and sell them to those who needed them for their private offerings]. And the profit from these sales would go to consecrated property. This is the statement of Rabbi Yishmael. Rabbi Akiva says: One may not generate profit by selling consecrated property, nor may one profit from funds set aside for the poor. What is the reason that one may not use consecrated property to generate a profit? For there is no poverty in a place of wealth. What is the reason that one may not use funds set aside for the poor to make a profit? For perhaps, one will encounter a poor person and there will be nothing to give him [as all of the money is invested].*

When the Beis Hamikdash stood, it was funded by donations from the people. Like other charitable institutions, some years were better than others. And so, on a good donation year, the Temple account would be in surplus. What would they do with the surplus funds? Rabbi Yishmael contends that the Temple leaders would purchase wine, oil, and flour, and sell it to the Temple attendees, thereby making a profit for the Temple account, which could then be used to purchase other Temple items. Rabbi Akiva disagrees. He maintains that "there is no poverty in a place of wealth." In his opinion, the Temple must always be run in a lavish manner. Therefore, one may not use Temple funds to generate small profits in the manner of paupers. It appears inappropriately frugal to be stretching the Temple *dinars*.

Many people claim to seek financial prosperity, but their mindset and behavior demonstrate that they are not ready to welcome Heaven's blessing. "There is no poverty in a place of wealth." If you truly seek wealth, you need to stop conducting yourself like a poor person and start acting and thinking as wealthy people do. When you adopt an attitude of *breitkeit*—open-mindedness and open-handedness—you create the right environment for blessing to manifest.

In the Rabbi Yishmael approach, you're constantly looking for little ways to stretch that dollar and hoping that one day, you'll miraculously become wealthy. In the Rabbi Akiva approach, you open your mind and heart up to the Almighty's unlimited bounty. When you recognize that Hashem has unlimited resources, you realize that it's just a matter of tapping into them and allowing His bounty to flow forth.

The Rabbi Yishmael-minded person looks for every little trick to become rich. He'll buy lottery tickets. He'll look for *segulos*—good luck charms—that will do magic for him, like being a *sandek* at a bris, overflowing the washing cup before a meal, *Maftir Yonah*, and putting *Havdalah* wine in his pocket. These *segulos* are all wonderful, bona fide elements of our tradition, but it's not how wealthy people think and act.

The *Sefer Hachinuch* teaches that there's one sure way of achieving God's blessing in your storehouse that's a greater guarantee than any *segulah*. What is it? Concentrating on *bentching* after your meal. Focus on the meaning of the words—they're filled with blessings of livelihood and sustenance. If we would merely have the right *kavanah* during *bentching*, we would need no other *segulah* for material prosperity![2] What the *Chinuch* means is that you don't need any special tricks to get rich. You simply need to recognize that Hashem provides. When you say that and mean it, your flow of wealth will come directly from Him; no *segulos* necessary.

How do you demonstrate your perfect faith in Hashem's ability and readiness to provide everything you need and more? You need to live like you mean it. Many people are not able to achieve wealth because they just don't maintain the right attitude. They're constantly playing the *nebbach* card, asking for handouts and being overly frugal in every aspect of their lives. There's no place for poverty if you seek wealth.

That means giving to others with an open hand. That will lead to the Almighty giving you with His open hand. It means spending lavishly on Shabbos and inviting an abundance of guests. When you do that, Hashem promises that you will never lack for supplies. And it means acknowledging the blessing that He's already given you. If you can afford

---

2 *Sefer Hachinuch* 430.

to eat in a restaurant, then you can afford a decent tip for the waiter. When you give abundantly, Hashem gives you abundantly.

The Almighty wants you to enjoy His bounty. He wants you to ask for His bounty. It's your choice if you want to live a life of stinginess and skimpiness. From Hashem's perspective, there's no shortage of blessing to bestow. You simply need to open your mind and start thinking big so that He can pour out His Heavenly blessing upon you. That means that when you ask Him for His blessing, don't ask for a two dollar an hour raise, ask for a promotion!

A friend of mine was still in law school when it came time for his kids to go to school. As everyone knows, it's not an inexpensive endeavor to give your children a good Jewish education. Thank God, most schools are very generous with their need-based scholarships. And so, he and his wife filled out all the forms and were offered a substantial break. Two years later, however, he had graduated and was starting to make decent money. Came the beginning of the academic year and the school sent him the scholarship forms that he had filled out previously. He called them up to thank them and declined their offer.

"Baruch Hashem I'm now able to pay full fees," he told them. "And I'm now ready to start paying back what I owe from the last two years," he added.

"You don't owe us anything," the chair of the scholarship committee responded somewhat bemused, "we assessed your fees based on your income and assets and you paid the right amount that we determined according to our formula."

"I'm sorry," my friend replied, "there must be some sort of misunderstanding. I never intended to take a hand-out. You're right that the last two years I couldn't afford to pay full board. But now I can. And I always knew that I'd eventually be able to pay. And now I'm ready to pay what I couldn't pay back then."

"Are you serious?" the committee chair responded incredulously. "In the ten years I've sat on this committee, nobody has ever come back to us offering to repay his tuition breaks!"

My friend has a Rabbi Akiva mindset. When you have a Rabbi Akiva mindset, you don't seek handouts. You take them if absolutely necessary, but you know that very soon, you're going to have more than enough Heavenly bounty to pay it all back. When you live with that perspective, Hashem will make sure that you have whatever you need in life.

Stop thinking like King Yehoram's trampled aide. Hashem has promised that He "will surely open the floodgates of the sky for you and pour down blessings on you."[3] May you open your mind and heart to His unlimited blessing!

---

3 *Malachi* 3:10.

DAF 107

Absolute Truth

A number of years ago, Rebeccah came to see me with her boyfriend, James. Her parents had asked her to chat with me because James wasn't Jewish. "Maybe I could help James with a conversion?" they were hoping. I explained to them that we can't just convert someone to get married. If James was independently interested in becoming Jewish, then we could explore that possibility. But he would really need to initiate the process, not them. At any rate, I was certainly happy to chat with them—my door is open to everyone.

Rebeccah and James came to meet with me. The subject of conversion, however, wasn't even on the table. "Look, Rabbi, James grew up Catholic. Imagine, his parents wanted me to convert to Catholicism! I wouldn't dream of it. So, why would my parents think that he would be interested in converting to Judaism? We've spoken about religion quite a bit and we both feel strong in our religious identities."

"That's great that you feel strongly about your religious identities," I said, "but how are you going to choose what you practice at home?"

"We don't have to choose. We've decided to bring up our children with both religions. If we have a boy, he'll have a bris. Then he'll be baptized. Then he'll have a bar mitzvah. And then a confirmation. You get the picture, Rabbi, right?"

אָמַר רַב זְבִיד הָנֵי מָאנֵי דְקוּנְיָא חִיוָּרֵי וְאוּכָּמֵי שְׁרוּ יְרוּקֵי אֲסִירֵי וְלָא אֲמַרַן אֶלָּא דְלֵית בְּהוּ קַרְטוּפָנֵי אֲבָל אִית בְּהוּ קַרְטוּפָנֵי אֲסִירֵי.

> *Rav Zvid said: Regarding glazed vessels, white and black ones are permitted. However, green ones are forbidden. And we said that [white and black ones are permitted] only if they do not have cracks. If they have cracks, they are forbidden.*

Earthenware vessels absorb food and drink cooked or contained in them. If they held forbidden food, such as wine poured as an idolatrous libation or chametz on Pesach, they are rendered forbidden and unable to be kashered. Rav Zvid teaches that black and white glazing prevents the vessels from absorbing the foods placed inside them, as long as there are no cracks in the vessel.

We live in very confusing moral times. Philosophically, ours has been dubbed the postmodern era. Postmodern ideology contends that there is no such thing as the absolute truth. All knowledge is situated and subjective. There's no right and wrong; it's all just opinions based on personal lived experiences. In such a climate, it's challenging enough to maintain one's personal moral compass, let alone convey values to one's children.

And yet, as Rabbi Sacks points out, it often doesn't take very long to see the consequences of such relativistic thinking.[1] A generation ago, marriage and traditional life was criticized as rooted in patriarchal conceptions of the right way to rear children. Single parenthood, we were told, was a valid choice that individuals could make. It didn't take much time, however, to witness the results of such a free-spirited attitude. Children from single-parent homes, we now know, are far more prone to poverty and criminal activity. In hindsight, it's not hard to see why. How can a single parent struggling to make ends meet be there constantly for the children? In a traditional family setting, parents do their very best to ensure one of them is around for the kids outside of school hours. It's not always attainable, but it's much more easily achieved than when all the responsibility falls upon a single individual.

Thank God, we have a guidebook for life given to us by the Creator to light the way and show us the path through the darkness of this world.

---

1 *Faith in the Future*, p. 24.

The Torah spells out our moral code, offering us instruction and clarity. We have values. We know the truth. And we can discern between right and wrong. We have been granted a black and white glazing that protects us from the moral ambiguity and confusion that surrounds us. As long as we make sure that we don't allow so much as a crack in our belief and convictions, we will be able to maintain that clarity for ourselves and our children.

It's not an easy demand. The world around says that belief in right and wrong is antiquated and bigoted. And so many people mistakenly believe that the way to avoid charges of bigotry and allegations of intolerance is to respond with the suggestion that everybody is right and that there's no absolute truth. That's the green glaze perspective and it only guarantees one consequence: that your children will be utterly confused and probably choose to try other approaches to life. After all, if everyone is right and there's no absolute truth, then why should they stick with your Jewish way of life?

But belief in the clear demarcation lines between good and bad, right and wrong, truth and falsehood, doesn't mean that you need to be intolerant of others. For starters, the advantage of Judaism over most other faiths is that we do not believe God wants everyone to be Jewish. You can be a good, right, true non-Jew, and we are absolutely OK with that. Second, however, the key distinction between intolerance and moral clarity is the acknowledgment in another human being's right to believe that he holds the absolute truth.

What do I mean? Postmodern thinkers would say, "I'm entitled to my views. You're entitled to your views. Nobody can make an absolute-truth claim because who knows what's really right or wrong?" By contrast, truth seekers respond to those holding contrary-truth claims, as follows: "I believe I am absolutely right. You are absolutely wrong. But, at the same time, I respect your right to believe that you are absolutely right, and I am absolutely wrong. We admit that we do not see eye-to-eye and we never will. But we tolerate one another's right to believe as we do."

Let's return to Rebeccah and James. Clearly, they hadn't given much thought to the contradictions that they were committing to in their lives and the lives of their future children. Take belief in God, for example. At its most basic level, Judaism and Catholicism are in opposition on the concept of God. Either one believes in unity, or one believes in trinity. You can't believe in both. It's one or the other.

The key to maintaining moral clarity in this very confusing world is to ensure there are no cracks in the vessel. There's no room to absorb forbidden influences that threaten to desensitize us from our moral clarity. That doesn't mean we cut ourselves off from the world and that our commitment to a black-and-white picture means we become inflexible. Of course not. What it means is that every idea that we encounter is processed through the lens of the truth of Torah.

In today's day and age, it's not easy to wear the badge of moral clarity with pride. But the Torah carries us through the haze of the world around us. May you become a vessel for the truth!

DAF 108

Moshe Would Be Nothing without You

Just as Moshe and Aharon are about to enter Pharaoh's palace for the second time to entreat him to let the people go, the Torah lists the names of the Hebrew families:

The sons of Reuven, Israel's first-born: Chanoch and Pallu, Chetzron and Carmi; those are the families of Reuven. The sons of Shimon: Yemuel, Yamin, Ohad, Yachin, Tzochar, and Shaul, the son of the Canaanite; those are the families of Shimon. These are the names of Levi's sons by their lineage: Gershon, Kehas, and Merari; and the span of Levi's life was 137 years. The sons of Gershon: Livni and Shimi, by their families. The sons of Kehas: Amram, Yitzhar, Chevron, and Uziel; and the span of Kehas's life was 133 years. The sons of Merari: Machli and Mushi. These are the families of the Levites by their lineage.

Amram married his father's sister Yocheved, and she bore him Aharon and Moshe; and the span of Amram's life was 137 years. The sons of Yitzhar: Korach, Nefeg, and Zichri. The sons of Uziel: Mishael, Eltzaphan, and Sisri. Aharon married Elisheva, daughter of Aminadav and sister of Nachshon, and she bore him Nadav and Avihu, Elazar and Isamar. The sons of Korach: Asir, Elkanah, and Aviasaf. Those are the families of the Korachites. And Aharon's son Elazar married one of Putiel's daughters, and she bore him Pinchas. Those are the heads of the fathers' houses of the Levites by their families.[1]

Why do we need to know the names of all these people? What difference do they make to the story?

הַמּוּדָּר הֲנָאָה מֵחֲבֵירוֹ שׁוֹקֵל לוֹ אֶת שִׁקְלוֹ וּפוֹרֵעַ אֶת חוֹבוֹ וּמַחֲזִיר לוֹ אֲבֵידָתוֹ וּבְמָקוֹם שֶׁנּוֹטְלִין שָׂכָר תִּפּוֹל הֲנָאָה לַהֶקְדֵּשׁ בִּשְׁלָמָא שׁוֹקֵל לוֹ אֶת שִׁקְלוֹ מִצְוָה קָעָבֵיד דִּתְנַן תּוֹרְמִין עַל הָאָבוּד וְעַל הַגָּבוּי וְעַל הֶעָתִיד לִגָּבוֹת.

If a person made a vow to abstain from any benefit from another individual, the other fellow may contribute his [half] shekel for him [to the annual Temple collection], and [the other fellow] may repay his debts for him. And [the other fellow] may return to him his lost object. And in a place where one is rewarded for returning a lost article, the reward is paid to the Temple treasury. It makes sense that [the other fellow] may contribute his shekel for him, as [the other fellow] thereby performs a mitzvah. For we learned: The Temple treasurers allocate the funds, taking into account donations that were lost, donations that were gathered, but not yet brought to the Temple, and donations that will be collected in the future.

When the treasurers in the Holy Temple would withdraw from the fund of accumulated half-*shekels* to purchase communal sacrifices, they would include donations that had been lost en route, donations that were still en route, and donations that were yet to be collected. Thus, all Jews have a share in the communal offerings brought in the Temple. The message here is that every individual's contribution counts. Even if, for whatever reason, an individual's half-*shekel* contribution did not make it to the Temple coffers, he is still counted and included.

When it comes to communal contributions, very often a person thinks that his efforts are worthless. He looks up at the "big *machers*"

---

1 *Shemos* 6:14.

and wonders whether his little contribution even counts. Either he thinks of himself as nobody special or he gets upset when his efforts don't quite make the mark.

Comes along the Mishnah to teach us that every individual's contribution is counted: those contributions that we see clearly, those contributions that seem to have gotten lost in the mix, those that didn't quite hit the spot, and even those who are behind in their pledges. Every contribution—financial or voluntary—is meaningful and significant, whether we see the impact clearly or not. There's no such thing as a meaningless contribution or communal role.

Who wouldn't like to be the next Moshe Rabbeinu? Everybody wants to feel that he's made a significant difference in the world. But here's the thing: Moshe Rabbeinu was only Moshe Rabbeinu because of the contribution of Machli and Mushi. Who? Machli and Mushi, his cousins. How do we know his cousin's names and what difference do their names make? Because the Torah tells us their names just as Moshe and Aharon are about to enter Pharaoh's palace. Why? Because without each of the individual Hebrews, Moshe and Aharon would have nobody to take out of Egypt. They were only Moshe and Aharon because there was a Machli and Mushi to redeem. And indeed, in order for the Exodus to take place, each and every Israelite had to play his part.

Broadly speaking, those specific roles included taking a sheep on the tenth of Nissan and slaughtering it on the fourteenth. It included circumcising all the males. It included smearing the blood on the doorposts and lintel. It included asking their Egyptian neighbors for parting gifts. And it included leaving Egypt with their families in an orderly fashion, taking their cues and instructions from Moshe and the Elders.

Think about it: Had any individual not played his part in the Exodus, it would never have gone smoothly. How do I know that? Because there were, in fact, individuals along the way who decided to do things their way. There was a group of Ephraimites who left Egypt a few years earlier and were slaughtered by the Philistines. There were various complainers and murmurers who stirred the pot along the way. There were the troublemakers who made the Golden Calf. There was Korach and his lot. All these characters weren't satisfied with the seemingly minor roles that they were assigned in the story. But their misbehavior simply demonstrates the important contributions made by all those who toed the line, sincerely and wholeheartedly donating their "half-*shekel*" to the history of our people, because they most certainly had roles that might have gone unnoticed.

The Torah doesn't mention the names of the Levites who heeded Moshe's call after the sin of the Golden Calf. It doesn't mention the names of all the Seventy Elders. It doesn't mention the names of the flagbearers. And it certainly doesn't mention every person who stood "behind the counter" to distribute the water from Miriam's well. But each of these contributors was essential to the success of Moshe and our national history.

Don't ever minimize the role that you play. Whether you're the person who greets people in shul on Shabbos or the volunteer who puts away the food after the *kiddush*, your contribution makes the shul and community work like clockwork and, ultimately, successful. There's no contribution that's not important.

Simply showing up to a community event is already a vital contribution. If Rabbi Akiva was the scholar-in-residence and nobody bothered coming, would he still be Rabbi Akiva? (Or would he be that tree in the forest?!) Hillel the Elder used to say, "When I am here, everyone is here," because if everyone imagined his contribution to be worthless, nobody would make any effort whatsoever.[2]

Make the effort, do your part. That's the only way that it will all come together. May you merit to be counted among those who serve the Almighty and His people faithfully!

---

2 Bunim, *Ethics From Sinai*, vol. 1, p. 111.

DAF 109

Twilight-Zone Judaism

What's the best method to ensure that you jump out of bed in the morning? Rabbi Shlomo Gantzfreid offers a guaranteed approach:

"You should realize that if you were called by any individual to participate in a business transaction in which there is profit, or to collect a debt, or if someone called with a plan to save your wealth from disaster, for example, if a fire occurred in the city or something similar occurred, you would certainly be quick to awaken immediately because of your concern for your wealth and you would not act sluggishly. Similarly, if you would need to go to the service of the king you would rise with alacrity."[1]

הַפּוֹסֵק מָעוֹת לַחֲתָנוֹ וּפָשַׁט לוֹ אֶת הָרֶגֶל תֵּשֵׁב עַד שֶׁיַּלְבִּין רֹאשָׁהּ אַדְמוֹן אוֹמֵר יְכוֹלָה הִיא שֶׁתֹּאמַר אִילּוּ אֲנִי פָּסַקְתִּי לְעַצְמִי אֵשֵׁב עַד שֶׁיַּלְבִּין רֹאשִׁי עַכְשָׁיו שֶׁאַבָּא פָּסַק מָה אֲנִי יְכוֹלָה לַעֲשׂוֹת אוֹ כְּנוֹס אוֹ פְּטוֹר אָמַר רַבָּן גַּמְלִיאֵל רוֹאֶה אֲנִי אֶת דִּבְרֵי אַדְמוֹן.

One who pledged money for his son-in-law as a dowry and subsequently went bankrupt, the betrothed woman may be left to sit unwed in her father's house until her hair turns white. Admon says that she can say, "Had I pledged the money myself,

1 *Kitzur Shulchan Aruch* 1:4.

I would agree to sit here until my hair turns white. But now that my father was the one who made the pledge, what can I do? Either marry me or release me!" Rabban Gamliel said: I concur with the statement of Admon.

Jewish marriage consists of two parts: the betrothal and the wedding. Nowadays, these two ceremonies are held sequentially at the same event. In Talmudic times, however, they were often months or even years apart. In today's Gemara, the bride and groom have celebrated their betrothal, but the wedding is delayed because the father of the bride is lacking the funds for the dowry that he had pledged. Meanwhile, the poor girl is sitting and waiting in a twilight zone between the betrothal and the wedding. Admon suggests that she should take matters into her own hands and issue her groom with an ultimatum: "Either we complete the marriage or let's call it a day. Living in this in-between stage is an unhealthy exercise in futility."

Sadly, many Jews live their Judaism in the twilight zone, enduring the worst of both worlds. They're married to their heritage, but they've never really thrown themselves into it. Instead, their commitment feels more like a burden. They're living with the "ball and chain" of *Judaism*, without the excitement and joy of *Yiddishkeit*. As some comedians like to quip, they're Jew-*ish*. They identify as Jews, but they're not particularly enthralled by it all.

A healthy spirit needs passion. To go through life in a state of inertia, when one is neither here nor there, is a heart-breaking life. If you're just going through the motions, but you have no passion, no spirit, no spirituality, no meaningful relationship with Heaven, then it's time to ask yourself whether it's really worth it. You're not doing Hashem any favors practicing a lifeless Judaism. It's time to let Him enter your life and embrace Him completely!

A joyous life is a meaningful life. Only when you have an overall purpose and goal is life manageable. Otherwise, the vicissitudes of life are way too tough to bear. It's easy to determine whether you're living in the twilight zone by your conduct first thing each morning. As soon as we open our eyes, we declare, "*Modeh ani lefanecha Melech chai v'kayam she'hechezarta bi nishmasi b'chemlah rabbah emunasecha*"—I thank you, living and eternal King, for returning my soul to me with mercy, great is your faith."

When you recite that line, what's going through your mind? Are you indeed grateful to Hashem for restoring your soul? Why? The most powerful word in that "prayer" is the one that's missing. There's actually no mention of Hashem's name. The traditional reason given for the glaring absence is the fact that we have not yet washed *negel vasser.* With our lingering *ruach ha'tumah,* it would be inappropriate to mention God's name.

But there's a more holistic basis for omitting His name. *Modeh Ani* is not really a prayer. It's a perspective with which we begin our day. Prayers require *kavanah,* but for the most part, if you prayed without *kavanah,* you've still fulfilled your duty (the exception being the first line of *Shema* and the first berachah of the *Amidah*). *Modeh Ani* intentionally omits God's name because it is *not* a prayer. Consequently, rattling off *Modeh Ani* with no thought is totally meaningless. The whole point of the *declaration* is to frame your own purpose for the day. A thoughtless *Modeh Ani* achieves nothing at all.

A focused *Modeh Ani*, however, is a decision to jump feet first into the marriage with Hashem. Twilight-zone Jews lie in bed hitting the snooze button again and again, letting their hair go white while essential minutes of their Divine mission tick by. If you find that happening, recall the sage words of Rabbi Gantzfreid about the million-dollar deal or meeting with the president that's happening this morning!

Let's return to the Gemara's scenario of the bride who is sitting in her father's home while her hair goes white. While our contemporary process of marriage doesn't allow that unfortunate twilight-zone situation to occur, sadly, twilight-zone marriages still happen. Instead of happening at the beginning of the marriage, however, they tend to arise after a number of years. The novelty and excitement have worn off and the relationship has become stagnant. Neither party is making much of an effort to move things forward and they're stuck in a situation of plodding along while their hair goes white. If that sounds like your marriage, it's time to declare, "Either we complete the marriage or let's

אֱלֹהִים אֲחֵרִים וְכִי מִי אָמַר לוֹ לְדָוִד לֵךְ עֲבוֹד אֱלֹהִים אֲחֵרִים אֶלָּא לוֹמַר לְךָ
כָּל הַדָּר בְּחוּצָה לָאָרֶץ כְּאִילּוּ עוֹבֵד עֲבוֹדָה זָרָה.

A person should always reside in Israel, even in a city that is mostly populated by gentiles, rather than residing outside of Israel in a city that is mostly populated by Jews. For anyone who resides in Israel is considered to have a God, and anyone who resides outside of Israel is considered not to have a God. As it is stated: "To give to you the land of Canaan, to be your God." And indeed, does anyone who resides outside of Israel have no God? Rather, it teaches that anyone who resides outside of Israel is considered as though he is engaged in idol worship. And so, it says with regard to David: "For they have driven me out this day that I should not cleave to the inheritance of Hashem, saying, Go, serve other gods." But who said to David "Go, serve other gods"? Rather, it teaches that anyone who resides outside of Israel is considered as though he is engaged in idol worship.

There's something about the environment outside the Land of Israel, explains Rabbi Yaakov Skili,[2] that leads to a laxity around mitzvah observance. It was this diaspora-mood that caused Yaakov to marry sisters. And likewise, it led to Yaakov turning a blind eye to the idolatry happening under his roof. Upon reaching the Holy Land, however, he immediately sensed the purity of the land and instructed the members of his household to remove all their idols.

It's tempting to be dismissive of the modern State of Israel as a secular country. While it is undoubtedly not run according to strict Torah law, it is, nonetheless, guided by Jewish values and tradition. My father tells the story of the time when he was teaching English in a school in Dimona. Each day, he would come into class and write the English date on the blackboard. One day, he enters and writes the date: 25 December, 1974. It suddenly occurred to him that it was the first time in his life that he'd worked on that date. He asked his students who knew the significance of that date in the calendar. He was pleasantly surprised

2 *Toras Haminchah.*

when not a hand went up. And this was in a state school consisting of non-religious children. Contrast that with every Jewish holiday, with which every Israeli child is basically familiar.

Indeed, it would be very difficult for Jewish Israeli children to encounter festive days of other faiths, as proselytizing is prohibited by law in Israel. Enshrined in Israel's Declaration of Independence is that it is a Jewish state. Thus, despite its secular foundations, the country is undeniably built on Jewish values. Jewish history and basic Judaism are taught as part of the state school curriculum. And it goes without saying that all Israelis can speak, read, and write Hebrew fluently. The intermarriage rate is far lower in Israel than in any other country. Shabbat is a special day—whether or not you keep everything, it's still called Shabbat! Pork is hard to find. Most Israelis fast on Yom Kippur and don't eat bread on Pesach.

When you think about the knowledge and experience of Judaism and Hebrew of the average Israeli compared to the average diaspora Jew, it's clear to see the Gemara's contrast between God's place in Israel versus the diaspora. Even today, a diaspora Jew is faced with all manner of idolatrous ideas to which most Israelis are simply not exposed. Even those Israelis who are furthest from Yiddishkeit are taught our values by the state. One of the most powerful experiences of my life was a shul mission to Israel. Shabbos afternoon, we ate *shalosh seudos* in the Old City at a warm and generous family that hosts *chayalim*—Israeli soldiers every week. The army brings them to Jerusalem to experience Jewish life first-hand in order to understand and internalize what they're defending and fighting for.

Nevertheless, despite its best efforts to keep its citizens in Israel, the country has one of the highest rates of emigration in the world. Today, there are close to a million former Israelis living in the Diaspora. From post-army kiosk workers to Silicon Valley geniuses to top university academics and everything in between, there is nowhere in the world that you won't find Israelis. One of the challenges that established diaspora communities struggle with is: How do you engage with them and get them to become synagogue members? In Israel, religious life is state-driven. Shuls are provided free of charge, and so, the concept of paying dues is completely foreign to them. Where do you begin in terms of changing that mentality and getting them to decide to join the mainstream Jewish community?

Sadly, many people's knee-jerk response to ex-Israelis is one of disdain. How could anyone choose to leave the Holy Land for life in the Diaspora? But isn't it a tad hypocritical to criticize so-called "*yordim*," Israelis who have left, if you've never even made aliyah to begin with? Others can't wrap their heads around providing community resources for Israelis who are not paying their way. But let me explain why that attitude completely misses the mark.

Most of us could never hold a candle to the average Israeli. Just think about the three-plus years they dedicated to the safety and security of the Jewish people on the frontlines of the battlefield. They've put their lives on the line for us. When I see an Israeli, I almost want to reach out and give him a big hug. There is no way I could ever repay him for everything that he's done for me and my family. He devoted his entire being to the Jewish people.

The very least that we can do in return is reach out to them and offer them perks like free membership in our shuls. We need to stop getting hung up on the fact that they won't become synagogue members anytime soon. Maybe some of them will, but most of them won't. Not today. Not next year. Probably never. They simply have no shul-membership culture—to pay for religion is almost sacrilegious to them!

Rabbi Eliezer teaches that one who lives in Israel is sin-free. Every Israeli who put his life on the line for the Jewish people is as holy as a Temple sacrifice. We could never repay him for his incredible devotion to the Jewish people. Until now, he hasn't experienced any faith but the one true God in his life. It's our responsibility to keep it that way. May we reach out and spiritually protect those who have dedicated themselves to our physical protection!

DAF 111

Uncontrollable Stimuli

Let me tell you about two young men who grew up before the war in Kosice, Czechoslovakia. Both grew up in very observant Jewish homes. These men survived Auschwitz, but lost their entire families. After the war, they moved out to Australia.

One man moved to Sydney, where he became active in the vibrant Jewish community. He joined a shul, went to minyan, and put on tefillin every day. He proudly wore his yarmulke all the time. And he told everyone about all the miracles that happened to him in the camps that enabled him to survive, and how grateful he was to the Almighty for choosing him as one of the few who were saved from the horrors of the Shoah. That man never stopped smiling and singing God's praises.

The second man moved out to rural Australia to be as far away from God and the Jewish community as possible. He rejected all Jewish observance and brought up his kids with very little Judaism. He was angry at God. He was bitter. And he was sure of one thing: he would never forgive Heaven for having taken everything from him. And so that's how this man spent the next few decades. Angry. Bitter.

I want to make it clear that we can never judge the decisions of people like this man who witnessed unspeakable atrocities. Who could question him for the anger that he harbored toward Heaven? But at the same time, how is it possible that two people who experienced the same horrors could have polar opposite responses?

I know what you're thinking. How do I know their experience was the same?

> וְאָמַר רַבִּי חִיָּיא בַּר יוֹסֵף עֲתִידִים צַדִּיקִים שֶׁיַּעַמְדוּ בְּמַלְבּוּשֵׁיהֶן קַל וָחוֹמֶר מֵחִטָּה מָה חִטָּה שֶׁנִּקְבְּרָה עֲרוּמָּה יוֹצְאָה בְּכַמָּה לְבוּשִׁין צַדִּיקִים שֶׁנִּקְבְּרוּ בִּלְבוּשֵׁיהֶן עַל אַחַת כַּמָּה וְכַמָּה.
>
> *Rabbi Chiya bar Yosef said: In the future the righteous ones will be resurrected in their clothes [levush]. We may derive this idea from wheat: If wheat, which when planted is a tiny naked seedling, but then blossoms adorned with beautiful clothing, then how much more so the righteous who were buried in their clothing!*

There are two words for clothing in Hebrew—*beged* and *levush*. *Beged* comes from the root "*beis-gimmel-dalet*," meaning "treachery." In fact, when you read the Hebrew alphabet backwards (utilizing the method known numerologically as *a-t ba-sh*), the word corresponds to the word *sheker*, meaning "falsehood." Clothes are false, a façade to hide one's true self. You can change your external appearance and dress up as anybody you want to pretend to be.

Before we get to the meaning of *levush,* let's examine Rabbi Chiya bar Yosef's comparison of the righteous to seeds. When a seed is planted in the ground, there are many external factors that will affect its ability to germinate, such as access to water, oxygen, light, as well as the soil temperature and depth. Given the same set of external conditions, some seeds will germinate, while others will fail to do so.

Think about all those little seedlings lying there in the ground complaining about how they could have made it if only they had better soil opportunities. Or if only they had better access to water and oxygen. It's not their fault they never took off. It's all the external factors beyond their control. They lie there *kvetching* away—and meanwhile the righteous seeds just take whatever comes their way and make the most of it. They know that they cannot control the air and sunlight. All they can control is their response to those external factors. Some environmental factors will be favorable to their growth. Others will be challenging. The key is to capitalize on the favorable elements and to overcome the challenging factors. If they can do that, they will sprout forth, clothed in amazing splendor!

That's the difference between righteous and not-as righteous people. It's tempting to think that righteous individuals have done well because they've had a good life. But that's not how this world works. We are all faced with a mixed menu of opportunities and challenges in life. Most of those are external to us and we have very little power to affect those external stimuli. What we can control is our response to those external stimuli. The righteous are those who have worked on mastering their ability to respond the right way.

At our inner spiritual core, we each consist of a pure, holy *neshamah*. But that *neshamah* is clothed in the physical body's faculties of expression, called *levushim*. The soul expresses itself through the three "garments" of thought, speech, and action. According to the *Maharal*, when the Gemara speaks of the righteous rising fully clothed, it is referring to these spiritual garments. The soul itself is absolutely pure; it is Divine. But it is clothed in the three spiritual garments, and we are tasked with refining those garments. The more a person refines his thought, speech, and action, the more he becomes one with his soul. Righteous people have refined their garments to the extent that they will rise with them.

Every time you withhold your anger, you refine your garment of thought. Every time you avoid gossiping, you refine your garment of speech. Every time you give tzedakah, you refine your garment of action. The more you refine, the greater the chance that they will shine upon you with splendor in the World to Come. During our present lifetimes, our job is to train our *levushim* to respond to external stimuli in a positive fashion. That doesn't happen to anyone naturally. We must all work on controlling ourselves. The righteous are those who have reached a level whereby any external stimulus evokes the purest, holiest reaction.

That's something for which we all must strive. And it begins by pausing whenever something external happens and pondering the source and meaning of the stimulus that we have encountered. Let me give you an example from the psychology of Cognitive Behavioral Therapy. You're lying in bed, and you hear noise downstairs coming from the kitchen. How do you react? Well, it all depends on how you perceive the source of the noise. Let's try a few different potential scenarios:

- It sounds like your place is being burgled. Are they armed? Will they enter your bedroom? You suddenly feel very scared.
- Actually, come to think of it, it sounds like your teenager is home from a late-night party. How many times have you told him to be quiet when he comes in? How dare he selfishly wake you up as he makes himself a midnight snack? You suddenly start feeling very angry.
- Wait a sec. Officially, your spouse wasn't due home from his business trip until tomorrow. It sounds like he might have been able to catch an earlier standby flight and is home early. You suddenly start feeling overcome with love and happiness at the thought of this pleasant surprise.

Three different responses to the same trigger situation. You can't control the stimulus. But you can control your interpretation and reaction to the stimulus.

Turning to an example from the Torah, let's say that I was to show you massive grapes, the size of tennis balls. What's the first thing that you would think? Amazing, delicious, out of this world, right? Prior to our entry into the Promised Land, Moshe sent twelve spies to spy out the country. Two of them, Yehoshua and Calev, saw these gigantic grapes and thought: Awesome, Hashem has given us blessings beyond our wildest dreams! But the ten others conclude: if the grapes are so huge, can you imagine the size of the giants who must be consuming them? We'll never manage to enter the land!

Same stimulus, two radically different interpretations.

I opened up today's *shiur* with the story of two young men who survived the Holocaust. One lived a life filled with joy. The other was bitter and angry. How did two people with exactly the same experience respond so differently? And then you asked me how I can be so sure their experiences were alike.

Let me tell you how I know. Because both stories were about my paternal grandfather. For many years he was angry and bitter. And then, one day, he woke up and decided that he didn't want to be this bitter, angry person. From that moment on, he spent the rest of his life going around telling everyone how grateful he was to Hashem for sparing his life, for saving him from the depths of hell on Earth. And he transformed into this deeply religious, faithful man.

Most stimuli we encounter in life aren't controllable. We can only control our reactions to those stimuli. May you merit the strength to refine your spiritual garments and rise up fully clothed in the World to Come!

DAF 112

You Are an Israeli Ambassador

Our Sages believed in the importance of promoting and displaying the beauty of the Land of Israel. Rabbi Abba would kiss the rocks of Akko. Rabbi Chanina would repair the potholes on the roads of Israel. When Rabbi Ami and Rabbi Asi would teach Torah in Israel, they would always make sure to find the ideal climate. Sometimes, that entailed taking their students from a sunny spot to a shady one. Other times it meant leaving the shade where it was chilly and holding the class in the sunshine. Rabbi Chiya bar Gamda would roll in the dust of the land of Israel.

רַבִּי אַבָּא מְנַשֵּׁק כֵּיפֵי דְעַכּוֹ רַבִּי חֲנִינָא מְתַקֵּן מַתְקָלַיָּה רַבִּי אַמֵּי וְרַבִּי אַסִּי קָיְימִי מִשִּׁמְשָׁא לְטוּלָּא וּמִטּוּלָּא לְשִׁמְשָׁא רַבִּי חִיָּיא בַּר גַּמְדָּא מִיגַּנְדַּר בְּעַפְרַהּ שֶׁנֶּאֱמַר כִּי רָצוּ עֲבָדֶיךָ אֶת אֲבָנֶיהָ וְאֶת עֲפָרָהּ יְחוֹנֵנוּ אָמַר רַבִּי זֵירָא אָמַר רַבִּי יִרְמְיָה בַּר אַבָּא דּוֹר שֶׁבֶּן דָּוִד בָּא קָטֵיגוֹרְיָא בְּתַלְמִידֵי חֲכָמִים כִּי אַמְרִיתַהּ קַמֵּיהּ דִּשְׁמוּאֵל אֲמַר צֵירוּף אַחַר צֵירוּף שֶׁנֶּאֱמַר וְעוֹד בָּהּ עֲשִׂירִיָּה וְשָׁבָה וְהָיְתָה לְבָעֵר תָּנֵי רַב יוֹסֵף בָּזוֹזֵי וּבָזוֹזֵי דְבָזוֹזֵי אָמַר רַב חִיָּיא בַּר אָשֵׁי אָמַר רַב עֲתִידִין כָּל אִילָנֵי סְרָק שֶׁבְּאֶרֶץ יִשְׂרָאֵל שֶׁיִּטְעֲנוּ פֵּירוֹת שֶׁנֶּאֱמַר כִּי עֵץ נָשָׂא פִּרְיוֹ תְּאֵנָה וָגֶפֶן נָתְנוּ חֵילָם.

Rabbi Chiya bar Gamda would roll in the dust of the land, as it is stated: "For Your servants take pleasure in her stones and love her dust." Rabbi Zeira quoted Rabbi Yirmiyah bar Abba: In the generation in which the son of David will come, there will be denouncements of Torah scholars. When I said this

> *before Shmuel he said: The generation will undergo refinement after refinement, as it is stated, "And if there be a tenth in it, it shall again be eaten up." Rav Yosef taught: Despoilers and despoilers of despoilers. Rav Chiya bar Ashi quoted Rav: In the future all barren trees in Eretz Yisrael will bear fruit, as it is stated: "For the tree bears its fruit; the fig tree and the vine yield their strength."*

Critics of Israel will jump at any opportunity to condemn the Jewish state. As Rav Yosef teaches, in the pre-messianic era, Israel will have an abundance of "Despoilers and despoilers of despoilers." We must be so careful that we don't give them any extra ammunition. There's a classic Winston Churchill line that Menachem Begin liked to use: "As I travel around the world, I pride myself on being the fiercest defender of every aspect of my country. I would never so much as whisper a criticism. Admittedly, when I get home, I've got a lot of catching up to do!"

There's no doubt that with two Jews and three opinions we all have different views of how Israel should look and what the country's priorities should be. But our Sages did whatever they could to enhance Israel in the court of public opinion. Ever wonder where the custom comes from to kiss the ground upon arrival in Israel? Well, Rabbi Abba would kiss the stones of Akko and Rabbi Chiya bar Gamda would roll in the dust of Israel!

Likewise, it's clear that Rabbi Ami and Rabbi Asi were concerned that people speak and feel positively about Israel. The country has some pretty warm weather and, at times, it can get chilly as well, but they worked hard to ensure the students would return home with a good report of life in Israel. It's not hard to view even the most beautiful land in an unkind light—we know that already from the story of the spies. The Gemara is teaching us that we are tasked with the mission of presenting Israel in the very best light possible.

There are very few Jews in the world today who do not acknowledge the great blessing of Jewish sovereignty in Israel. Even those in the non-Zionist Chareidi camp understand that the magnitude of Torah learning today is unparalleled throughout most of the history of our people. And that may be counted as one of the major successes of the modern country of Israel.

But as Rabbi Chanina makes clear, it's not enough to just support the yeshivos in Israel. Without the physical infrastructure—roads, airports, parks—Israel wouldn't operate as efficiently as it does. Israel is a modern miracle, spiritually and physically, and we must be prepared to support and highlight all of its achievements.

Israel has been fighting to defend its international legitimacy since its inception. A number of years ago, however, the focus of Israel advocacy switched from playing defense against the onslaught of anti-Semitic accusations to highlighting all the wonderful achievements of the State of Israel. Israel is a beautiful tourist destination; the state provides equal rights for all; it is a leader in science, technology and medicine, and boasts a number of the world's top universities and hospitals.

And it has become a powerhouse of Jewish learning. But as Rabbi Yirmiyah bar Abba predicted, "In the generation in which the son of David will come, there will be denouncements of Torah scholars." Notice how his statement is juxtaposed to the teachings about the potholes and other physical aspects of Israel? Defending Israel before its critics means standing up for Israel's success in every area of life. Whether or not you personally would prioritize mandatory army service for all or automatic exemptions for yeshiva students is immaterial to Israel advocacy. When you're abroad, your task is to defend Israel.

What is the meaning of Rav's teaching, "In the future, all barren trees in Eretz Yisrael will bear fruit?"

In the *Shabbos Mevarchim* prayer we declare, "He will gather our dispersed from the four corners of the Earth; all of Israel are *chaverim*." The Gerrer Rebbe explains the meaning:[1] in the messianic era, every single Jew will be a *chaver*. In Talmudic language, *chaver* means a learned and halachically trustworthy individual. Both men and women were entitled to earn this appellation. Today we are witnessing a flourishing of Torah learning unparalleled in history, emanating primarily from

---

1 Cited in *Likutei Yehudah*.

the Land of Israel. It has become a right of passage for young men and women to spend at least a year learning in yeshivos and seminaries in Israel, and the numbers of previously unaffiliated Jews attending *baal teshuvah* institutions is growing by leaps and bounds.

The Talmud enjoins us to be part of Israel's marketing team. Wherever you are, you should be an advocate for the Jewish state, singing its praises in every facet of its existence, from the spiritual to the physical to the material to the cultural. May you forever strive to be a proud ambassador of our Promised Land!

About the Author

Rabbi Daniel Friedman is currently on his fourth *daf yomi* cycle. He received *semichah yadin yadin* from Rav Gedalia Dov Schwartz, *zt"l*, Av Beis Din of the Beth Din of America. He has served communities in the US, Canada, Australia, and the UK. His articles have appeared in the *Journal of Halacha and Contemporary Society*, *YU Lamdan*, the *Jewish Press*, the *Jerusalem Post*, Aish.com, and numerous other outlets. He was the inaugural chair of the National Holocaust Monument of Canada and is a world-renowned expert on the intersection of halachah and international relations.

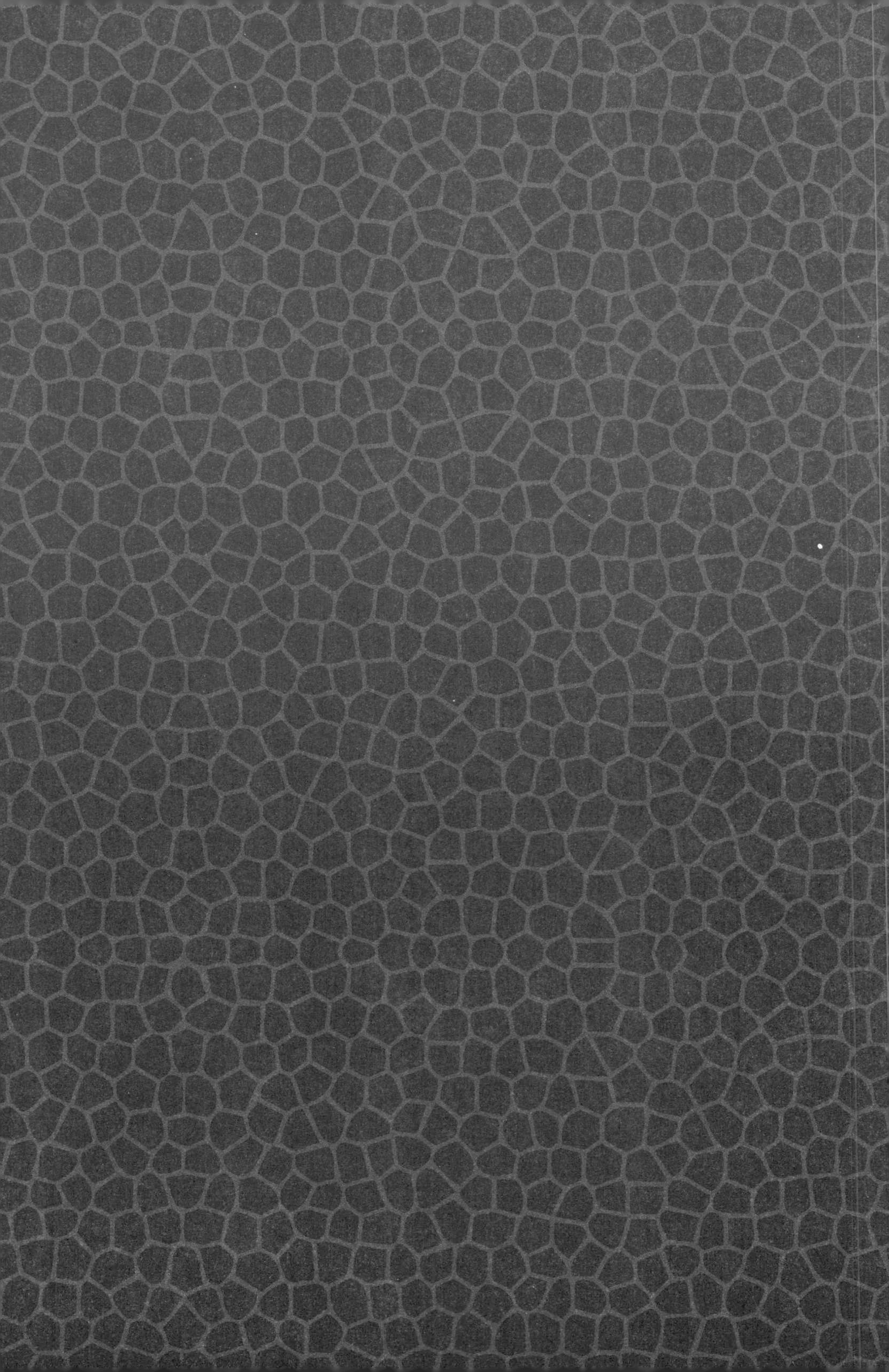